SUCKING EGGS

Patricia Nicol was born in Aberdeen, Scotland, and was brought up there, in the United Arab Emirates and England. She now lives in London, where she works as a journalist for the *Sunday Times*.

PATRICIA NICOL

Sucking Eggs

What your wartime granny could teach you about diet, thrift and going green

VINTAGE BOOKS
London

Published by Vintage 2010

2 4 6 8 10 9 7 5 3 1

First published in Great Britain in 2009 by Chatto & Windus

Vintage
Random House, 20 Vauxhall Bridge Road,
London SW1V 2SA

www.vintage-books.co.uk

Addresses for companies within The Random House Group Limited can be found at: www.randomhouse.co.uk/offices.htm

The Random House Group Limited Reg. No. 954009

A CIP catalogue record for this book is available from the British Library

ISBN 9780099521129

The Random House Group Limited supports The Forest Stewardship Council (FSC), the leading international forest certification organisation. All our titles that are printed on Greenpeace approved FSC certified paper carry the FSC logo. Our paper procurement policy can be found at: www.rbooks.co.uk/environment

FSC
Mixed Sources
Product group from well-managed forests and other controlled sources
www.fsc.org Cert no. TT-COC-2139
© 1996 Forest Stewardship Council

Printed and bound in Great Britain by
CPI Bookmarque, Croydon

CONTENTS

PART FOUR
REBELLION

AFTERWORD
LESSONS FOR TODAY AND MY APPLICATION OF THEM

For my parents

INTRODUCTION

Buy nothing for your personal pleasure or comfort, use no transport, call on no labour – unless urgent necessity compels. To be free with your money today is not a merit. It is contemptible. To watch every penny shows your will to win.
Wartime government poster

It wasn't difficult in 1940 to persuade people to make sacrifices because everyone knew there might not be a 1941.
Peter Hennessy[1]

When I started working on this book in the summer of 2006, Britain's economic situation was outwardly healthy. It was a strange time, then, suddenly to develop a fascination with an era when Dame Austerity reigned supreme. Two unrelated incidents had piqued my interest. First, while idly flicking through Jane Grigson's classic *English Food* (1974),[2] I was struck by a passage in which she bemoaned the loss of traditional recipes during the period of rationing because difficulties in obtaining ingredients had eroded the culinary skills of the past. Around the same time, I was writing an article commemorating the fiftieth anniversary of the first performances of John Osborne's play, *Look Back in Anger* (1956). Those I interviewed reminisced about post-war Britain. Through the smog of time they conjured up a threadbare land where everything had been hard to come by and even the food was grey. One man spoke passionately of his infuriatingly insipid female contemporaries – all, he claimed, educated no further than a level of simpering idiocy. But, he added, to coax one of them into bed had been any evening's primary objective.

My Britain, half a century on and before we toppled into recession, seemed eye-poppingly different – a colourful, multicultural country with its position apparently secure in a globalised world. A place where, at least in my own overall experience, the two sexes operated on an equal footing. A country that – if not exactly the New Jerusalem some had dreamt of building post-war – was nonetheless a land of soya milk and acacia honey, where computer-tracked chains of supply criss-crossed the world to meet our every insatiable demand.

But Grigson's lamenting of the blow butter shortages had dealt to Sunderland patisserie chefs would never have made me pause had I not already been having doubts about the sustainability of our own lifestyles in twenty-first-century Britain. Our well-fed nation is overfed. We have become a nation of malnourished fatties and thus a burden to our beleaguered National Health Service. The government's projected figures suggest that a fifth of all British children will be obese by 2020[3] and yet its headline-grabbing attempts to instil healthy eating habits in the young appear to be failing.

Worst of all, the scientific consensus is that our consumerist lifestyles could literally cost us the earth. Already the environmental damage of our rapacious appetites is sending out shock waves. We are an island nation surrounded by seas that, marine experts say, could be stripped of fish stocks by 2048.[4] On the land, meanwhile, decades of intensive farming have denuded acres of once arable soil of their nutrients and, in livestock farming, introduced abnormalities into the food chain. The pernicious impact of our gluttony does not stop at our own shores: the leaching of the soil of southern Spain through over-farming, the drying up of rivers in Africa, the destruction of tropical rainforest, even the melting of the polar caps – all, environmentalists claim, could in part be blamed on First World consumption. Moreover, concerns about our excesses are not confined to the supermarket's food aisles. Third World sweatshops clothe many of us. The way we eat and shop produces more rubbish than we have space for in this country, yet the economic alternative, which is to pay some poorer country to bury it for us, leaves us stuck in a moral quagmire.

Also debatable is how we consume energy to fuel our homes and workplaces, to travel and to pursue leisure. In the first cold snap of the winter of 2006 a power surge cut off electricity to millions of homes across Germany, France and Italy, as well as parts of Spain, Portugal, the

Netherlands, Belgium and Austria.[5] It was the first time in decades that lights had gone out all over Europe. Afterwards it was announced that such blackouts would become more frequent in the near future. Shortages of fuel and water, futurologists tell us, will be the basis of new global conflicts.

It was these grim warnings that first prompted me to further my interest in a wartime era when the government intervened at a day-to-day level to curb consumption and increase self-sufficiency. So my *Look Back in Anger* interviewees, and Grigson's indifferent cakes, took me to the archives of the Imperial War Museum where I expected a depressing day's reading. But instead I found myself almost immediately immersed in research materials that moved, inspired and excited me. Here was a patched-up New Jerusalem, yes; but a happier, more hopeful place than the one depicted by my interviewee, who had been a sex-starved, angry young man in the 1950s. And the values of the people whose letters and diaries I read there had a specific resonance. At the time, I was both failing to make ends meet and trying to pursue a greener lifestyle, while finding modern manuals for ethical living either off-puttingly apocalyptic or plain smug. There was nothing in the wartime manuals advocating prudence and providence over profligacy that could not be applied to today, but somehow they did it all with much more can-do conviction.

It was then I realised that we do not have to look far back in our own history for a timely lesson in making seismic lifestyle changes. The grandparents at whom we may once have scoffed for hanging on to leftovers and hoarding pieces of string and Green Shields stamps were, in contrast to us, model global citizens. Their carbon footprints barely left a mark. They wasted almost nothing and what they had no use for they recycled. They bought locally because, with a world war on, they had to think globally. They dug for victory and grew their own vegetables, as we are now being encouraged to do. They abandoned their cars and did not dare light a fire, flick a switch or turn on a tap without thinking of the energy that would be consumed. Theirs was not a disposable culture; they made do and mended. In 'the great saucepan offensive', they salvaged. Decades before No Logo became an international rallying cry, they were pioneering anti-consumerists dressed in Utility clothing, with Winston Churchill leading the way. They 'did thrift' years before it became a fashion model's fad; they invented the second-hand shop and the recycling bin.

Most important and inspirational, their heroic self-sacrifices on the Home Front made a huge, almost immediately recognisable impact. At the outbreak of the Second World War two-thirds of Britain's food and raw industrial materials came from overseas. By 1943 less than a third did. Britons, by following government-imposed rationing and productivity measures, had become largely self-sufficient.[6]

The years of austerity were threadbare, but they had their rewards. The wartime coalition government's tight control over production and consumption, industry and the individual, paved the way for the Welfare State with its stated aim to care for its citizens 'from the cradle to the grave'. If no housewife mourned the final end of rationing nine long years after the end of the fighting, nearly all grudgingly acknowledged that it had seen them through the war well. The austerity measures, to save food, materials and labour, not only gave Britain the most efficient Home Front of any country involved in the global conflict, they also improved the nation's health. In the period of rationing (8 January 1940 to 3 July 1954) the weight of newborn babies increased; the life expectancy of non-fighting males went up; Britons had better teeth, stronger bones and grew taller. Less alcohol, tobacco and fats were consumed, due to rationing, higher prices and lack of supply. The dietary gap between rich and poor narrowed. Children, especially those from poorer homes, benefited from the National Milk Scheme, the provision of cod liver oil and orange juice and, in particular, the increase in the provision of nutritious school meals, which went up from about 160,000 before the war to 1.6 million in 1945,

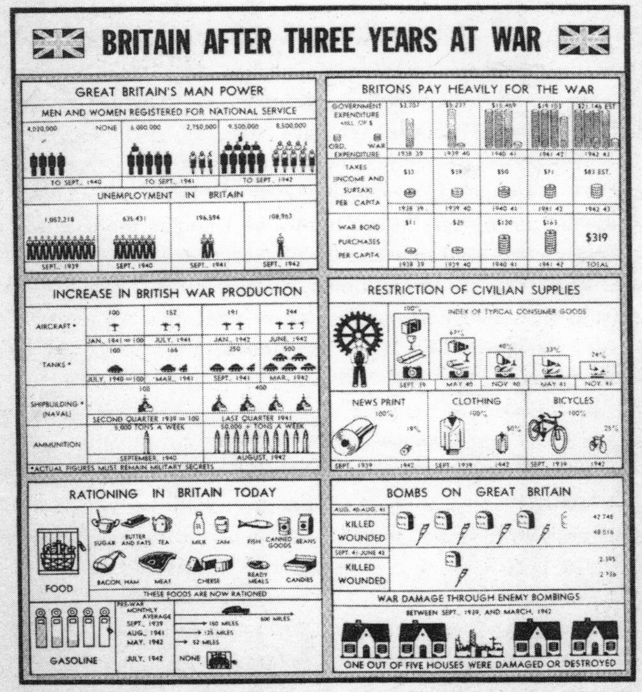

This pictorial chart gives just a slight idea of the three years of fighting and sacrifice which the people of Britain have dedicated towards smashing the Axis.

It would be impossible to show every restriction that Britain has submitted to gladly and willingly during these first three years of war. To show how even the limited supplies of food available are not always obtainable by the public, how unrationed foods are frequently so scarce that few people can obtain them at all, how furniture and household linen, pots and pans are practically unobtainable.

But as civilian supplies of food, clothing and fuel grow smaller, Britain's war effort grows larger. Savings campaigns exist in every village, the sale of certificates and war bonds is ever on the increase, interest-free loans are made to the government.

Every factory is working at top speed, twenty-four hours a day turning out an ever-increasing number of tanks, aircraft and munitions with which to deal the death blow to Hitler and his Axis partners.

The British can laugh at shortages and rationing because they know that by doing so they are contributing to victory.

Ministry of Information poster

when 40 per cent of pupils received a subsidised meal providing as many as 1,000 calories a day.[7]

Of course, 'lifestyle' is a relatively new coinage. Life and death presented themselves much more starkly in our grandparents' day. Unlike most of my generation, which has grown up accustomed to endless options, they were given little choice. They lived frugally, because the government imposed austerity. Ours was the promised land they fought for, but soon its rich resources may run dry. In the early years of this decade Andrew Simms, of the New Economics Foundation think tank, wrote a paper advocating an 'environmental war economy'. He argued, 'For decades, poor countries around the world have suffered austerity programmes imposed with the excuse of tackling dubious foreign debts. In the face of climate change, rich countries should now be getting their environmental budgets in order and starting to make huge cuts in consumption.'[8]

But would we ever stomach such government measures again without the common goal of a war to win? Many of us may already buckle under the moral pressure not to fly by asking, as that wartime generation did, 'Is your journey really necessary?' before booking an air ticket. But when hot running water is available at the flick of the switch, would we really forgo power showers to share baths with plimsoll lines round them as did even the residents of Buckingham Palace? We now pay lip service to green issues, which are seen as vote winners, but would we respond positively if a government we had voted in imposed austerity measures? Or is firm government intervention exactly what we need as we face the double whammy of recession and the depletion of our environment's natural resources?

Does our past hold that lesson too? In 1945 the British population gave a surprise landslide victory to a Labour government promising a Welfare State. In 1949 Attlee's Labour administration was re-elected, but with a tiny majority. In 1951, with the nation at a near standstill due to strikes and fuel shortages, Attlee was forced to call another election, which the Conservatives, under Churchill, walked. A key factor in the pioneering post-war Labour government's loss of support was that the nation's housewives had had enough of self-sacrifice. British women wanted the Welfare State's promise of protection 'from the cradle to the grave', but not to live post-war in a weary nation of three-day weeks, industrial strikes, queues that could occupy an entire morning and the depressing monotony of continued rationing. They voted, not for frugality, but for the Conservatives' promise of prosperity. It is no coincidence that the British cinematic successes of the period were the Ealing Comedies, *Passport to Pimlico* and *Whisky Galore*, both made in 1949, and both of which mocked austerity and made heroes of those who mutinied against the stifling, soul-sapping bureaucracy that maintained it.

In writing *Sucking Eggs* I have used historic records and contemporary sources to explore the oddly neglected subject of wartime rationing: its gradual imposition from 1940; people's response to it, both positively (the huge success of campaigns including Dig for Victory, Make Do and Mend and the Great Saucepan Offensive) and negatively (the Black Market and post-war discontent); and its long-term effects in terms of health and way of life. In looking at the dramatic lifestyle changes made on the Home Front in that period I have discovered valuable lessons we could relearn today. Should we have listened more closely to our grandparents, who had much to teach us about austerity? Or were they – in their own longing to replace tapered-in Utility wear for the swoosh of Christian Dior's New Look, to buy a refrigerator and then a run-around for Sunday motoring – complicit in the collective stamping out of frugality? Have they left us to reinvent, if not the wheel, then the wheely bin?

It is not just credit-crunch Britain's economic downturn, or international shortages of staple foods such as rice, that are new since I started researching this book; my personal circumstances have altered dramatically too. In the summer of 2006 I was single and living alone in east London. By the time *Sucking Eggs* was first published in hardback I was a married mother of a two-month-old baby, living at the opposite end of town. I now have more of a vested interest in this world's future and in furthering the lifestyle changes that, inspired by what an older generation achieved in the war, I have started to make. Like my grandmother, I'm dreaming of a safer future in a New Jerusalem.

PART ONE

FOOD

PREFACE

People were largely ignorant of anything except their appetites and had no knowledge of food values. As a nation, it was broadly true to say that we were indifferent to both our agriculture and our horticulture. We could get cheap food abroad: refrigeration had largely solved the problem of transport: meat from Australia, New Zealand, and the Argentine was very good – and cheap – and so were the dairy products of the southern hemisphere. There was, in fact, little except potatoes that we grew in this country that somebody else could not produce either cheaper or earlier – excepting, of course, the 'good English beef', the best of which was said to be produced in Scotland!

From the memoirs of Lord Woolton, Minister of Food 1940-3, published in 1959[1]

It's called the Fife Diet and . . . the 'Fife' in the name is not a magic ingredient, but refers to the region of Scotland just north of Edinburgh. Next month, 14 valiant pioneers there will celebrate a year-long dietary experiment which doesn't involve cutting out certain foods, only food miles . . . In Britain, 80 per cent of food is currently imported, and only 20 per cent locally produced. The idea was to reverse those percentages and the dieters have found it surprisingly easy.

Cassandra Jardine, *Daily Telegraph*, 27 October 2008[2]

Britain's food culture in the first half of the twenty-first century proves that you can have too much of a good thing. Many foods once regarded as luxuries – chicken, salmon, prime cuts of meat, butter and cream – or seasonal delicacies – most fruit and vegetables – have been devalued by year-round over-familiarity. We should be aroused by English asparagus and its delicate signalling of summer in May; then, having feasted on berries in June and July, we should be bracing ourselves for the plum time of late August and September. These local seasonal delights – with their unique perfume and texture – are the essence of a ripening then cooling British summer. Instead, tasteless, woody asparagus, flown in from Latin America, is available all year; Mexican strawberries can be bought in the depths of our winter; and from spring to autumn South African plums crowd out juicier native varieties on our supermarket shelves. A friend of mine used regularly to serve her pre-school son a meal she billed as 'toddler tapas': a few olives; guacamole; tiger prawns; baby tomatoes labelled as having been plucked on the vine; then a pudding of banana and blueberries. Fifty years ago most of this food would have been prohibitively expensive exotica; but today, thanks to airfreight and the buying might of our supermarkets, it is extravagant but commonplace.

The processes by which our food reaches us – especially in our non-agrarian cities – is a wonder of our age. In the past the growth of cities was checked by their ability to feed themselves. In the twentieth century improved transportation and refrigeration seemed to resolve this problem and cities expanded accordingly. By 2006 the world's population could be identified as predominantly urban for the first time. Today's cities use up 75 per cent of the world's resources, while our urban population is currently set to double by 2050.[3]

Yet our ability to feed ourselves in the supercities of the future is not guaranteed. Indeed, it will falter if we continue to deplete the world's natural resources. Food is fuel. It is fuel in that it powers each one of us, but it is also fuel in the sense that grown food is, at its most basic level, energy captured through photosynthesis. 'Harnessing solar energy in edible form is basically what farmers did until about 1850; and it is more or less what they have done since, too, except that since that date, they have supplemented the process with the use of fossil fuels,' writes Carolyn Steel in her book *Hungry City*.[4] Modern food production is heavily dependent on oil. On farms it is used in machinery, fertilisers and pesticides, and to transport, process and preserve foods. The majority of us shop in brightly lit, air-chilled supermarkets that we drive to in fuel-guzzling machines. These supermarkets use up oil to transport foods over vast distances and to package, preserve and display them in the fuel-inefficient ways that their extensive research has shown them consumers expect. The carnivorous among us – and that is an ever-increasing number of us globally – have far more energy going into our foods than those who eat a predominantly vegetarian diet. And the more dependent we are on processed foods – which use up more fuel in pre-preparation, packaging, preserving, even pre-cooking and display – then the more oil-squandering our diet will be. Oil is the undeclared ingredient in almost all our foods. Carolyn Steel claims that a Briton consumes an average of four barrels of oil per year, while the average American consumes almost double that amount. She concludes, 'When we eat today, we are effectively eating oil.' That means that as the oil runs out, so could our food, or at least the way we eat now.[5]

The end of cheap food?

We are currently experiencing an international food crisis that the United Nations has called 'a silent tsunami'. Since 2005 the costs of wheat, rice and other staple grains have risen steadily. Between January and April 2008 alone the price of Thai rice – a world benchmark – nearly doubled. Prices will probably continue to escalate as a result of the unpredictability of the world's markets: fluctuating oil prices; farmers producing grain for biofuel instead of feed for humans and animals; water crises; rising population. In rapidly developing and urbanising countries such as India and China an increased affluence is leading to new patterns in consumption. In 2008 food price hikes sparked riots in more than thirty developing countries as geographically and culturally remote from one another as Yemen and Haiti – where five were killed in protests that brought down the government.[6] In more affluent economic areas, such as Hong Kong, fears for food security led to hoarding. In rice-producing lands such as Egypt, Cambodia, Vietnam and India fears of unrest brought in emergency protectionist government measures, banning or drastically reducing grain exports. Even the US felt the impact of such shortages: the retail giant, Wal-Mart, rationed its customers' rice purchases. And the prognosis for future food security does not look rosy here in Britain: a 12 per cent increase in the cost of an average shopping basket is predicted to put £750 extra on the average family of four's annual shopping bill.[7]

The end of wasted food?

Perhaps it will be a good thing if food in the West becomes more expensive. We cannot survive without food, but its cheap and easy availability has made us shamefully profligate with it. In 2008 the government-supported body WRAP (Waste and Resources Action Programme) revealed that almost a third of all the food we buy annually in Britain was being thrown away without being eaten, at an individual cost to the average British household of as much as £640 annually.

Britain's eaters are in terrible shape. As food prices declined steadily throughout the post-war era, our consumption grew. Now, for the first time, children in Britain – still the world's sixth-largest economy – are projected to have a lower life expectancy than their parents. Obesity and weight-related diseases are being detected in progressively younger sufferers. If we looked up from our TV dinners for long enough we would see an epidemic all around us. Scientists have said that as many as 6 per cent of Britons could be malnourished, despite being obese.[8]

How do you persuade a nation to live more healthily? In modern Britain that could be the most important question for any politician to ask. And how to answer it may be the greatest welfare challenge. *Healthy Weight, Healthy Lives: A cross-government strategy for England*, published in 2008, claimed that in 2007 overweight and obesity had cost the National Health Service an estimated £4.2 billion and the wider economy £15.8 billion. And if our national bingeing continues as projected those figures will spiral. The study estimated that by 2050 the cost could be as high as £9.7 billion to the NHS and £49.9 billion to the wider economy (2007 prices).[9] Too much of the wrong sorts of food and too little exercise has made Britain the sick man of Europe.[10] The published figures confirm what you can see in any street or on any bus: most of us have been piling

Ministry of Information poster

on the pounds. Since the 1980s the prevalence of obesity has trebled in England alone, where in 2006 23.7 per cent of men and 24.2 per cent of women were deemed obese and almost two-thirds of all adults (61.6 per cent, approximately 31 million) were either overweight or obese.[11] Obesity levels of the young are rising at an alarming rate. The 2006 figures for England show that among children aged two to fifteen, almost one-third (29.7 per cent, nearly three million) are overweight (including obese) and approximately one-sixth (16 per cent, about 1.5 million) are obese. The figures projected, should current trends continue, are terrifying: by 2010, one-third of adults and one-fifth of children aged two to ten could be obese, while by 2050 60 per cent of adult men, 50 per cent of adult women and 25 per cent of all children under sixteen could be obese.[12]

In the UK, for all our fear of flu epidemics and hospital infections, gluttony is the greatest health hazard we face. Obesity-related illnesses range from the most obvious – high blood pressure, heart disease, osteoarthritis, type 2 diabetes – to the less expected yet just as personally devastating, including infertility.

All this is known. Yet as a nation we don't seem to want to help ourselves. The 'five-a-day' fruit and vegetable message has been hammered home, as has the basic guideline that exercise should be as habitual a part of our lives as television watching. Our doctors warn us when we tip the scales and TV chefs exhort us to eat more healthily, while demonstrating how to shop and cook. Yet in 2006 only 40 per cent of men and 28 per cent of women met the recommended guidelines for exercise (at least thirty minutes of moderate-intensity physical activity at least five times a week). And while women are marginally more likely to eat fruit and vegetables, those who met the 'five-a-day' target accounted for only 32 per cent of the female population. And it does not look as if the next generation is poised to show us couch potatoes a better way: while children remain sportier than the adult population there are still 30 per cent of boys and 41 per cent of girls who do not meet the government's recommended levels of physical activity for two- to fifteen-year-olds. It is the diet of the young that is really worrying, though: only 19 per cent of boys and 22 per cent of girls eat five portions of fruit and vegetables daily.[13]

An unhealthy lifestyle is linked to low income. The poorest sectors of any society have always been more likely to be malnourished. To be malnourished in modern Britain, however, does not mean that a person is underfed, but weighted down with non-nutritious junk. In developed countries there is an inverse relationship between obesity and socio-economic status, among women especially. For example, the prevalence of obesity in women is far lower among managerial and professional households in England (18.7 per cent) than in households with routine or semi-routine occupations (29.1 per cent). The children of low-income families also get less exercise than those of high-income ones. There are ethnic variations, too, that could be genetic but are also certainly environmental and dietary: among women, in England the BMI (Body Mass Index) is markedly higher for those of Black Caribbean ($28.0kg/m^2$) or Black African ($28.8kg/m^2$) origin than in the general population ($26.8kg/m^2$), and markedly lower in Chinese ($23.2kg/m^2$).[14]

In January 2009 the government launched the Change4Life campaign, at a cost of £75 million to the taxpayer, plus a further £200 million drawn-in sponsorship, predominantly from the food and drinks industry. The campaign has womb-to-tomb fat-fighting ambitions that include targeting 'at-risk' pregnant women to promote healthy eating and breastfeeding. In schools, cookery lessons for all eleven- to fourteen-year-olds will be back on the curriculum from 2011; while pupils should by then be benefiting from an increased investment in school meals and sports provision. The government will work with the food and drinks manufacturing industry to promote healthier choices and will work against the proliferation of fast-food outlets near state-supported places including schools. If, however, improvements in national obesity levels have not been noticed within three years, the government has not ruled out introducing more stringent regulations against the food industry. There will be 'healthy towns', apparently, and the nationwide promotion of basic motor skills we might have 'forgotten', such as walking.

The mighty Finns

It is difficult not to be cynical about this profusion of governmental initiatives. But go to the website of the embassy of Finland in London and, under the banner of lifestyle, you will find a proud account of how a government-sponsored public health campaign transformed Finland from one of the world's unhealthiest nations.[15] In the 1970s the combination of a diet rich in saturated fats and an inactive lifestyle had made Finland the coronary heart disease capital of the world. Today obesity is still a problem but it is one that the whole country is aware of and fighting against. By 2005 the number of men dying of heart disease and lung cancer had dropped by at least 65 per cent, while life expectancy had risen by seven years for men and by six years for women. Finland now has Europe's lowest rate of child obesity, suggesting that the lessons of healthy eating are being passed from one generation to the next.[16]

The Finnish authorities achieved this by asking whole communities to work together to quit smoking, curb drinking, reduce intake of butter and salt, and to eat more fresh fruit and vegetables. Villagers ran 'quit and win' competitions for smokers, while towns competed against one another to reduce their cholesterol levels. Meanwhile, everyone was encouraged to exercise more. To ensure inclusiveness, and to make the transformation from being a couch potato more palatable, all forms of exercise from skiing to ball games were made either free or subsidised heavily. From these schemes, a new form of sport – Nordic walking – was developed.[17]

The kind of community health initiatives that are only now being introduced in Britain – amid grumbling that they amount to a nanny-state erosion of civil liberties – have been active in Finland for decades. The Finnish government is involved on a daily basis: parents-to-be are given lessons in nutrition; schools monitor children's weight throughout the year; junk food and sugary drinks are banned from school sites; lessons in nutrition and cookery, and provision of physical activity are core elements of the curriculum. School lunches are free and created under nutritional guidelines. In the universities, workplaces, institutions and hospitals, canteen lunches are subsidised and prepared to nutritionists' specifications. Since the average Finn eats 2.6 meals per week provided by mass catering services, this government-sponsored healthy eating should be hugely beneficial. The government has intervened in agriculture by increasing subsidies to farmers producing healthier crops, such as berries and canola oilseed rape – while dairy subsidies are now decided by protein rather than fat content. Legislation exists to force the fast food industry to adopt clear labelling of high salt contents, though the approach has mostly been 'softly softly', whereby the public health campaign has created a demand for the food industry to come up with more nutritious products.[18]

Some who have studied the Finnish model to see if it could be applied to Britain have expressed scepticism, largely because the more urbanised Britain has a far greater population (60.6 million) than Finland (5.24 million). But those who have studied wartime Britain will see many parallels. Strict government rules were introduced in 1940 to a British population of 48.2 million (1940 statistic). Then, as now, we needed to preserve fuel and to reduce dependency on imported foods. Our wartime coalition government succeeded in doing so through 'fair shares for all' rationing and growing our own food. The results were spectacular. Between 1934 and 1938 two-thirds of the British population's intake of calories and half of its protein supplies had come from imported food. Between 1939 and 1944 food imports were halved from an average of 22 million tons per year to an annual average of between 10.6 and 11.5 million tons between 1942 and 1944.[19]

Britain stood isolated in 1940. By 1945 it also stood stronger thanks to its comprehensive nutritional policies, effectively maintained by the Ministry of Food's huge bureaucracy. Britain ate better and more equally than any other European country involved in the war. The Ministry of Food's nutritionists were responsible for the then radical decision to expand communal eating. They fortified margarine and flour with nutrients, and brought in a vitamin welfare scheme. A diet rich in vegetables, vitamins, milk and slow-energy-releasing carbohydrates, and low in saturated fats, sugars and red meats, improved the strength of bones

Calling all mothers
The right food and good eating habits lay the foundation of health and happiness
THE CHIEF FACTS to remember in feeding children of any age are that, in proportion to their size, children need more of the body-building foods (milk, meat, fish, cheese and eggs, dried milk and dried eggs) than do adults: And to gain their fair chance in life children must have their full rations and allowances. So no giving part of their meat and cheese, for instance, to grown-ups, and no putting their priority milk into the family tea-cups!
Use nearly all the Points coupons in the children's books for foods of body-building and protective value: tinned milk, meats, and fish, peas and beans, dried fruits (including prunes), etc. And—this is equally important—make sure the children have a good helping of green vegetables, either raw in salads or lightly cooked, every day.
FREE LEAFLETS. There is a series of leaflets—just published—which tell the "why's" and "how's" of planning meals for children from 1 to 17 years of age. The leaflets contain recipes as well as many useful hints. Why not send a postcard for those of interest to you? Please ask for "How to plan meals for Children," and be sure to give the ages of your children. Address: Ministry of Food, (Dept 625L.) Food Advice Division, London, W.1.
Do you know . . .
Orange juice alternatives: What to give instead of orange juice when children are no longer on the Green Ration Book.
What to use for sweetening when sugar is short?
How to classify foods making menu-planning easier?
How to introduce good feeding habits without tears?
How to make delicious and nourishing mock cream?
These are just a few of the subjects covered in the "How to plan meals for Children" leaflets. See free offer in paragraph above.
An extra for young workers up to 18:
It is National Milk Cocoa: a grand food and a most delicious drink. Supplies are limited, so for the time being, at any rate, National Milk Cocoa is available only to young people up to 18 years of age, and at their place of work. If your young people are not getting National Milk Cocoa please urge them to ask about it. It is so important for them, and so nice.
ISSUED BY THE MINISTRY OF FOOD

and teeth, and all but eradicated diseases associated with child poverty such as rickets (which was, in June 2008, reported to be again on the rise in Britain[20]). Subsidies for the poorest members of society, specifically targeting expectant mothers and young children, had dealt a blow to the hunger and malnutrition once endemic in the poorer sectors of the country. The 1945 statistics showed the lowest ever rates for infant, child and maternal mortality, along with a reduction in the numbers of still-born babies and of deaths from serious diseases associated with poverty such as typhoid and diphtheria.[21] In nutritional terms the differentials between rich and poor had been eroded, while, crucially, the Ministry of Food's huge powers of propaganda meant that their target audience began to develop an understanding of nutrition – of why potatoes were better for them than sugar and why the carrot was a resourceful kitchen companion.

CHAPTER ONE

GO TO IT:

Towards victory on the kitchen front

*I think the credit-crunch is making everyone have a re-think about how they shop and cook so people are tightening their belts and are becoming much more conscious about waste.**

Gill Holcombe, *Daily Telegraph*, December 2008.

It's not fair to get more than your fair share.

Wartime Ministry of Food advertisement

In September 2008 a girlfriend mentioned that departmental colleagues of hers had started stockpiling tinned foods. We had met, for my hen night, within days of the collapse of the US banking giant, Lehman Brothers. If anyone else at that gathering had promoted panic hoarding we would have fallen about laughing. This friend, however, works as an economic projectionist for one of the few lending institutions that is being predicted to survive this financial crisis relatively unscathed. Her department's role is to map out our economic futures – what on earth were we to make of the fact that her boss was now bean-counting in bulk?

It only takes a bout of baleful weather – such as the flooding in the summer of 2007 that drove 17,000 Britons from their homes – or a shortage of vital items – the strike at Grangemouth oil refinery in April 2008, for example, which held up North Sea oil delivery – to expose the

* Her first book, *How to feed your whole family a healthy balanced diet, with very little money and hardly any time, even if you have a tiny kitchen, only three saucepans (one with an ill-fitting lid) and no fancy gadgets – unless you count the garlic crusher . . .*, became a surprise best-seller in late 2008.

fragility of the chains of supply on which the majority of us are dependent. Were there to be a collapse in either our energy supplies or our banking systems, would our government be able to stop a rapid descent into chaos, characterised by rioting and looting? Well, they would if they had planned for these eventualities with the meticulousness of Britain's pre-wartime government, working on the basis that when supplies are threatened, fairly administered universal rationing is the only guarantee against social insurrection and the only means of securing fair shares for all.

Pre-war

In the 1930s Britain was largely dependent for its nutritional needs on imports: 90 per cent of its cereal grains and fats, about 50 per cent of its meat supplies, 70 per cent of its cheese and sugar, and as much as 80 per cent of its fruit was brought in from overseas. In the by now heavily urbanised and industrialised country what was left of its agricultural land was predominantly for livestock farming – but animal feed was imported. Then, as now, how Britain fed itself was a subject of national debate.

In the early nineteenth century Britain's significantly smaller population had been a largely self-sufficient one, with a diet dominated by bread grains, not least because high duties discouraged food imports. Following the repeal of the Corn Laws in 1846 living standards rose, and food became more affordable due to the freeing up of trade and improvements in transport. These changes powered the workers of the Industrial Revolution, the nineteenth century's population explosion and Britain's rapid urbanisation. Britain drew on the resources of a huge overseas empire. From the mid nineteenth century through to the mid twentieth her citizens benefited from an ever improving and more varied diet, rich in wheat, meat, fats, dairy, fruit, sugar and tinned foods. Refrigeration methods, first pioneered in the meat-packing districts of America's Midwestern cities in the 1920s, made it possible to import even meat in bulk. Refrigeration was to revolutionise freight and storage, and thus the transportation of perishable foodstuffs.

By the outbreak of the Second World War, with the grim years of the Depression and mass unemployment beginning to fade into memory, Britain was, for all but the poor, a land that cherry-picked its foods globally. But those far-sighted enough to plan for the coming war knew that in a period of widespread international upheaval such dependence on imported foods would never be sustainable. In their minds – and the public's collective memory – stalked the spectre of the lean late years of the First World War, when German submarines targeted supply ships in an attempt to starve Britain into surrender. The resultant breakdown in food distribution led to a doubling of some prices and long disgruntled queues for even basic staples such as bread. Anger at the food situation was reported as a principal cause of industrial unrest. And this was resentment that no government could afford to ignore, when at the time their ally, Russia, was losing control to the mob. From June 1917, the government took complete control of imports and home production, and the British civilian population was, according to Sir William Beveridge (of Beveridge Report fame), permanent secretary to the then Ministry of Food, 'catered for like an army'.[1] From 1918 there was rationing of sugar, fats and meat, which continued until 1920. Rationing, if not exactly popular, was perceived as the only sensible means of guaranteeing supplies and ensuring their fair distribution.

The Chamberlain administration (1937–40) followed a political policy of appeasement; but behind the scenes civil servants prepared for war. Beveridge – as one of the architects of the First World War's rationing scheme and author of a volume of the Carnegie Endowment history of that war, *British Food Control* (1929) – was, in 1936, the obvious person to appoint as chairman of a subcommittee of the Committee of Imperial Defence (CID). Asked to investigate rationing and food supplies in times of war, they stressed that rationing would only succeed if the necessary bureaucracy was in place well in advance and if there was a government-guaranteed availability of fair shares for all. Their findings led, in December 1936, to the forming of the Board of Trade Food (Defence Plans) Department, which, on the outbreak of war, was expected to evolve into a Ministry of Food.

The committee took advice from nutritionists and formulated a diet that was to be lower in rationed sugar, meat and fat, but to have a guaranteed buffer of non-rationed native vegetables ('energy foods' such as potatoes, corn and grains). An increase in catering establishments that would remain non-rationed was also suggested.

Nutrition was a new field. Calories had only been discovered in the 1900s; the first vitamins in the 1910s and 1920s, essential amino acids and minerals in the 1930s. It was fortuitous for wartime Britain that not only was it home to some of these pioneer scientists, but that nutritional discoveries had gone hand in hand with a reforming impulse to improve the lot of the poor through diet. In Aberdeen was Sir John Boyd Orr, regarded by many as the founding father of modern nutrition science and among the first to establish a clear link between poverty, poor diet and ill health. The publication of his *Food, Health and Income* (1936), which estimated that the diet of half the UK population was deficient in some nutrients while at least a third were too poor to eat healthily, was to have international repercussions. On the back of it he was asked to mastermind the Carnegie Survey of Diet and Health, which was used as a foundation for food rationing.

Boyd Orr was a veteran of the First World War, who would go on to be awarded the 1949 Nobel Peace Prize for his work in keeping the people of post-war Continental Europe from starvation as a controversial first director general of the United Nations Food and Agriculture Organisation. Like Lord Woolton (the Minister of Food from 1940, who insisted that the British rationing scheme be promoted for its nutritional benefits), Boyd Orr was an educated middle-class man who had seen poverty and hardship for himself. After gaining a first degree from Glasgow University he had taught in that city's slums. This work had soon prompted him to return to the university to study medicine, then biology, despite financial difficulties. On the eve of the First World War he had taken up a post as director of the Rowett Institute, which monitors human and animal nutrition to this day. He served as a medical officer in the trenches and in 1919 was awarded the Military Cross and Distinguished Service Order, before returning to the Rowett to lead its pioneering research.

Boyd Orr and the Rowett Institute (devoted wholly to the war effort between 1939 and 1945) were among those to whom the pre-war planners turned when formulating the nation's rationing scheme. Other key figures were Elsie Widdowson and her scientific partner Robert McCance. Co-authors of a standard text, *The Chemical Composition of Food* (1940), these two were responsible for such innovations as the addition of calcium into bread. Having helped to formulate rationing, they tested their diet by taking a group of young fellow scientists to the Lake District where they all adhered strictly to the programme while energetically hiking and cycling.

After the Munich crisis of September 1938 the pace of pre-war planning for rationing accelerated. In order to increase yields of grains and vegetables the Department of Agriculture first audited Britain's farmland and then, from May 1939, tried to put more of it to active use with the 'Ploughing-up Campaign', which offered farmers the incentive of £2 per acre to plant fields that had been left fallow. The ambition was, in the space of one or two harvests, to reverse the farming trends of the past two centuries and convert the British landscape from being predominantly dedicated to grazing to mostly arable. Meanwhile the Board of Trade Food (Defence Plans) Department was already purchasing additional stocks of food, making logistical plans for transport and storage, and drafting food control legislation. By the summer of 1939 50 million ration books had been printed.

The Ministry of Food

The second Ministry of Food was established by Emergency Powers Act in the first days of the war, to Beveridge's blueprint. At its peak in 1943 it would directly employ 50,000 civil servants, plus a huge force drawn from the ranks of voluntary and charitable bodies such as the Women's Voluntary Services (WVS), Women's Institute (WI) and Salvation Army. These women – they were mostly, but not all, women – ran British restaurants; helped out in canteens; drove soup kitchens;

distributed pies to rural workers, and provided evacuees and the bombed-out with the makings of a meal.

The Ministry's HQ was in central London but it delegated to nineteen Divisional Food Officers (eighteen in Great Britain and one in Ulster), which in turn supervised 1,500 local Food Control Committees made up of representatives of the consumer and the retailer, and appointed by local authorities. Reporting to these committees were about 1,300 Local Food Offices, which would eventually do all the detailed hands-on work of distributing and renewing ration books, licensing food dealers, enforcing orders and supplying extra rations of limited goods such as orange juice and cod liver oil to those happy few designated as 'priority customers'. These Local Food Offices were to be in time the harassed front desk of what one newspaper would bill accurately as 'the biggest shop in the world', with an annual turnover of £600 million. Back at the ministry some offices dealt only with securing supply of a single commodity. The Food Ministry was the sole importer of some basic foodstuffs, with negotiators working all over the world to secure the best prices for huge bulk buys. In Britain itself it was the sole purchaser of livestock for slaughter and milk.

Debates over the introduction of rationing

National registration for rationing began in September 1939. In the course of the following weeks every member of every household in Britain received his or her own ration book. But it was not until November that the government confirmed there would be rationing of bacon and ham (at 4 oz per person per week), butter (4 oz) and sugar (4 oz) from 8 January 1940.

The delay was due to debate. Those who opposed rationing pointed out that the country was not experiencing very many shortages. This was thanks to pre-war stockpiling, a strong harvest the previous year and a record amount of slaughtering in the immediate aftermath of the declaration of war in order to save on animal feed. If the war were to be a speedy one, rationing would be a wasted effort, they argued. This was the period of 'the phoney war' and for most civilians, including members of the Cabinet, the conflict was still being regarded as simply an inconvenience. Only a month after Germany's invasion of Poland a world-weary article in the *Daily Telegraph* was already complaining that instead of the expected 'blitzkrieg', the British people were being bombarded by regulations, exhortations and petty officialdom. The sandbagged civilian population, only just getting the hang of struggling out of bed for another false air raid warning, were already feeling ennui.

But those who argued in favour of rationing saw a bigger picture and were not prepared to take the risk of stretching Britain's chains of food supply to breaking point in a naïve belief that the war would be over within months. Without rationing, its proponents argued, an irregularity in the arrival of one vital supply could spark off panic buying, giving the rich an unfair advantage in terms of stockpiling. One East End grocer claimed, 'The shortages are bringing in the rich people from the West End to take the poor people's food. They come in their cars . . . and buy . . . nightlights and candles, tinned goods, corned beef and that sort of thing . . . they go mad on sugar. I've been rationing sugar for the last three or four days. A good shopkeeper keeps some back for his regular customers.'[2]

But through the autumn of 1939 the Cabinet remained divided between conservative elements who felt that rationing would be a further infringement on civil liberties and those who argued that state control was the only means to ensure fair shares for all. And both branches of opinion found support for their arguments within the national press: '. . . the public should revolt against the food rationing system . . . There is no necessity for the trouble and expense of rationing, merely because there may be a shortage of this or that essential commodity. Why should old women be forced to wait here and there before shops for their supplies? This form of folly is difficult and almost impossible to understand.'[3]

There was further dithering as the Cabinet decided what sort of rationing system Britain should adopt. The choice was between a 'differential scheme' – whether, for example, as happened in wartime Germany, a heavy industrial worker should get a bigger meat ration than a desk worker, or a teenage boy more food than his female sibling – or a 'flat-rate individual' scheme such as the one introduced in Britain during the First World War. The Ministry of Food, working on recommendations from the TUC, advocated against introducing too many different elements, stressing that the difficulties in identifying individual workers would lead to resentments and that such a scheme would be more difficult to administer. They also argued that there was no need for extra rations for individual manual workers since one of the guiding virtues of their proposed scheme was to ensure a guaranteed buffer of non-rationed bread, vegetables and potatoes, and cheap, subsidised or free meals in schools, works canteens and restaurants.

As it turned out, the Cabinet and the right-wing press need not have exercised themselves so strenuously over civil liberties and troubled visions of insurrection. The public, especially those housewives who remembered the severe inflation and shortages of 1917 and 1918, were supportive of rationing, even expressing gratitude for the government's forward planning. The clarity and parity of the scheme became its saving grace and key selling point: all understood the propagandists' argument that fair shares for all meant that a maid-of-all-work would receive the same rations as her mistress. (Though, in reality, the mistress was in a far better position both financially and opportunistically legally to supplement her food stipend with off-ration goods.)

The ration book

In the first wave of food austerity measures there were four variations of ration book: the buff-coloured RB1 (Ration Book One) was issued to everyone aged more than six years old, although that age limit was later reduced to five. Small children received the green RB2, which gave provision for extra milk and preferential treatment for orange juice and oranges, but less meat. At the back of the green ration book there were also the extra allowances for pregnant and nursing mothers. For those

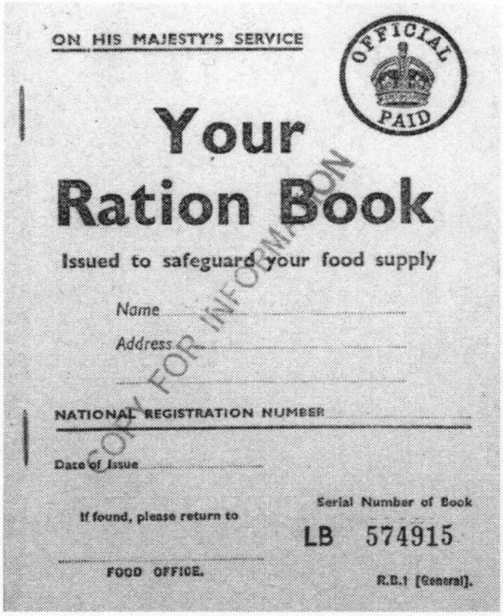

ON HIS MAJESTY'S SERVICE

OFFICIAL PAID

Your Ration Book

Issued to safeguard your food supply

Name

Address

NATIONAL REGISTRATION NUMBER

Date of Issue

If found, please return to

FOOD OFFICE.

Serial Number of Book

LB 574915

R.B.1 [General].

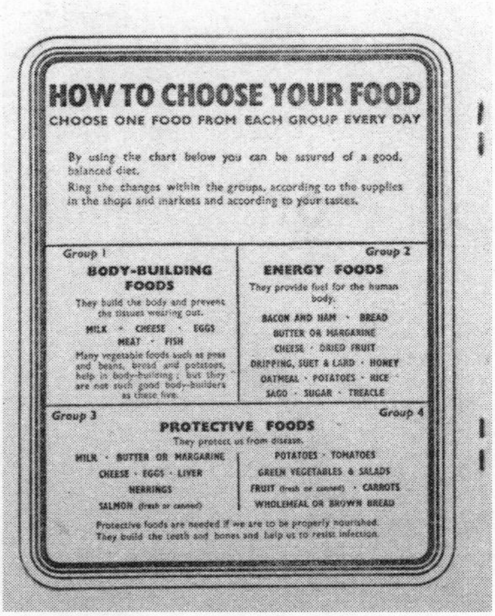

HOW TO CHOOSE YOUR FOOD

CHOOSE ONE FOOD FROM EACH GROUP EVERY DAY

By using the chart below you can be assured of a good, balanced diet.

Ring the changes within the groups, according to the supplies in the shops and markets and according to your tastes.

Group 1

BODY-BUILDING FOODS

They build the body and prevent the tissues wearing out.

MILK · CHEESE · EGGS

MEAT · FISH

Many vegetable foods such as peas and beans, bread and potatoes, help in body-building; but they are not such good body-builders as these five.

Group 2

ENERGY FOODS

They provide fuel for the human body.

BACON AND HAM · BREAD

BUTTER OR MARGARINE

CHEESE · DRIED FRUIT

DRIPPING, SUET & LARD · HONEY

OATMEAL · POTATOES · RICE

SAGO · SUGAR · TREACLE

Group 3 / Group 4

PROTECTIVE FOODS

They protect us from disease.

MILK · BUTTER OR MARGARINE

CHEESE · EGGS · LIVER

HERRINGS

SALMON (fresh or canned)

POTATOES · TOMATOES

GREEN VEGETABLES & SALADS

FRUIT (fresh or canned) · CARROTS

WHOLEMEAL OR BROWN BREAD

Protective foods are needed if we are to be properly nourished. They build the teeth and bones and help us to resist infection.

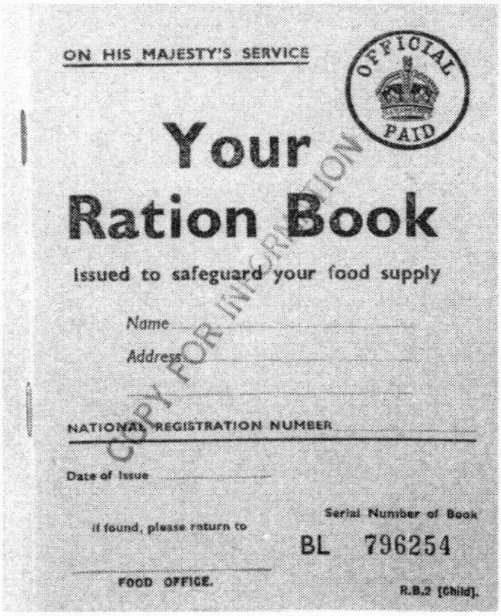

ON HIS MAJESTY'S SERVICE

OFFICIAL PAID

Your Ration Book

Issued to safeguard your food supply

Name

Address

NATIONAL REGISTRATION NUMBER

Date of Issue

If found, please return to

FOOD OFFICE.

Serial Number of Book

BL 796254

R.B.2 [Child].

Ration books were green, beige and white. The clothing ration book was pink.

whose itinerant lifestyles made it impossible to register with a single retailer there were variations on the RB1: the RB3 for travellers and the RB6 for weekly seamen. Finally, from 1943 onwards there was the blue RB4 for those aged five to sixteen (extended in 1944 to eighteen). Each serialised book contained a space for the holder's name and address, and coupons that the shopkeeper would retain in exchange for goods (though later these were replaced by a rubber stamp).

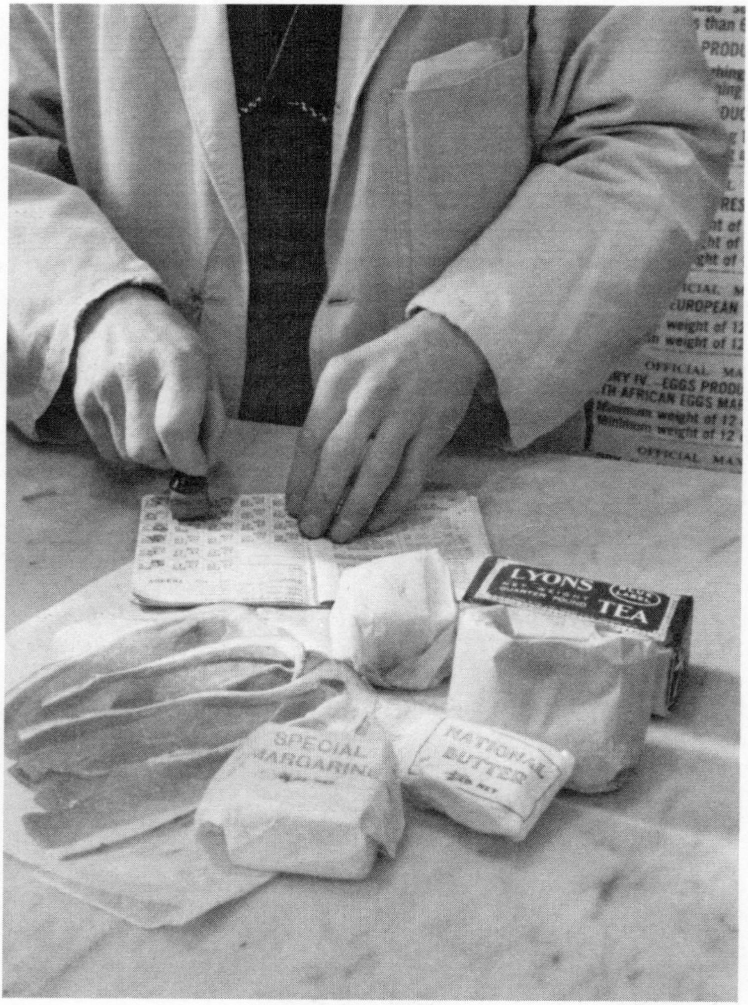

A grocer stamps a ration point.
On the counter, some examples of a weekly ration.

These coupons were for meat, bacon and ham, butter and margarine and cooking fats including lard and dripping, and sugar.

Once rationing was introduced, the choices of the housewife, the shopkeeper and indeed the supplier (the newly established Ministry of Food) were curtailed sharply because of the pressing need to reduce imports. Coveting foreign goods, unless recognised staples, became unpatriotic. The housewife on her regular rounds could no longer exercise choice; she had to elect particular retailers to receive her ration. This was one of the principal tenets of the British scheme and was designed to combat corruption: everyone received his or her full share, but no more. Shops, meanwhile, were only supplied with sufficient supplies of rationed goods to cater for their registered customers. Non-rationed goods could be bought anywhere without the exchange of coupons or a retailer's rubber stamp. However, there was far less choice to be found on the shelves. The concentration of the market into the hands of one supplier (the Ministry of Food) meant that most luxury goods disappeared from the shops for the duration. Many well-known brands gradually vanished too, as the Ministry rationalised stocks: of 350 varieties of biscuits available pre-war, for example, only twenty survived in wartime. Rationed goods such as margarine and bacon were manufactured and distributed by the Ministry, which took over formerly independent wholesalers to create its own goods: MARCOM (margarine), BINDAL (bacon) and, perhaps confusingly, BACAL (butter and cheese).

Most housewives elected to register their households with a small number of shops, which then received their groceries. Meat (at a price not weight value of 1s 10d) was put on the ration from March 1940 and tea (2 oz weekly) and cooking fats (2 oz) from that July. In 1941 rationing was extended to cover cheese (though with vegetarians and agricultural workers getting an extra supply) and preserves. This was the extent of 'straight rationing' as opposed to 'points rationing'. Levels of the actual ration available for products would fluctuate throughout the war depending on supply and inflation – cheese, for example, which started at a meagre 1 oz weekly, increased to 8 oz per week in July 1942, but was reduced to 6 oz, then 4 oz, then 3 oz by May 1943.

Lord Woolton: the popular face of the Ministry of Food

A vast bureaucracy interfering in people's lives in the most intimate way on a day-to-day basis needs a human face. From April 1940 the Ministry of Food was, in the general public's mind, embodied in the figure of Frederick James Marquis, the first Baron Woolton, better known as Lord Woolton.

The Ministry's success, in asking for so much forbearance from so many, was in no small part due to this middle-aged – he was fifty-eight when he arrived at the Ministry of Food – yet dynamic figure. When Churchill took over as Prime Minister in 1940 he confided to his cronies, 'We shall have to be ready with a rescue squad for Woolton.' As it transpired, Woolton twice rescued Churchill (in 1943 by agreeing to become Minister of Reconstruction, despite his misgivings, and as Party Chairman in the post-war period). After Churchill's return to power in 1951, Woolton served in his Cabinet for four years.

'A cheerful cove' according to Geoffrey Dawson, wartime editor of *The Times*, Woolton was an accidental rather than a career politician; a man of the people rather than a patrician; one whose educational background was Manchester Grammar School and his local red-brick university, rather than Eton and Oxbridge. He hailed from the Midlands rather than the south and had a background in an entrepreneurial business environment, and before that in social welfare. It was his most recent experience in retail that had initially recommended him to the government. During the inter-war years he had built up the Midlands department store chain Lewis's (not to be confused with John Lewis), for its owners, a Liverpool-based Jewish family, the Cohens. This gave him an understanding of markets, consumer trends and the logistics of retail – and also of the absolute need to keep the customer onside.

There was, however, an implicit irony in his being at the helm of so protectionist an organisation. At Lewis's he had been a pioneering, market-liberalising retailer, the Sir Terry Leahy or Philip Green of his day.

During a fact-finding trip to America in the aftermath of the First World War he had taken inspiration from the competitive agility of that market. And on his return he had introduced cheap, ready-to-wear, fashionable frocks to the British market in what must be seen as a forerunner of today's Primarks and Topshops. On the food front he had endeavoured to bring his customers a wider choice at more competitive prices by buying from abroad: he undercut the prices charged by British egg farmers by shipping eggs from as far afield as China; while British bacon manufacturers were forced to raise their game after his shops offered customers cheaper bacon sourced from Poland as well as superior, if more expensive, cuts from Denmark.

In peacetime he had made buying British the housewife's choice. But as war approached he took a more politicised, protectionist stance. In 1938, shocked by the situation in Germany – not least the sudden change in circumstances of many of Lewis's Jewish-German suppliers – he led a national boycott, telling all his sales managers that they were to sell off their German stocks quickly and then cease to trade with that country. His memoirs recall:

> It was what the public wanted . . . a means of expressing their emotion . . . It was not long before people were coming into the stores and asking if the goods they were considering buying were German; they were prepared to pay more for British goods and many other retailers followed the same line of policy. For the first time, people were given the opportunity of registering a protest in a form that the Germans, apart from their Government, would understand. They did – and they were very angry about it, and months afterwards 'Lord Haw-Haw' threatened that Lewis's stores would be bombed out of existence . . . our lead was taken up not only here, but in the Dominions and the United States.[4]

With what today might be seen as a background incompatible with big business, Woolton had earlier worked as a teacher in a northern industrial town, then a social worker in Liverpool's slums. His financial acumen informed the practical side of his wartime work, while his personal

Lord Woolton accepts a cup of tea from a mobile canteen.

experiences of helping the poor laid the foundations for the paternalistic side of the Ministry of Food. As a young man, working in a hostel in Liverpool's docklands, Woolton had been deeply shocked by the fate of a woman neighbour who had fallen on hard times – she had died from starvation. Since then he had taken a passionate interest in nutrition and child welfare. He and his wife had raised funds to establish Liverpool's first free pregnancy clinic and dentistry service. As he writes in his memoirs:

> It was this early experience in a poverty-ridden district of Liverpool that gave me the stimulus to use the powers of a war-time Ministry of Food to make provisions for the health of children which I believe now to be a permanent part of our national life. . . . I determined to use the powers I possessed to stamp out the diseases that arose from malnutrition, especially those among children, such as rickets. The health of the children today is the reward of that policy.[5]

Thus Woolton arrived at the Ministry of Food in 1940 with a determination that his department would not only be a model of cost-effective efficiency, but also powered by a reforming zeal. He suggested that a sign be put above the main entrance saying 'We not only cope, we care'. His interest in nutrition meant that his first question on being appointed to the ministry was to ask who his scientific adviser was. From then on he worked closely with Professor Jack Drummond, the biochemist whose dramatic death* has since overshadowed his lifetime's achievements. Drummond, like Woolton, was a wartime draftee to government. He helmed the Ministry of Food's science unit, but in guiding the formulation of a ration scheme to keep Britain's Home Front fighting fit he drew not only on his knowledge but also on the experimentation and indeed goodwill of fellow scientists now regarded as pioneers in the field of dietetics. One of their influences on the formulation of wartime national food policy was to take heed of the then newfangled, but now commonplace, idea of differing needs. As Woolton later put it, 'With this highly skilled advice of widely different approach, we worked out a diet for the nation that would supply all the calories and all the vitamins that were needed for the different age groups, for the fighting services, for the heavy manual workers, for the ordinary housewife, for the babies and the children, and for pregnant and nursing mothers. That was large-scale and all-embracing planning.'[6]

Subsidies were put in place to ensure that those in most nutritional need, termed 'priority classes', got preferential treatment. So the first sign to the outside world that a woman might be pregnant would probably not – as it is today – be that she was no longer knocking back booze, but that she was taking delivery of more milk or being allowed orange juice.

* In the 1950s he became the victim, along with his wife and young daughter, of one of France's most notorious unsolved murders.

Variations to the ration

Among the first to complain of being badly served by the basic ration were those who did not eat meat. Vegetarianism had been a growing trend in the 1930s, but Adolf Hitler was a vegetarian and this was poor PR for non-carnivores. Nevertheless, the government listened. Britain's 500,000 vegetarians were able to register for a special supplementary ration of cheese, nuts and usually an extra egg a week, in lieu of a meat ration. Jews and Muslims could exchange their bacon and ham ration for extra cheese, though Orthodox Jews were never able to insist on kosher cheese because the bureaucrats worried that such a level of specialist catering might fuel anti-Semitism. Kitchen propaganda, meanwhile, often encouraged cheap, healthy vegetarian fare.

The Ministry found it more vexing to decide how to feed industrial workers. Having rejected the German method of differentiating between different classes of workers as too bureaucratically cumbersome and liable to provoke discontent, it was decided that some heavy workers should receive a larger cheese ration, while others, such as miners, would benefit from government-sponsored on-site canteens providing a solid lunch. Agricultural labourers in the field, for whom canteens were impractical, were given extra cheese and in some areas benefited from the Rural Pie Scheme, launched in 1942 and administered by the WVS. Pies, each containing a pennyworth of meat (or sandwiches if time and shortages were biting), would be prepared by a village baker or else by some Samaritan familiar with shortcrust techniques, then distributed by volunteers to workers in the field. At the peak of its popularity the scheme accounted for more than 1.25 million snacks being distributed weekly from around 5,000 villages.

The luckiest beneficiaries of extra rations were pregnant and nursing mothers, babies and small children. And soon the public health benefit of this was seen in declining infant mortality rates and stillborn births, and in the virtual eradication of diseases associated with child poverty, such as rickets. Generous means-tested subsidies ensured that even the poorest benefited and this narrowed the nutritional gap between different classes. For too many the previous decade had indeed been 'the hungry Thirties'. In the 1940s children from even the poorest classes were drinking as much milk as middle-class children had in the 1930s. Today's public health administrators could only dream of such improvements in so short a time.

It helped those at the ministry with a socially minded agenda that they had the ear of the minister in charge. Woolton took a great personal interest in the nutritional welfare of future generations. Indeed, he later wrote: '. . . it became one of the more ribald jokes of the department to say that they could get anything out of the Minister if it was for the ladies whom they disrespectfully described as "the preggies"'.[7] After his scientific advisers told him that milk, fruit juices, cod liver oil, halibut oil and eggs were the principal special foods required by pregnant women, nursing mothers and infants, he gave them the first right to these limited supplies. In order to secure sufficient fruit and fruit syrups for Britain's future generations, Woolton made a personal appeal to the fruit growers of the United States to supply oranges. These were then converted into juice by Boots the Chemist at a most 'patriotic' price.[8]

The largesse of the ministry when it came to the priority groups could cause resentment. For some, milk was a particularly sore point. During much of the war the adult RB1 allowance was between two and three pints per week. In the same period, however, a pregnant woman could benefit from a pint of milk a day, a baby in its first year from a pint a day (this presumably has much to do with fashions in breastfeeding) and a young child from between three to seven pints weekly, to be consumed at home or through free school milk. In households where people were not keeping their own chickens, eggs were similarly controversial. Whereas a pregnant mother or small toddler might expect as many as three eggs a week, an older sibling would be lucky to see a shell egg from one month to the next. Adults grumbled about having to stand by and watch small children squander foodstuffs, but when they came crying to the ministry about spilt milk, Woolton sought reassurance from Lord Horder, the King's physician. Horder told him that while milk was essential for the young, it was possibly even detrimental to the old. Thus the policies stuck.

In time the milk and juice lobby was, however, buoyed by the PR gained from those serving in the Armed Forces. The ministry received many letters of thanks from soldiers who had left their families at home and were relieved that they were being looked after. Most letters were addressed directly to Woolton. Indeed, as he recollected jauntily in his memoirs: 'Not a few of their wives sent me photographs of their babies, apparently bursting with food and good health. But it was thoughtless of so many to write on the photograph "One of Lord Woolton's babies"! What a joy they were to my private secretaries!'[9]

Logistics of food distribution

Though it was Woolton's proudest achievement of the wartime period that never once did he and his ministry fail to deliver the ration, they sometimes came perilously close. His negotiators showed a brand of international derring-do that would have impressed James Bond. In office, Woolton took inspiration from a book he had read to his children, written by General Jack Seeley, later Lord Mottistone, called *Fear – And Be Slain*. At one point when the country's wheat supplies were running low he secretly instructed a colleague, James Rank – who, like him, was a civilian recruited from business – to buy up options on the world's wheat markets without revealing that he was purchasing for the British government, for to have done so would have raised the price exponentially. Rank followed instructions; then, some weeks later, came to Woolton to say that he was ready to complete the transaction and would need £100 million in dollars by 3 p.m. that very afternoon. Woolton, who had done nothing to secure the currency, telephoned the Chancellor of the Exchequer, who angrily refused to help, rebuking Woolton for flouting usual Cabinet procedure. Woolton replied,

> 'I will not write a paper about a commercial transaction of this magnitude; it would be impossible to keep it secret and the loss to the Treasury would not be less than twenty millions if the markets knew

> what was happening.' He asked me if this was the way I normally conducted my business affairs: I told him it was. He then asked me what responsibility I expected him to carry: I told him none except to tell me whether the dollars would be available. In short I was using him as a banker . . .[10]

After some toing and froing Sir Kingsley Wood grudgingly agreed to underwrite the deal within an hour of Rank's deadline. The deal was done. At 4 p.m. Woolton went to Wood's office to apologise and explain what he and Rank had been doing, and at what saving to the British government.

> We had bought all the wheat that this country would want for six months, at a price of seventy-two cents a bushel, and I said to him – prophetically, but unhappily – 'and you will never live to see wheat at seventy-two cents again.' . . . I assured him that if anybody had known that it was the British Government that was buying, we would have had to pay a much higher price, that it had been bought under every possible sort of disguise . . .[11]

A similar moment of brinkmanship occurred with the Ministry of Food's speculation on the world's meat markets. The Argentinians, knowing they had a stranglehold on meat supplies, falsely pushed the prices up in an attempt to bully the British into paying more. Woolton refused to play ball and instead rerouted British shipping through Australia and New Zealand. After months of bluffing it out, the now-troubled Argentinian government were forced to offer supplies at a more competitive price.

To rule the waves had never been more important to Britain, which, despite the success of its austerity measures, still required almost a million tons of food and materials to be delivered each week. The Axis was targeting civilian and military supplies. An intensification of U-boat attacks had, by May 1941, led to the loss of 142 Allied merchant ships, while air attacks had sunk 179. In what Churchill named the Battle of the Atlantic, the Allied sea forces did not gain the upper hand until May 1943, by which point various technological developments, including sonar, had given the British the advantage. Meanwhile, Britain's fight to control the seas had cost the lives of 30,248 merchant sailors and seen the sinking of 3,500 merchant vessels and 175 Allied warships.

Woolton would later claim that finding cargo space posed almost as great a problem as the U-boats. Many British ships had been converted to war, others signed over to bring in war supplies. On the few remaining vessels the Ministry of Food could afford only to license shipping space for staple foodstuffs. So, because it would have been illogical to transport water through perilous seas, it ruled against importing much fresh or tinned fruit and instead drained it at source and imported dried fruit. Since there was a huge pressure on refrigerated shipping space, meat carcasses were deboned in the southern hemisphere and then telescoped, to save on space and weight. 'Many are the housewives who were brought up in those years who never knew what parts of the animal they were buying,'[12] Woolton was to recall cheerfully, without speculating what a knock-on effect this might have had on the standards of post-war British cooking.

For those ships that made the journeys the seas were dangerous. In the course of two hours on one Friday afternoon the ministry received five separate signals from the Admiralty informing them that food ships had been sunk in the Atlantic. It was an unhappy coincidence that the cargo of all of these ships was predominantly made up of bacon. The Ministry's priority was to ensure that the ration was fulfilled. Several warehouses full of bacon in the Liverpool area, which had been intended to supply Lancashire for the month ahead, were reallocated across the country. 'As the one solitary ship that had bacon on board came in to the port of Liverpool, a special squad of men was charged to bring off the bacon with all speed, load it into lorries and send it straight off into distribution. We honoured the ration, but it was a near thing.'[13]

A special department checked the arrival time in every port of all vessels carrying food. Any delay was queried. Yet even when imported food succeeded in making its way through the submarine-infested waters to Britain, it was not safe in harbour. For obvious reasons most warehouses had been built on sites near ports, but these soon came under air attack from the Luftwaffe. The bombing depleted the country's stocks of refrigerated meat stored in dockland cold storage. The ministry persuaded the Treasury that the solution was to fund the building of cold storage and grain warehouse units – some underground – in eight different remote and thus, theoretically, safe parts of the country, which would be better protected from attack.

Lend-Lease

Of course, one of the greatest boosts to British supplies during the Second World War was American Lend-Lease. By the terms of the loan – for which Britain made its last repayment of $83.3 million (then £42.5 million) on 29 December 2006 – the US government shipped food and military supplies to Britain and other Allied powers in exchange for deferred dollar repayment and the use of territories for military purposes. Later there would be bitter resentment in Britain at the American government's abrupt and unexpected termination of Lend-Lease in August 1945 and at the United Kingdom's decades of indenture to the new world superpower. It is undeniable, however, that when supplies first started arriving in May 1941 they were a lifesaver. In the next four years Britain was to benefit from $31.4 million worth of goods (which, at today's prices, would be the equivalent of at least $400 billion). And crucially,

Lend-Lease solved the problem of Britain paying for goods at a time when its government had actually run out of dollars. Without the US policy piloted by Roosevelt, food would have had to be imported from further afield at greater risk to shipping and at no business advantage to the Allies.

When the first consignment arrived in the UK on 31 May 1941, Woolton went along with Roosevelt's personal representative to the UK, Averell Harriman, to greet the ship. Woolton later wrote, 'He formally transferred the cargo to me. It was four million eggs, one hundred and twenty thousand pounds of cheese, and one thousand tons of flour. To celebrate, I broke my own regulations – and handed over, for division amongst the unloading staff of two hundred and forty, a twenty pound cheese.'[14]

CHAPTER TWO

WISE EATING IN WARTIME

There is only so much a government can do for its people. 'Move! Live!' is the message of New Labour's latest expensive campaign directed at its dissolute and feckless electorate. Next there will be continual television adverts urging us 'Breathe in, you useless monkeys! Now breathe out! Now breathe in again!' They think that without their help, we will all die, suffocated beneath a brown mountain of fast food, our poor arteries clogged and our guts about to burst. They want us to eat less. The campaign, unveiled with great cruelty on January 2 . . . is called Change4Life. The mere presence of that numeral in the middle made me want to head for McDonald's and order a triple cardiobypassburger with cheese and extra fries – but hell, kowtowing to the most cretinous aspects of our culture is seen as obligatory by politicians of all parties, so one shouldn't be too hard on the government.

Rod Liddle, *Sunday Times*, 4 January 2009

Appetite is a good guide to our needs . . . and if we take more than we require, we generally store the surplus as fat.

Cautionary note from the Ministry of Food's leaflet 'Foods for Fitness: An ABC of Choosing Foods'

Does a surveillance culture undermine our freedom of movement? We feel as worried as we are comforted by CCTV cameras, credit reference agencies and security forces; by the vigilance of our employers; by snooping, whistle-blowing and even delving through our rubbish. Such measures have, some claim, made us the most watched country in the West. 'Nanny state policies' are called for, and then repulsed as an abuse of basic liberties.

There was no more nannying a state than the one that thrived during the Second World War. The degree to which the wartime government involved itself in even the most finite details of day-to-day existence – how

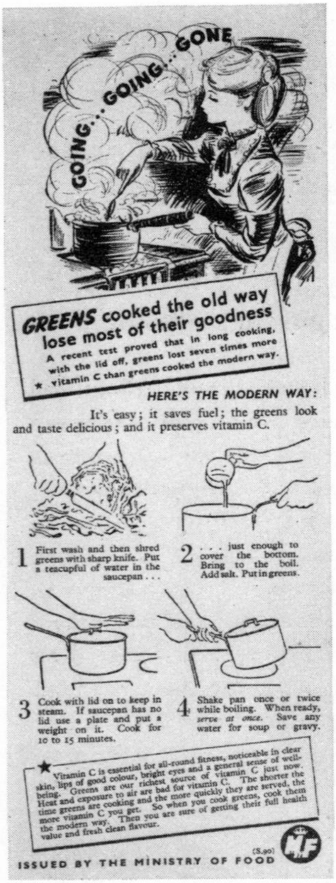
GOING... GOING... GONE
GREENS cooked the old way lose most of their goodness
A recent test proved that in long cooking, with the lid off, greens lost seven times more ★ vitamin C than greens cooked the modern way.
HERE'S THE MODERN WAY:
It's easy; it saves fuel; the greens look and taste delicious; and it preserves vitamin C.
1 First wash and then shred greens with sharp knife. Put a teacupful of water in the saucepan . . .
2 . . . just enough to cover the bottom. Bring to the boil. Add salt. Put in greens.
3 Cook with lid on to keep in steam. If saucepan has no lid use a plate and put a weight on it. Cook for 10 to 15 minutes.
4 Shake pan once or twice while boiling. When ready, serve at once. Save any water for soup or gravy.
★ Vitamin C is essential for all-round fitness, noticeable in clear skin, lips of good colour, bright eyes and a general sense of well-being. Greens are our richest source of vitamin C just now. Heat and exposure to air are bad for vitamin C. The shorter the time greens are cooking and the more quickly they are served, the more vitamin C you get. So when you cook greens, cook them the modern way. Then you are sure of getting their full health value and fresh clean flavour.
(S.90)
ISSUED BY THE MINISTRY OF FOOD
MF

to cook vegetables, say, or manage your washday – was extraordinary. Take cakes: in 1941 the Ministry of Food issued a regulation against cake icing, which also decreed that in icing's stead only one layer of either chocolate or jam would be permissible as a cake topping. People adapted their party food accordingly. Indeed, this edict had a surreal follow-up story: in October 1942 the popular press reported that cardboard wedding cakes with icing made from chalk or fabric were now available for hire and display.

Why didn't our forebears rebel? They did, of course. But only when Britain was no longer threatened. The quintessential post-war novel is George Orwell's *Nineteen Eighty-Four*, written in 1948, published in 1949, with its portrait of a downtrodden, grey London and its grim warning against a state-controlled and monitored society, chivvied into obedience by coercive propaganda. But Orwell had earlier written the equally quintessential account of the British spirit under attack, *The Lion and the Unicorn* (1941), in which he observed, 'England is . . . a land of snobbery and privilege, ruled largely by the old and silly. But in any calculation about it one has got to take into account its emotional unity, the tendency of nearly all its inhabitants to feel alike and act together in moments of supreme crisis.'[1]

And so, at a time of supreme crisis, the British accepted the guidance of the wartime coalition government's Big Brothers. These Big Brothers were not what we have come to regard as strictly 'Orwellian', but rather trustworthy, supportive, almost avuncular elder siblings, who had the public's best interests at heart. But it wasn't just an accepting faith in the authorities that made the majority of Britons obey a vast number of restrictions on their day-to-day consumption. That they did so with a grumble but without rebelliousness is surely down to the fact that self-sacrifice was 'sold' to them with immense chutzpah.

The kitchen is the key to victory: Lord Woolton and the Ministry of Food's propaganda machine

Woolton (nicknamed 'Uncle Fred' by ministry underlings) had an innate sense of how to sweeten a bitter pill. He was a showman but the showmanship was based on a retailer's knowledge of a housewife's hopes and needs: if lemons were to appear at all it would be just before Shrove Tuesday, while the ministry would try to get dried fruit into the shops in the run-up to Christmas. He had the empathetic intelligence to grasp that it would not be enough simply to administer austerity with rigorous efficiency; he saw himself as a crusading general in a battle for hearts and minds. When he first toured his new ministerial department, he immediately discovered that '. . . it was suffering from a general depression. The press was against them and they were dejected, and frankly puzzled, by their unpopularity'.[2] So Woolton invited the King to visit the ministry in the hope that the monarch's public recognition of the vital work being undertaken there would boost morale.

He next launched a charm offensive on the press. He had dabbled in journalism himself and therefore had some understanding both of the workings of the media and of how frustrating it is for a reporter to feel he is being fobbed off with partial information instead of being given the full story. Woolton invited Fleet Street's editors and home correspondents to a meeting at which he assured them that he would always deal as honestly with them as was within his power – that his only reason for refusing to answer a question would be on grounds of national security. He asked them to show him and his department the same respect. Soon afterwards he gave his first press conference on the subject of waste avoidance:

> I was fortunate in managing to use one or two homely phrases that pleased my audience: I appealed to the women of Britain to 'mobilise themselves on the Kitchen Front', to use their skill to make use of what was available and to avoid the more comfortable habits of peace-time. I was so kindly received, both by the public and the Press . . . I sensed that if I could so administer the department as to keep the public reasonably informed as to the reason for my actions, they, in turn, would give me the support that was essential for my success.[3]

He broadcast regularly, spending hours at a desk in his shirtsleeves fine-tuning his radio speeches. He encouraged the public to write to the Ministry of Food with problems, ideas and praise, and he answered much of the correspondence himself.

Wartime celebrity chefs

The only time when radio listening figures trounce television viewing ones is 8.15 in the morning, hence it is known to radio broadcasters as the most important point of the day. On BBC Radio 4's agenda-setting *Today* programme it is the time slot reserved for the day's key interview. During the Second World War 8.15 was when the *Kitchen Front* radio programme went out for five minutes daily, 'before the housewife sets out to do her shopping'. Usually presented by either the cookery writer Ambrose Heath or the popular broadcaster Freddie Grisewood (known affectionately as 'Ricepud'), it attracted up to 14 million listeners, significantly more than any other daytime talk programme. In the first week alone the BBC received 1,000 letters, along with parcels of cake and other gifts from housewives responding to its tips.

Its contributors included Marguerite Patten, a food writer still popular today, and Woolton himself, who in his occasional visits to the studio of the *Kitchen Front* sometimes sparred with 'Gert and Daisy' (Elsie

A compendium of recipes by celebrity chefs.
For the radio's popular *Kitchen Front* programme.

and Doris Waters). These Cockney sisters, part of a theatrical dynasty as the siblings of Jack Warner of *Dixon of Dock Green* fame, were, at the outbreak of war, already the biggest female double act in British comedy – the French and Saunders of their day. Headliners on the music hall circuit, they were radio stars on the Light Programme's *Workers' Playtime* as well as the *Kitchen Front*. Their characters, Gert and Daisy, were a pair of sensible but sparky charladies able to cope with whatever life threw at them. Their first piece of cheery propaganda was a series of routines to promote the Ministry of Food's 'Feed the Beast' Economy Campaign, in which they extolled using up leftovers, eulogised greens and gave tips on how to save fuel and stretch – or even leave out – your meat ration, while still producing a satisfying meal. For Christmas 1941 they presented 'murkey', stuffed mutton, to replace hard-to-come-by turkey. Daisy recommended that for the stuffing 'you use your imagination'. Gert responded, 'Do you get that at the butcher's too?' This might fall flat on the page sixty-eight years later, but in the dark days of war Gert and Daisy were a huge hit with women whose struggles at the stove they represented with a humorous, can-do, but never patronising attitude. Within a fortnight of their first broadcast, 30,000 listeners had written in for their recipes.

Another regular on the *Kitchen Front*, and a man in fact obsessed with regularity, was Dr Charles Hill, aka the 'Radio Doctor', 'with the greatest number of patients in the world'. His comments about bowel movements shocked those listeners who found him unnecessarily vulgar. Pastiches of his exhortations to 'visit the throne at the same time each day' were enjoyed on the variety circuit. Immediately after Christmas 1940 he commented, 'Another of Boxing Day's little troubles is constipation. Too much food and too much arm-chair and the body's reply is: "What I have I hold."' When he spoke of 'that humble black-coated worker', some listeners must have sat aghast in anticipation – he was referring to the prune. Most of them, however, relished his robust good sense and the clarity with which he explained how ingestion related to nutrition and digestion. He advocated such freely available foods as dandelion leaf as a salad vegetable, dismissed sugar as a 'menace' and exploited his position to launch several attacks on British cooking habits. He railed against the 'assassination' of vegetables by over-boiling and rejoiced that the traditional British Sunday roast joint was so hard to procure in wartime ('Hot on Sunday – cold on Monday – and if there's anything left, hashed or murdered on Tuesday').

The recipes broadcast on the *Kitchen Front* radio programme were developed in the Ministry of Food's Portman Square kitchens, minutes from Broadcasting House. There they produced a regular supply of pamphlets incorporating recipes, top tips and stern warnings.

> Grow fit . . . not fat on your war diet! Cut out 'extras'; cut out waste; don't eat more than you need. You'll save yourself money; you'll save valuable cargo space which is needed for munitions and you'll feel fitter than you ever felt before.

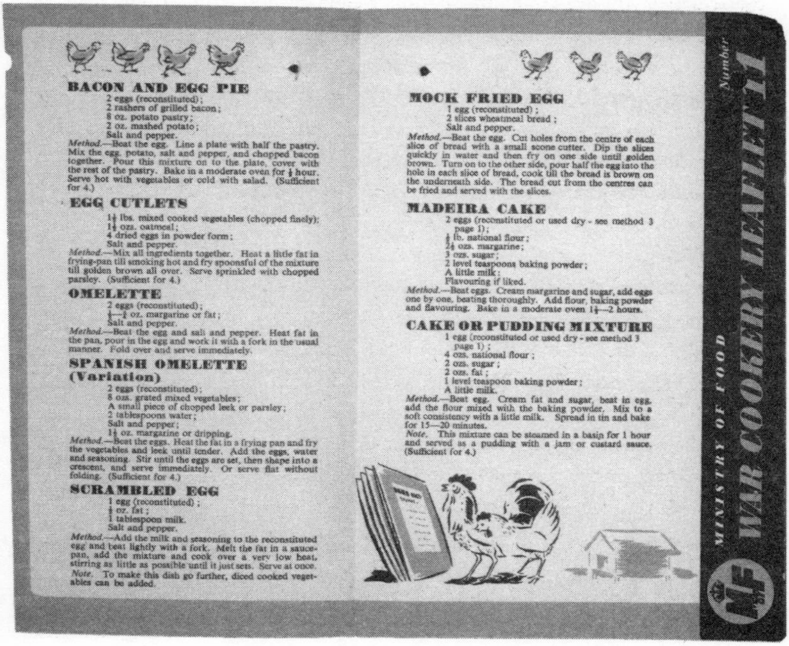

BACON AND EGG PIE

2 eggs (reconstituted);
2 rashers of grilled bacon;
8 oz. potato pastry;
2 oz. mashed potato;
Salt and pepper.

Method.—Beat the egg. Line a plate with half the pastry. Mix the egg, potato, salt and pepper, and chopped bacon together. Pour this mixture on to the plate, cover with the rest of the pastry. Bake in a moderate oven for ½ hour. Serve hot with vegetables or cold with salad. (Sufficient for 4.)

EGG CUTLETS

1½ lbs. mixed cooked vegetables (chopped finely);
1½ ozs. oatmeal;
4 dried eggs in powder form;
Salt and pepper.

Method.—Mix all ingredients together. Heat a little fat in frying-pan till smoking hot and fry spoonsful of the mixture till golden brown all over. Serve sprinkled with chopped parsley. (Sufficient for 4.)

OMELETTE

2 eggs (reconstituted);
¼—½ oz. margarine or fat;
Salt and pepper.

Method.—Beat the egg and salt and pepper. Heat fat in the pan, pour in the egg and work it with a fork in the usual manner. Fold over and serve immediately.

SPANISH OMELETTE (Variation)

2 eggs (reconstituted);
8 ozs. grated mixed vegetables;
A small piece of chopped leek or parsley;
2 tablespoons water;
Salt and pepper;
1½ oz. margarine or dripping.

Method.—Beat the eggs. Heat the fat in a frying pan and fry the vegetables and leek until tender. Add the eggs, water and seasoning. Stir until the eggs are set, then shape into a crescent, and serve immediately. Or serve flat without folding. (Sufficient for 4.)

SCRAMBLED EGG

1 egg (reconstituted);
½ oz. fat;
1 tablespoon milk.
Salt and pepper.

Method.—Add the milk and seasoning to the reconstituted egg and beat lightly with a fork. Melt the fat in a saucepan, add the mixture and cook over a very low heat, stirring as little as possible until it just sets. Serve at once.
Note. To make this dish go further, diced cooked vegetables can be added.

MOCK FRIED EGG

1 egg (reconstituted);
2 slices wheatmeal bread;
Salt and pepper.

Method.—Beat the egg. Cut holes from the centre of each slice of bread with a small scone cutter. Dip the slices quickly in water and then fry on one side until golden brown. Turn on to the other side, pour half the egg into the hole in each slice of bread, cook till the bread is brown on the underneath side. The bread cut from the centres can be fried and served with the slices.

MADEIRA CAKE

2 eggs (reconstituted or used dry - see method 3 page 1);
½ lb. national flour;
2½ ozs. margarine;
3 ozs. sugar;
2 level teaspoons baking powder;
A little milk;
Flavouring if liked.

Method.—Beat eggs. Cream margarine and sugar, add eggs one by one, beating thoroughly. Add flour, baking powder and flavouring. Bake in a moderate oven 1½—2 hours.

CAKE OR PUDDING MIXTURE

1 egg (reconstituted or used dry - see method 3 page 1);
4 ozs. national flour;
2 ozs. sugar;
2 ozs. fat;
1 level teaspoon baking powder;
A little milk.

Method.—Beat egg. Cream fat and sugar, beat in egg, add the flour mixed with the baking powder. Mix to a soft consistency with a little milk. Spread in tin and bake for 15—20 minutes.
Note. This mixture can be steamed in a basin for 1 hour and served as a pudding with a jam or custard sauce. (Sufficient for 4.)

MINISTRY OF FOOD
WAR COOKERY LEAFLET Number 11

The imaginations of these kitchen workers – who, incidentally, included Eileen Blair, George Orwell's first wife – were fed by a continual dialogue with the public who sent in requests for advice as well as their own tips, recipes and food parcels. A few of those recipes may today read like a joke, such as the one for Blitz Broth (dust and plaster optional), but the inventive 'mock' dishes were all too practical. At the outbreak of war many people did not know how to cook. Wealthier women had never before lifted a finger in the kitchen. Others were ignorant of science and nutrition. The ministry explained which foods were 'body-building' or 'protective' or 'gave you energy'. It also instructed everyone – even competent cooks – in the new arts of preparing and cooking wartime exotica such as spam and whale meat.

Sausages were off-ration (their ingredients and contents the subject of much ribald humour) and women were taught how to make Toad in the Hole, with sausages and dried egg powder. They were encouraged to experiment freely with off-ration meats such as offals and rabbit, which could be flavoured with herbs from hedgerows and slow-cooked for hours in an oven preparing several meals at once, thus minimising the use of fuel while maximising flavour. Women were also taught how to cook over open fires, while the WI organised cookery demonstrations.

The ministry's cookery leaflets ranged freely from No. 1 (suggestions on cooking with oatmeal) through to No. 27 with its tips on drying and salting. Pamphlets in between explained how to stretch the sugar ration to make jam; how to can tomatoes and where to find what vitamins. Others advocated a salad a day throughout the year; championed herring as the king of fish, made suggestions for 'What's Left in the Larder' and demonstrated how to cook cuts of meat. Most of these recipes would still have some relevance to home cooks today – especially the ones looking to cook more economically, environmentally and fuel-efficiently. And many of the dishes, for those adherents to British revivalist cookery – with its championing of traditional puddings, seasonal native vegetables and cheaper 'forgotten' cuts of meat and fish – are even fashionable.

A multimedia approach

At the cinema, there were 'Food Flashes' whose advice ranged from the threatening ('Food is a munition of war. Don't waste it') to the chiding ('It's not clever to get more than your fair share') through to the praising ('Carry on Fighters on the Kitchen Front. You are doing a great job'). Meanwhile newspapers charted the national obsession with supplies and passed on advice from the Ministry of Food billed as 'Food Facts'; they also carried advertisements from the manufacturers of products such as Bovril or Horlicks, which had been allowed to remain in production because of their energy-giving properties. Many newspapers, such as the *Daily Express* and the *Daily Telegraph*, also produced their own recipes and ultimately recipe books. Women's magazines were fully signed up to the propaganda war. A chunk of the editorial space in each issue of *Woman's Own*, *Woman's Journal*, *The Lady*, *Mother and Baby*, *Good Housekeeping*, even *Vogue* was devoted to keeping up home morale in your kitchen – or your drawing room, should you have successfully retained any staff. And meanwhile enterprises such as the Good Housekeeping Institute flourished.

Dr Carrot and Potato Pete

Those that have the will to win
Cook potatoes in their skin
Knowing that the sight of peelings
Deeply hurts Lord Woolton's feelings.

Wartime Ministry of Food advertisement

When, in 2009, the British government launched their £75 million Change4Life campaign they did so with a cartoon television advertisement commissioned from Nick Park's Aardman Animations. Similarly, Woolton was often assisted by cartoon figures, most of which – including the fretting Mrs Doubtful, the obtuse Mrs Simple or the exemplary Mrs Lightfoot ('works in a factory all day . . . doing her bit . . . but even in wartime conditions is seldom tired, never ill, never nervy on account of eating potatoes and carrots every single day') – are now largely forgotten. But Dr Carrot and Potato Pete are remembered by those who were children during the war. These two starred in their own poster campaigns, fronted recipe books, inspired doggerel and even had popular nursery rhymes adapted to accommodate their mythical status.

Potatoes provided vitamin C, when fresh fruit was in shortage, and served as a native-grown, energy-giving alternative to wheat, which could then be imported in smaller quantities. Cooks were encouraged to experiment with potato flour in pastry and scones. The potato-dedicated Ministry of Food leaflet, No. 27, trumpeted the versatility of the humble tuber and included useful tips. Cooks were encouraged to eat the skins of potatoes, to preserve potato water for stock and never to throw away leftovers. There were suggestions for stuffed baked potatoes (a wartime legacy), potato and watercress soup; potato and bacon cakes, potato salad, potato and cheese flan, potato curry, savoury potato sandwich spread, potato pastry and even sweet potato biscuits. No surprise, then, that a *Modern Home* editorial from 1941 should complain of the heaviness of the wartime diet: 'You would think war conditions might make all of us thinner, but that isn't the way it works. Maybe it's the greater proportion of starch in our diet; at any rate, lots of quite young women are having to let out their buttons.'

It wasn't just housewives who were courted by the tasty tuber, but their children too.

> There was an old woman who lived in a shoe.
> She had so many children she didn't know what to do.
> She gave them potatoes instead of some bread,
> And the children were happy and very well fed.

Potato Pete pulled it off. By the end of the war, potato consumption in Britain had gone up by 60 per cent, the largest increase of any commodity.

The twinkly, bespectacled, spats-wearing Dr Carrot ('the Children's best friend'), often depicted carrying a doctor's bag with VIT-A written on it, always spoke with kindly words: 'Call on me often enough and I'll keep you well.' Carrot cake first became popular during the war. Dr Carrot's promotion of carrots as an alternative source of sweetness ('Carrot flan . . . reminds you of apricot flan – but has a deliciousness all of its own') may not have always convinced, but his finest hour came with the promotion of carrots as an aid to seeing in the dark of the blackout. Dr Carrot suggested that carrots were what gave the famous fighter ace 'Cat's Eye' Cunningham the edge over the Luftwaffe's best. Suddenly small boys were keen to gobble up their carrots in emulation of their hero.*

At Christmas time the Ministry of Food released a Food Facts Quiz. Families were invited to guess the price of fresh-salted cod per pound, to explain how to mix milk powder or to answer such teasers as: what is (or are) Rose Hips? (Answer choices: A Russian folk dance? The name of a famous woman spy? An Eastern dance? Pods of wild roses rich in vitamin C?)

Norman Longmate suggests: 'The Kitchen Front was the only one where Great Britain never lost a battle.'[4] If, before the war, most housewives had known nothing of nutrition, by the end of it many were prepared to write in complaint to the Ministry if they felt their children were not getting the vitamins, minerals, protein and carbohydrates they now knew were necessary for robust health. And Woolton's role as both the ministry's figurehead and a popular public person granted him the honour of having a dish named after him: Woolton pie, a vegetable concoction bound in a white or gravy sauce and topped with oatmeal. The dish was universally unpopular, but the businessman turned public servant who had lent it his moniker was not. Though surveys show that the popularity of rationing varied during the war, Woolton's approval rating rarely went below 79 per cent.

* What was really helping the RAF was the invention of radar.

The day-to-day of life on the ration

I wish I were Queen Victoria: then I could thank you – From the depths of my Broken WIDOWED heart. Never NEVER NEVER have we had such a rapturous ASTOUNDING GLORIOUS – no, I can't get the hang of the style. All I can say is that when we discovered the butter in the envelope box we had in the household . . . That's a whole pound of butter I said. Saying which I broke off a lump and ate it pure. Then in the glory of my heart I gave all our weeks ration – which is about the size of my thumb nail – to Louie – earned undying gratitude; then sat down and ate bread and butter. It would have been desecration to add jam.

. . . Bombs fell near me: trifles, a plane shot down in the marsh: trifles; floods damned – no, nothing seems to make a wreath on the pedestal fitting your butter.

Virginia Woolf writing to Vita Sackville-West, 29 November 1940[5]

'Fair shares for all'

It is a common modern misunderstanding of the wartime scheme that everything was rationed and that the ration book somehow replaced the cash economy. In fact, most goods were off the ration and those that were rationed still had to be paid for – though the poorest could benefit from subsidies to ensure their health did not fall behind. In the first weeks of the war especially, the beleaguered housewife had to contend with a dramatic rise in inflation. This was, however, later mitigated by almost full employment and raised income levels. Meanwhile, the Ministry of Food's price controls ensured that key commodities remained universally affordable. Despite intermittent grumbling about always having to queue for extras or resentment that some seemed more equal than others in the eyes of certain shopkeepers, the general public recognised the need for rationing and responded positively to its administration. This was largely due to its perceived justness. The Ministry of Food sold the policy to the public as 'fair shares all round' and key to that was the decision to ration only foods for which a supply could be guaranteed. 'I [Woolton] planned not to be driven to rationing by realised shortages, but to "put something in the cupboard" for the days when supplies might fail – which earned me the nickname of "Squirrel" amongst the cartoonists.'[6]

Wartime food was healthy but dull, and required inspired cooking and planning. The Mass Observation diaries of Nella Last – immortalised on television by Victoria Wood as Housewife 49 – are full of delicious-sounding meals assembled judiciously from unpromising pieces of meat stewed for hours or making clever use of ersatz flavourings (dried carrot gratings to replace candied peel and fruit zest). The diaries of Mrs Milburn, meanwhile, heap praise on the home economies of her cook Kate who, even in the war's darkest days, seems to have always managed to produce a decent pudding. Less skilful housewives, however, or those who, having entered or returned to the workplace, found themselves fighting a daily struggle to make the time to collect their ration – let alone queue for any extras – often found it hard towards the end of the week to come up with anything more promising than a dried-egg omelette.

Queues formed for extras. Fish, even in coastal towns, was in intermittent and often rather aged supply, because most fishermen were now engaged more directly in the war effort as sailors, merchant seamen or by working in coastal defence. Tomatoes, unless you grew and canned your own, were a luxury item. Those who did not keep their own hens were forced to accept American powdered eggs. Many fruits were difficult to source. But perhaps the most notorious shortage, at least in the early years of the war, were onions, the supply of which dwindled after the occupation of France and the Channel Islands. An onion became a luxurious present for a house warming or even a wedding. A 1½ lb onion raffled among the staff of *The Times* newspaper raised £4 3s 4d. A presenter on the *Children's Hour* radio show said wistfully of a birthday gift, 'I did hear of a lucky girl the other day who was given some onions, but we can't all expect a lovely present like that.'

Introduction of points rationing

Has anyone with an organic delivery box ever moaned to you about how boring the choice can be in the depths of winter? Imagine if you were never able to supplement it through the Hungry Gap months of spring, before nature became bounteous again.

By wartime rationing rules, households were asked to nominate local retailers, such as a butcher and a greengrocer, where they wished to do their shopping. Having made their election, it was then illegal to buy rationed goods anywhere else. Shopkeepers received supplies according to the number of registered customers they had. Customers exchanged ration book coupons for their allowances. These coupons were date-specific, which meant that you could not save up any commodity from one week to the next. As the war progressed, the levels to which basic food-stuffs were rationed adapted according to supply and further products were gradually added to the ration. By the summer of 1941 products on the basic ration included bacon and ham, sugar, tea, preserves (jam, marmalade, syrup, treacle), meat, cheese, butter, margarine and cooking fats.

Shoppers did not have many choices and grumbled that 'a fair share for all' meant that the rich had a fairer time of it than others. For the instinctively conservative Woolton and the Tory Churchill a problem with the concept of rationing was that it was anti-Free Market. Woolton later recalled,

> There were constant demands that more and more commodities should be rationed. People who found that their neighbours had occasionally been able to get tinned salmon or sardines, various tinned meat, or dried fruit, demanded that the Ministry of Food should ration all these things. They did not realise the impossibility of this task; it is only possible to ration if there are sufficient supplies for everybody to have some, and this multitude of different articles that indeed made life tolerable for people, were all in such short supply that it would have

MEALS *without* MEAT

Seven appetising meals without using the meat ration

ALL RECIPES FOR 4 PERSONS **ALL SPOONS LEVEL**

FOODS TO USE INSTEAD OF MEAT

Meat is a body-building food and can be replaced only by one of the other body-building foods.

1. The best are: Milk (fresh, household or canned), Cheese, Fish (fresh or canned) and Eggs (fresh or dried).

2. Second best are: Soya flour, Dried Peas, Beans and Lentils, Oatmeal and Semolina.

Our bodies use a mixture of the two kinds very well.

No. 29

> been impossible for everybody to get even the smallest quantity. Small consignments of them had sometimes been put into a little space that happened to be available when a ship was being loaded, and they were all very useful, but on the whole they produced more irritation than pleasure . . . I was determined that we would not ration unless we could ration successfully: on this issue I was not prepared to risk public confidence in the coupons for essential foods. Also I was chary about burdening a somewhat exhausted department with further claims on their administrative efficiency.[7]

The solution was the more flexible points system, unveiled by the Ministry of Food on 1 December 1941. This scheme, which actually borrowed, adapted and aimed to improve on a system in place in Germany, involved totting up a weekly allocation of points rather as those dieting with WeightWatchers do. Some luxury foodstuffs that had a small and intermittent supply, such as game in season and fresh salmon, still remained off-ration. But goods that came into the country in sufficiently regular, albeit small, quantities – such as spam or tinned fruit – were now given a points value. As a rule it was a luxury item in short supply (such as tinned salmon) that commanded the highest points value, while a humbler commodity (such as corned beef) might be bought for fewer points. If the Ministry of Food's officials suddenly realised that they had a greater than usual supply of, say, tinned sardines they would adjust the points down accordingly.

Each customer was allotted weekly points, which he or she could then 'spend' as wished. The wise housewife was empowered with the right to decide whether she saved or splurged. Although, as with rationing, points could not be held over for long periods, it was possible to save up a few for a birthday or a special meal for a husband returning home on leave. Points could also be given as gifts to friends or relatives. Woolton likened his points scheme to a Stock Exchange and (just as, after its 1980s liberalisation, following the shares markets became a passion for a wider public) people watched its movement with a beady eye for bagging a bargain. The government made it its practice to announce the points on a Sunday when most people were at home with nothing much to do and, more importantly, the shops were closed, so there was little chance of a run on them. This also gave the housewife time to plan her points spending sensibly.

Points were instantly popular and this was in no small part due to some canny planning on the part of Woolton and his Ministry of Food bureaucrats. As he recalled,

> The whole scheme depended upon the success of the first two months and on this I took no risks. For several weeks before it came into operation I reduced the public supply of nearly all of these extras. Meanwhile the shopkeepers built up heavy stocks of nearly all of them, on the strict understanding that they were not for sale until released by order from the Ministry. With great patriotism they legitimately kept these goods 'under the counter'. When I announced the scheme, I assured the public that it would work and that the next day they would be able to get these goods in the shops . . . Thus when they went to test the points rationing scheme they not only found that the goods were there but they had the agreeable task of deciding how much 'luxury', in terms of points, they wanted – salmon, sardines, dried fruit, tinned meat, golden syrup, etc. For the women it became 'shopping' instead of 'collecting the rations', and this gave them a little pleasure in their harassed lives and an exercise in their natural skill. If the demand for any one article became excessive the points value of it was put up until consumption had been checked.[8]

The points system, which reintroduced a type of active consumerism within the rationing scheme, was one of Woolton's greatest successes, attracting admiration even today. As Aubrey Meyer, director of the Global Commons Institute, an environmental think tank has said, 'National unity flowed from the government, whose key achievement was to introduce a rationing scheme based on points equality. This was transparent, simple and accountable. It meant that those who were making the effort to be frugal were not undermined by those who were not.'[9]

Woolton certainly felt that by the time the war appeared to be turning in the Allies' favour, the Ministry of Food had established a system that was working in both administrative and humanitarian terms. Indeed, it could be argued that it worked so well that it was maintained for much longer than was necessary.

> By 1943 . . . supplies were not only widely distributed in the shops and the normal food warehouses, but we had established emergency warehouses throughout the country, using cinemas that had been closed, old church halls, and the like. We had gone further than this: throughout the villages of England we had appointed, to operate in emergency, Voluntary Food Officers, who kept, under their own control, emergency rations of food sufficient to keep the village alive for a few days in the event of a failure of supply either because communications had been destroyed, or in the event of invasion, when normal sources of supply might well have been cut off. To prepare for this possibility, in association with the military services, we held exercises to test the strength of our reserves in the event of invasion or action by parachutes, or the complete disruption of supplies through bombing of roads, or of bakeries, or of power-stations, that might affect the food manufacturing industries. It became, in fact, a constant battle of wits against the enemy, with the harrowing certainty that if we failed the people would go hungry.[10]

What we could learn from their wartime experience

When food rationing finally ended on 3 July 1954 – with the return of meat as a free market commodity – the occasion was marked by ration books being burnt in Trafalgar Square and London's Smithfield Market opening at midnight, instead of 6 a.m., for the first time in almost fifteen years. The fearsome-sounding British Housewives' League patrolled butchers' shops to monitor prices.

More than five decades later such scenes now seem extraordinary. But have we today ventured too far from those bureaucratically bound austerity years to a food economy geared too much towards bottom-line savings? Is it time to stop eating the globe and instead to eat in a more globally aware way? Our need to eat imported rice, for example, is nothing compared with the need of any housewife in south-east Asia or subcontinental India to buy rice for her family. We have our own national staples – potatoes, oats and wheat – to source locally. And when an ongoing fuel crisis has created a world food crisis, surely it is time to ask some searching questions about the amount of fuel expended in importing, transporting and preserving the food that we eat? Yet for those British consumers struggling to feed their households on a limited income, or for those who do not prioritise quality over quantity when it comes to food shopping, there is little financial incentive to source produce locally. Local food is rarely less expensive food. Lamb or apples imported from the southern hemisphere are frequently cheaper than their English cousins. Thai chickens can knock pence off even battery-reared British ones. Vegetables imported from Holland's efficient markets tend to cost less than the ones grown here.

But the wartime experience proves that a government *can* intervene in a nation's food economy and manipulate it to serve its own purposes. If, for example, the spectre of an energy crisis were to frighten British politicians into trying to increase this country's self-sufficiency, financial incentives could be used to promote home production and produce, while taxes and penalties were used to increase the prices on imported items. If the government's priority were to promote health, similar measures could be introduced – with farmers receiving higher subsidies for lower-fat produce, for example, and fast-food manufacturers being penalised in cost terms that they would inevitably pass on to the consumer. Indeed, with so many British citizens fighting food-related diseases, is now the time to readopt free nutritional supplements for the needy and for children? Another wartime lesson would be to use propaganda to campaign more effectively for food that is both better for us and better for our environment. With that kind of muscle manipulating the way we shop and eat, we might become better consumers of food that isn't going to cost us the earth.

CHAPTER THREE

DIG FOR VICTORY:
Towards a more self-sustaining nation

In total war-time, the plough is as essential as the sword,
and food is the fuel on which our war machine depends.
Minister of Agriculture, 19 February 1944[1]

The highways and cars
Were sacrificed for agriculture
I thought that we'd start over
But I guess I was wrong . . .
This was a discount store,
Now it's turned into a cornfield
Don't leave me stranded here,
I can't get used to this lifestyle.
'(Nothing But) Flowers' by Talking Heads,
lyrics by David Byrne[2]

In 1970s Scotland power cuts seemed to happen almost nightly. My mother recalls that every time the lights went out, and candles were found to light us towards bed, I would misunderstand what was going on and break into 'Happy Birthday'. But there can't have been a power cut every evening because another enduring childhood memory is of a television programme, first aired in 1975, and a companion ever since.

It was to be almost another twenty years before I discovered it borrowed its title and theme tune from Fellini's 1960 classic *La Dolce Vita*. *The Good Life*'s allusion was gently ironic: the Goods and the Leadbetters, the sparring Surbiton neighbours who were the hit sitcom's protagonists, were a world removed from Fellini's louche Roman aristocrats. Their story was simple: Tom (Richard Briers) and Barbara Good (Felicity

Kendall) were middle-class refuseniks who had dropped out of the rat race to pursue a life of self-sufficiency. The joke was that they had not moved to Mull or North Wales to do this, but had stayed put in Surbiton where their neighbours and friends were the unapologetically aspirational Jerry (Paul Eddington) and Margo Leadbetter (Penelope Keith). The comedy was in the cultural clash between the couples.

Tom's and Barbara's back-to-basics hippy philosophy was one shared with 1970s entrepreneurial heroes such as the Body Shop's Anita Roddick, the *Food for Free* writer Richard Mabey and the vegetarian restaurateurs behind Cranks. The Goods were also cranks. Barbara wore dungarees and bandanas, and kept a stroppy goat. Now, in 2009, her do-it-yourself ways have become aspirational in their turn for a new tribe of 'Frugals', for whom success does not necessarily mean excess. Think of the Tory luminary David Cameron, with his *zeitgeist*-savvy advocacy of pedal power and growing his own vegetables in his garden. There are even comic moments rich in bathos, just as in our favourite sitcom, like the chequered history of the controversial, but reportedly near useless, wind turbine on the roof of his Notting Hill home.

The upper classes have fielded Hugh Fearnley-Whittingstall, a man-and-home brand, to berate us for buying 'standard' supermarket chickens instead of free-range ones. The People's Cook, Jamie Oliver, has been doing his bit with tub-thumping campaigns showing us that since we are what we eat we are, too, what we buy to eat. Commentators as diverse as the Radio 4 *Today* programme presenter John Humphrys, who has hill-farmed in Wales, and Rosie Boycott, the former *Spare Rib*, *Independent* and *Daily Express* editor (who surely at one point was of the Shirley Conran school of thought that life was too short to stuff a mushroom, but today probably forages for them from the smallholding she works in the West Country) are champions of organic production methods.

Seventy per cent of Britain is farmland,[3] yet we source an ever decreasing amount of our food from there. According to DEFRA (Department for Environment, Food and Rural Affairs), 38 per cent of the food we eat is imported from overseas, including half our vegetables (triple the amount we imported in 1961) and a surprising 95 per cent of all our fruit (double what we imported in 1961). What really shocks is that we are importing fruit and vegetables that are indigenous to Britain – and importing them when they are actually in season in Britain.[4] A British farmer could have earned a living growing the stuff here, but instead we expend fuel bringing apples and onions from New Zealand, plums from South Africa and strawberries from Spain, primarily because that works out cheaper. Who's to blame? Well, most of us feel more comfortable when we blame the supermarkets. But 80 per cent of us choose to do our groceries shopping in supermarkets.[5] And those supermarkets carry out a lot of market research: they know the British customer intimately and they know that our shopping habits are dictated – as are theirs – by cost above all.

That Britain would have to increase its self-sufficiency was obvious long before 1939. Pre-war planners had first to address the fallow state of British farming and the fact that the country's million-strong agricultural community felt undervalued – and not without justification, since many were impoverished. The Second World War was to transform their lot. Over the next decade farmers were the recipients of status-improving financial incentives, machinery and teaching. They were lionised through propaganda. And they repaid these investments with a transformation of their industry in an impressive drive for efficiency and productivity. The government's priority was for more land to be given over to growing staple energy crops such as wheat, corn, barley, oats, potatoes and cattle fodder, but first they had to audit what farmland was available and how much of it was in active agricultural use.

The real work of the 'Ploughing-Up Campaign' then began in the late spring of 1939, with farmers being offered £2 per acre to cultivate fallow land and fields that had been left to grass for at least seven years, the first in a number of lucrative grants and incentives introduced throughout the wartime period. In the autumn of 1939 the ministry stated its target: to have 1.7 million more acres producing crops by harvest time 1940. The farmers rallied to the cause, ploughing round the clock with tractors where they had them, with horses where they did not, often staying out long after blackout.

Some of the fallow land, such as water-logged fenland in Norfolk, stone-strewn Welsh uplands and rabbit-infested downs in Sussex, had always been deemed unfarmable but now, with the incentive of government cash and the call of patriotic duty, farmers set about trying to convert as much as possible to arable use.

For a few specialists the ploughing-up was soul-sapping – destroying dreams and laying waste to generations of hard work. One such farmer was a rose grower, Harry Wheatcroft:

> We put the plough through a field of some hundred thousand trees – a heartbreaking job. We tore from the greenhouses the bushes that were to give us blooms . . . and so made room for the more urgent bodily needs of the nation.
>
> Pigs now wander about where our Polyantha roses bloomed. There's wheat and barley where acres of Hybrid Teas coloured the land – even the humble cabbage stands where our standard roses once held majestic sway. The odour of our greenhouses has changed too. Here half a million onion plants have taken the place of the roses. They in turn will be succeeded by tomato plants and fruit; then lettuce, while the light still holds, and afterwards the humble mustard and cress.[6]

In April 1940 farmers such as Wheatcroft were rewarded with some good news statistics, a rarity at that stage in the war, and the nation's thanks and approbation. The ministry was able to announce that the farmers had done their bit magnificently and the autumn's harvest would be a bumper one. It was indeed a record breaker and throughout the war each year's harvest bettered the previous one. By 1944 the amount of land under cultivation had increased from 12.9 million acres to 19.8 million, while food production had risen by 91 per cent.[7]

Suddenly, from being marginalised figures, farmers and their families were courted by the government and praised by the media. In Soviet-style propaganda posters they and their hoes were raised up as national heroes. It was a second agricultural revolution – with the mechanisation of farms (the numbers of tractors rose from 56,000 pre-war to 203,000)[8] and growth in the use of fertilisers contributing to the huge rise in yields.

Machinery pools were formed, which meant that many collaborated, for perhaps the first time, with their neighbours, farming not as rivals but as a team working towards a common cause. Organisations such as the Young Farmers' Club flourished. Events such as 'Neighbours' Day', when a farmer would host a weekend visit to his lands and steadings, became a regular country practice. Machinery, equipment, knowledge and workers were often shared if it meant crops being harvested earlier.

As one Surrey farmer would later recall, 'Farmers found themselves promoted from the rather poor relation to a much sought after and respected member of the family. These things completely changed their output and they put their heart and soul into the job.'[9] A Norfolk woman focused on the financial benefits: 'Farmers were as poor as church mice, but before the war was half over they had not one but two cars in the garage. It made most of them. The government were generosity itself.'[10] This was borne out by salary increases above inflation. In the 1930s the average weekly wage for a farmworker was seldom more than 30 shillings, with no allowance for holidays, sick leave or unemployment benefit. By 1945 the minimum weekly payment was 70 shillings, plus extra money for overtime, a week's paid holiday and the benefits of the Welfare State. Even allowing for the war's high inflation rate, this was a significant improvement. Before the war many young men, seeing no future on the land, had headed for the cities; now the wartime improvements in salary and status gave even the lowliest agricultural workers a renewed pride in their work. One Oxfordshire smallholder would later remember 'feeling for the first time in my life the food we were producing really mattered and whatever we had for sale someone was waiting to buy it'.[11]

But not every countryman woke up to a golden dawn in a bucolic Arcadia. Enthusiasm for government-driven changes was not universal. The Emergency Powers Act gave the Ministry of Agriculture the right to take possession of farms or dislodge tenant farmers; to levy prices; to decide what was grown. To save on feed, financial incentive was offered to encourage sheep farming over cattle, while livestock for slaughter had to be sold to the state for an agreed price. To carry out their bidding at a local level the ministry, in conjunction with the National Farmers' Union, appointed County War Agricultural Executive Committees throughout the country. An 'Ag' position was voluntary and generally went to someone from the yeoman landowning and farming classes rather than a tenant farmer. In other words the Archers and Aldridges were running the rural show, emphatically not the Grundys.

Though most Ags worked peaceably with those farming in their jurisdiction, there were occasions when tenant farmers felt that an Ag had abused its position. By the Emergency Powers Act the Ags were the ones who advised the ministry to evict tenants at short notice if they felt that a farm was not working to its maximum yield, or if a ministerial edict had been carried out ineptly. In truth, though, the whole system was reliant on goodwill and back-breaking work, and sometimes the tenant farmer might not have had the funds available to implement the ministerial instructions. There were tales of tenant farmers being evicted from lands their forebears had worked on for more than a century, and yeoman farmers exploiting their roles to widen the boundaries of their own farmland. Even so, a campaigning body set up in 1944 to redress the alleged wrongs against the tenant farmers, many of whom ended up working in industry after a lifetime on the land, the Dispossessed Farmers' Supporters Association, achieved very little, despite attracting 5,000 members.

The everyday story of country folk during wartime, however, did for the most part seem to be that of a productive idyll where everyone did his or her bit for the war effort to ensure that the nation had sufficient food to fight its good fight. And the figures spoke for themselves. The Ministry of Information's *Home Front Handbook*, first published in 1943 and revised in 1945, states, 'As a result of the ploughing-up policy, the area of arable land in the United Kingdom has increased by 50 per cent, and of tillage by 66 per cent, since before the war. By the end of 1944, no less than five million acres of grassland had been ploughed up . . . Some percentages of crop acreage increase in the United Kingdom since 1939 are: Wheat 83; Oats 52; Barley 95; Rye 594; Potatoes 101; Sugar Beet 26; and Flax 669. Half the wheat in national flour is home produced, and Britain grows her whole domestic sugar ration.'[12]

Another impressive statistic is that whereas in 1939 the average yield of wheat was thirty-three bushels, within four years, by the harvest of 1943, it was fifty and in some areas as much as eighty. The nation did not go hungry, even when Allied shipping was losing in the Battle of the Atlantic. By 1944 Britain had halved imports from 22 million tons to between 10 and 11 million tons. That we could rely on home-grown food in such circumstances was due to heroic effort all over rural Britain.

Lend a Hand on the Land

Lend a Hand on the Land at an agricultural camp . . . Our farmers and farm workers will do their utmost to ensure that we don't go short of essential foods – bread, milk, potatoes and sugar. But labour is short and to do all that needs to be done they must have help from the public – and that means YOU.

You'll need a healthy holiday and you'll get paid for it. What's more you'll enjoy good comradeship and fun when the day's work is done. There's a BATTLE FOR BREAD to be won. YOU can help to win it and save our people from want.

Leaflet recruiting for agricultural camp volunteers in the south-east region, issued by the Ministry of Agriculture

Of course, all the work was not done in the countryside alone, nor was it done only by country folk. Throughout the war, and for years afterwards, rural communities benefited from an influx of city dwellers lent from elsewhere to help them increase their productivity.

Today, one of the few organisations in Britain that offers working holidays in the British countryside is the National Trust. For as little as £70 a week, including accommodation and food, volunteers can work on a farm or on a project to preserve our national heritage. Of course, for £170 a week, full board, one might be able to buy a bucket and spade Mediterranean holiday on lastminute.com. But previous generations did not have the option of bucket-shop flights and backpacking tours. Thus farm holidays, endorsed and championed by a wartime government that

ordinarily demonised holidays and leisure travel as unpatriotic, were a popular option for everyone from poor urban families to liberal types who idealised the pastoral, to those who had grown up on the land and wanted a sense of continuity.

As a medical student, my father spent several holidays working in the potato fields of Aberdeenshire. For many schools in the region the October half-term holiday was not so much a break as the exhausting time of 'tattie picking'. That was in the 1950s, but the heyday of the working farm holiday came in the 1940s when the government made a special allowance for agricultural breaks, giving them their ringing endorsement. With so many younger farmworkers having seized the opportunity to sign up with the Forces in the initial call-up, the farms needed volunteers to help achieve their increased agricultural targets. A general appeal went out to 'Lend a Hand on the Land', which was answered enthusiastically.

Children formed a sizeable part of this voluntary agricultural work-force. Indeed, so many rural school pupils were being pressed into working on farms that at one point MPs in the House of Commons expressed concern. In 1943, a memorably bumper harvest year, 70,000 pupils spent at least a week of their holiday at a farm camp. In 1944 and 1945 the Ministry of Agriculture's School Help target was 73,000. To house these tyro farmers, 1,200 school camps were established around the country. A Ministry of Information book published in 1945, *Land at War: The Official Story of British Farming 1939–1944*, has a photograph of a work gang of boys, some of whom look no older than ten, carrying pails. It is captioned: 'Potato Race: In spare time and holidays they have done good work, sowing, reaping, picking up pocket-money in their stride. Farming for them has been a worthwhile game.'[13]

The book explains further:

> Great numbers came from town and city too, from public and council schools alike – boys and girls to whom the produce of the farm had never been much more than items on a shopping list . . . They helped with every kind of job: the boys potato-planting and lifting, tractor-driving, harvesting, flax-pulling, root-hoeing and singling, the girls potato-planting and lifting too, weeding, pea-picking, fruit-picking, flax-pulling – their neat swift fingers unrivalled at such labour. In 1942 the boys and girls of Britain worked nearly 10,000,000 hours in the fields . . . Surrounded by the clamour of war, they appreciated very well the reality of what they were doing; they knew their work was important, and, of course, they were being paid for it.[14]

It was not just children, though, who attended agricultural camps. In 1944, 107,000 British civilians – two-thirds of them women – spent at least a week of their annual holiday entitlement working the land at one of about 150 farm camps across the country. Many of the volunteers were students, who were expected to undertake some public service and who benefited from the pay of between about 24 shillings and 30 shillings a week, plus bed and board. Civil servants could take a week's, or even a fortnight's, extra holiday if they signed up for farm work. In 1943 10,000 desk-bound pen pushers swapped the stale air of bureaucracy for a rake or hoe in the open countryside. Back at the Ministry of Agriculture the propagandists were keen to advertise the camps' unstuffy egalitarianism, making much of one that had berthed a dustman, two typists and a bishop. It was this rustic classlessness that the book *Land at War* was keen to shout about:

> To these camps the workers came in their thousands; they forgot Blackpool and Clacton; they forgot coal-dust, oil-waste, buzzing lathes, blackout-boards; they tore off their shirts, took a good swig of country air, and plunged into the corn and cabbage as if for a salt-sea bathe . . . And they got a smell of the land; they saw what a crop looked like, what it was like to handle, and what labour went into the raising of it. When at last they got back to their desks, counters and work-benches, stiff as they were, blistered, burnt red with the sun, their food tasted better to them, the countryside had more significance, and the farmer's life – his problems and the tasks with which he is faced – seemed more real to them, less of a fable, because they had shared it with him.[15]

Other sources of assistance came from the Emergency Land Corps, organised in forty-seven counties, which contributed nearly 50,000 itinerant workers, many of them retired people or the families of those already at work on the farms and those employed elsewhere locally. The WI also encouraged its members in the countryside to lend a hand where they could. Soldiers stationed at home and American GIs helped out with the harvest. And, by 1944, 74,000 German and Italian prisoners of war were employed on the land, working alongside British agricultural labourers and volunteers. The PoWs seem to have impressed with their efficiency, although the GIs were more popular.

The Women's Land Army

Instead of silks and georgettes she wears wool and corduroy and clumping boots; her working hours seem never definitely to end . . . she lives among strangers, and the jolly atmosphere of homely love or outside fun is replaced often by loneliness and boredom. She gets up when most people are still warmly asleep . . . she goes to bed with aching muscles after a dull evening, knowing that next morning the horrible alarum will shrill through her sleep calling her back to damp boots, her reeking oil skin, and the mud and numbing cold outside. All this she has done, and is doing so that we can eat.[16]

Vita Sackville-West, in her official history of the Women's Land Army

With good reason, the most famous of those who lent a hand on the land were the Women's Land Army (WLA), which in its 1943 heyday counted 84,463 among its ranks.[17] The WLA was both the most romanticised and the most exploited of the wartime women's organisations.

Subsequent generations of women owe a debt of thanks to the WLA for proving once and for all that women can endure physical hardships in the workplace. But these women were poorly trained and inadequately kitted out; paid significantly less than the men they worked alongside (in 1945 a maximum of 48 shillings weekly, compared to the 70 shillings per week their male colleagues were receiving); had to put up with much ribald humour of the 'backs to the land' variety; and had fewer chances of promotion and less leave than other servicewomen. Most humiliating and infuriating of all, land girls were excluded from the benefits and resettlement grants offered to other Civil Defence Workers and Forces women after the war. Their president, Lady Gertrude 'Trudie' Denman, resigned in protest in February 1944, but by then most of her army had already decommissioned itself, although the WLA was not dissolved officially until 1950.

But the WLA, which had actually been founded in the First World War,

started the second global conflict with heady aspirations. As war broke out, British farmers found themselves in an unenviable position. The young men working on the land in the then depressed farming industry had been among the first to sign up. Now farmers were being asked to increase their productivity dramatically, but they had also lost key workers in all sectors. When it was suggested that women might be able to do the jobs that the men had done, they were at first sceptical. However, when the first land girls arrived on the farms, they soon realised that keenness could be a good match for experience for all but the hardest physical undertakings.

THE WORLD FOOD
SITUATION IS GRIM
SERIOUS SHORTAGE
FACES US AND THE
PEOPLES OF EUROPE
20,000
VOLUNTEERS
ARE NEEDED IMMEDIATELY
BY THE
WOMEN'S LAND ARMY
Apply:- MINISTRY OF LABOUR EMPLOYMENT EXCHANGE

The media made much of the social diversity of the WLA. Photographers were urged by their editors to return from the fields with pictures such as one that appeared in the *Daily Herald* portraying an ex-beautician giving Buttercup, a Jersey cow, a pedicure.[18] Even official commentators enthused about 'the young, sun-tanned, cord-breeched army of one-time shop girls, typists, mannequins, mill girls, hairdressers, parlourmaids . . .'.[19] Though middle-class girls did sign up in order to escape stultifying home lives, they were not the target recruits. The majority of WLA soldiers were fleeing a different kind of monotony – that of assembly-line work in the factories and mills of Lancashire and Yorkshire. They signed up for fresh air, comradeship, the physical beauty of the countryside and the chance to pursue another type of life. As one girl, who spent the war in remote north Wales, wrote, 'Before joining the Women's Land Army . . . I worked for five, long, dreary years in an office in Brixton . . . Always I dreamt of hills and stars and green free spaces, and sometimes, leaning over a ledger in springtime, I could actually smell the primrose of my imagination.'[20]

But if the land girls came to the countryside with high expectations, they often had to confront the low expectations of their hosts.

> The coming of the Land Girl in the early days, was a source of some perplexity to the farmer. To his wife also . . . Compared with the ruddy, strong-limbed village lasses, these paler, streamlined, town-bred girls seemed much too fragile for the rigours of outdoor work. But . . . the girls . . . soon surprised everyone . . . by their almost obstinate fanaticism . . . Lancashire girls . . . adapted themselves readily to the subtleties of farm mechanisation. As a Wiltshire farmer said of another type: 'I was a bit doubtful . . . when I found I was let in for a couple of actresses off the stage. But let me say this – if actresses can make such good Land Girls, let me have actresses again!'[21]

The work undertaken by the 'girls' entirely broke the mould of society's expectations of 'the weaker sex'. In Lincolnshire two land girls, aged twenty and nineteen, were responsible for the deaths of 12,000 rats in one year.[22]* Four land girls working for the Pest Control Department and deployed to north Wales, travelling between farms on their bicycles, were responsible for exterminating 35,545 rabbits, 7,689 rats, 1,688 foxes and 1,901 moles.[23]

Miss Mary Tetlow's unpublished letters and handwritten account of her wartime experiences, housed at the Imperial War Museum, offer a typical survey. In 1943 Mary, an assistant librarian, was sent from her home in Bradford to RAF Catterick to grow vegetables for the airmen stationed there.

> Prospective LA members had to go to their own doctors. Mine didn't approve of land work for girls: 'Do you realise you will be out in all weathers?' . . . A word about my uniform; the dress uniform consisted

* At this point in the nation's history when every bushel of wheat had to be accounted for and when just one of the 50 million rats estimated to be living in Britain could eat a hundredweight of food annually.

> of a fawn hat, with wheatsheaf badge, and a matching greatcoat (two pairs of dungarees were sent on later . . .). To complete this outfit, I received a pair of shoes and two pairs of knee-length woollen stockings. I was given also a raincoat (stiff, very long, shiny and khaki-coloured), a pair of canvas leggings, and a pair of leather ankle-boots. These boots were marvellously comfortable – I wished I'd worn trousers all my life. But the dressed-up landgirl was ill-at-ease. But the materials were of the best. Every landgirl had to buy her own green tie. . . .

The other land girls with whom she shared her new life were Kathleen ('who looked like an actress even in dungarees'), Ida and Amy (who had been carpet weavers near Dewsbury), Doreen (who had managed a shop in Huddersfield) and a Yorkshire lass straight from school. 'The vegetables we grew were cabbage, lettuce, potatoes, onions, peas, carrots and beans; and the hundred or so rabbits inhabiting a Nissen hut were intended for consumption also. I can say this fine, hot summer of 1943 was the happiest of my life. The food was wonderful (why did the airmen grumble?) and my weight rose to around 9 stone for the first and only time. Our social life never flagged.'

After an altercation with a bullying male commanding sergeant, Mary was transferred to tougher farm work near Ripon, working threshing machines. It was filthy work and her 'downfall' there (and indeed that of many a land girl) was to be the dust, which gave her a stubborn chest infection and rash that eventually led to her being invalided home. Her 1985 memoir concludes,

> Regarding the lack of gratuity [resettlement grants, given to other Civil Defence workers], I didn't miss it at the time. It was such a relief when the war was over; and my return to the books and the readers, and old colleagues was so enjoyable . . . But one colleague was missing. She had gone on to university from service in the WRNS, eventually becoming a head teacher, thus achieving what had been a hopeless ambition before the gratuity came her way. So it seems now that the Land Girls were denied a chance to get on in life. Worse, some of us who were injured

> or who became permanent invalids – I heard there were many victims of arthritis – had little hope of compensation.[24]

About 6,000 women worked in a subdivision of the WLA, the Women's Timber Corps, established in April 1942, helping to fell trees for use as telegraph poles, fuel and building materials. Before the war most timber had been imported and when war broke out many foresters had joined up. 'Lumber Jills' or 'Pole Cats', as they were nicknamed, wore WLA uniforms, but were distinguished by a green beret with a badge of a fir tree sewn on it and a pair of brass miniature crossed axes, worn on the overcoat sleeves. The Home Timber Production Department of the Ministry of Supply undertook the administration, discipline and welfare of members.

The unpublished memoirs of Mary Dowzell offer an insight into the lives of these trouser-clad Rosalinds turned Ganymedes, hard at work in the nation's forests:

> I was nearly 19 when I volunteered . . . in the summer of 1942 . . . I was one of a small gang of six men and three girls. The men did the felling, crosscutting of pit roofs and haulage work, while we, the three girls, cleared and burnt tops and stripped bark from selected tree lengths for telegraph poles . . . We were always hungry, and ready to eat whatever there was in our lunch tins. Pasties were of course the Cornish standby, they together with the 'manual workers' extra cheese allowance, and spam, was our mainstay on most days until our evening meal back at our billet.[25]

Mary Dowzell, like many who served in the WLA, came away with happy memories, but later came to resent that other female military and Civil Defence workers had benefited more from resettlement grants in the post-war period. In 1951 King George VI told Lady Denham, on awarding her a medal, 'We always thought that the land girls were not well treated.'[26]

The wartime urban farmers

Now is the time to plough up the park and make over flower beds for vegetables.
Vogue, 1940

We can justly congratulate ourselves on what we have achieved. But we must on no account relax our efforts. The war is not yet won. Moreover, even if it were to end in Europe sooner than we expect, the food situation, far from becoming easier, may well become more difficult owing to the urgent necessity of feeding the starving people of Europe. Indeed in many ways it would be true to say that our real tasks will only then begin. Carry on therefore with your good work. Do not rest on your spades, except for those brief periods which are every gardener's privilege.
Lord Woolton, 1944

In April 2008 British newspapers reported that vegetable seed sales were up 60 per cent on the previous spring. Prices of some types of lettuce had risen by 17 per cent in the year from April 2006, potatoes by 19 per cent and tomatoes by 6 per cent. A growing environmental awareness was making being green-fingered fashionable.[27] People were keen to grow their own veggies.

It seemed these would-be Toms and Barbaras had been planning their seed purchases for a while. One of the best-selling cookery books of 2007 was *Jamie Oliver at Home: Cook Your Way to the Good Life*. The most bought gardening book was Carol Klein's *Grow Your Own Veg*, which sold more than four times as many copies as the second favourite gardening manual, *The Allotment Book* by A. M. Clevely. Among the most critically acclaimed cookery books in the year's Books for Christmas recommendations was *Moro East* by Sam and Sam Clark, the London restaurateurs' description of – and recipes for – the produce they and their neighbouring leaseholders grew on a network of East End allotments before they were bulldozed to make way for the London 2012 Olympics site.

Tending an allotment in Kensington Gardens.
(The Albert Memorial in the background.)

What the success of these books tells us is that for the first time since the era of rationing there is a hunger in Britain to reconnect our larders to our land; our kitchens to our gardens. The wartime Dig for Victory campaign did not confine itself to the countryside. It took its battle right to the heart of Britain's bombed-out city centres. An evocative photograph from the period shows a middle-aged Londoner using his lunch hour to hoe onions in the garden converted from his office block's roof. In the background is the blast-damaged dome of St Paul's Cathedral. Another shows a uniformed waitress outside what looks like the Ritz Hotel in Piccadilly, watering the tomatoes and lettuces that have usurped the flowers from its window boxes.

In the UK today there are roughly 330,000 allotment holders, while a further 100,000 people are on a waiting list that grows longer by the day.[28] Popularity of allotment gardening had been strong throughout the nineteenth century and had surged in the First World War, but had fallen further and further out of fashion in the 1920s. During the Depression years of the 1930s, religious and charitable bodies, such as the Society of Friends and the Land Settlement Association, had tried to promote working on allotments as a way for the unemployed to be self-sufficient smallholders. But it was to take another war to remind the British they were a nation of gardeners. The Minister of Agriculture, then Sir Reginald Dorman Smith, said in a speech on 4 October 1939, 'Half a million more allotments properly worked will provide potatoes and vegetables that will feed another million adults and one and a half million children for eight months out of twelve . . . So, let's get going. Let "Dig for Victory" be the motto of everyone with a garden and of every able-bodied man and woman capable of digging an allotment in their spare time.' Meanwhile the Cultivations of Lands (Allotment) Order allowed councils to put derelict land to work producing vegetables. Even the church, far from discouraging Sunday gardening, sanctioned it in a pastoral letter from the Archbishop of Canterbury. Appropriately – given its namesake – St Martin-in-the-Fields church in Trafalgar Square went a step further. It held a special allotment service during which prayers went up for nature to be bountiful and a lesson was read by the BBC gardener, Mr Middleton.

Vast tracts of land that had formerly been used for leisure purposes – from school playing fields to municipal flowerbeds, to residential gated squares and the private parklands of stately piles – were converted to war work. The grassland of Windsor Great Park became the country's biggest cornfield. In Hackney, thirty-three acres of oats were planted across land that had in more carefree days accommodated seventeen football pitches.

Young school pupils being taught how to garden.

Kensington Park Gardens showed the way by planting cabbages in its flowerbeds. The grass borders of the moat of the Tower of London, the Albert Memorial and the forecourt of the British Museum were planted with vegetable seeds. Factory owners encouraged their workers to garden on company land in their breaks and spare time, while many rail workers cultivated sidings. In the city centres, where bombs had flattened properties, the rubble was cleared and new vegetable life encouraged. In Bethnal Green, a Bombed Site Producers Association had, by August 1942, some '300 members working on 30 sites, sieving soil with punctured dustbin lids to clear the ground of bomb debris'.[29]

The allotment movement was reborn. At the outbreak of war there had been approximately 800,000 in the country. By 1945 there were at least 1.5 million, though the official statistics handbook claimed 1.7 million, all co-opted into the task of increasing Britain's self-sufficiency. By the summer of 1941 Bristol had more than 15,000 allotments, Nottingham had 6,500, Norwich had 4,400, while in the London borough of Tottenham alone there were almost 3,000.[30] In 1943 it was reported that 2.5 million gardens were producing food worth about £12 million. By 1945 the government estimated that 5 million private gardens were growing vegetables.[31] At the war's end it was estimated that 10 per cent of all the food produced in Britain (and not just fruit and vegetables, either) was coming from private endeavours.[32]

To fuel the British people's enthusiasm for self-sufficiency the government's propaganda machine went into overdrive. In September 1939 'Growmore Bulletin No. 1', a pamphlet produced by the Ministry of Agriculture and the Royal Horticultural Society, was published. Unfortunately, being a rush job, it contained misprints guaranteed to waste novice gardeners' time and money, for example mixing up three inches and three feet when describing how to plant marrows. But it soon improved and became the blueprint for all subsequent Growmore and Dig for Victory propaganda. The campaign was deemed so important that in later reprints both the Minister of Agriculture, now the Rt Hon. R. S. Hudson MP, and the Minister of Food, Lord Woolton, wrote forewords. Hudson's noted:

> Before the war the Royal Horticultural Society concentrated a large share of its attention on making the home beautiful with flowers . . . But with the war came a new need: the cry for food, and for food in increasing quantities, to defeat the menace to our shipping and to replace supplies from territories overrun by the enemy . . . It is fitting that the Society should now produce a manual for the vegetable gardener, and in commending this to the public the only point I would stress is that of orderly planning. The objective of the amateur gardener should be to supply his household with vegetables **all the year round**, and not – as has so often happened in the past – to produce unwanted quantities in summer, but only bare soil in the dark days of winter, when the food problem reaches its most acute phase.

On the opposite page Woolton added:

> 'This is a Food War. Every extra row of vegetables in allotments saves shipping. If we grow more Potatoes we need not import so much Wheat. Carrots and Swedes, which can be stored through the winter, help to replace imported fruit. We must grow our own Onions. We can no longer import ninety per cent of them, as we did before the war. The vegetable garden is also our National Medicine Chest – it yields a large proportion of the vitamins which protect us against infection . . . The battle on the Kitchen Front cannot be won without help from the Kitchen Garden.'

By the time the campaign's updated pamphlet was published in 1940 the slogan 'Growmore' had been sidelined by the zingier, more inspirational and memorable 'Dig for Victory', a newspaper man's coinage. The campaign's symbol was the booted foot of Mr W. H. McKie of Acton atop a spade. The twenty-six subsequent Dig for Victory campaign pamphlets, improved upon with each reissue, remain models of clarity. The first, eventually called 'Dig for Victory leaflet No. 1 (new series) VEGETABLE PRODUCTION in private gardens and allotments', included a rallying foreword from the Prime Minister, Winston Churchill – who had made it known he was growing potatoes in his garden at Walton Heath – stating, 'Every endeavour must be made to . . . produce the greatest volume of food of which this fertile Island is capable . . .'. It contained handy diagrams illustrating a cropping plan. Next came, 'No. 2: Onions, Leeks, Shallots and Garlic', to fight against the dire onion shortage of the war's early years. The following leaflets included, 'No. 3: Storing Vegetables for Winter Use', 'No. 7: Manure from Garden Rubbish (Compost Heap)' and a few that crossed into the Kitchen Front's remit, such as 'No. 10: Jam and Jelly Making', 'No. 11: Bottling and Canning' and 'No. 14: Drying, Salting, Pickles, Chutney'. There were at least three leaflets that dealt with combating common diseases and pests, and three others that advised on how to make the most of smaller spaces such as allotments, roofs and window box gardens, the latter with the can-do opening: 'Town dwellers who possess no garden and are unable to cultivate an allotment need not despair of being able to add to their food supplies through their own effort.' Rather late in the day, perhaps, came 'No. 20: How to Dig'. While, the last in the series was 'No 26: How to use Cloches'.

Of course, wartime gardeners suffered the vagaries that beset all of their tribe, as when a cabbage patch was eaten by rabbits, or potatoes were destroyed by blight. On 28 July 1942 Clara Milburn recorded in her diary, 'This afternoon, I sadly decided to take up all my beautiful bed of onions, badly attacked by the onion-fly grub. It was no use to leave them to be eaten off, Hitler fashion, and I shall not grow them again. They were a back-aching job to plant out, and I have spent many hours on their culture – all for nothing. Most disappointing. In fact – and I might as well record it – I am at the moment fed up with the garden. Every year we slave in it, take years off our life with overwork . . .'[33] In fairness, though, on 11 July 1942 she had described having 'our own lovely spinach, just gathered'[34] for supper. Then, on 12 July 1942, there was 'a little potter round the garden, getting a lettuce and carrots for supper . . .',[35] all of which sounds immensely rewarding. Those who grew their own tended to eat better and more cheaply than those who were dependent on the limited stocks in the shops.

Chicken, rabbit and pig clubs

It was not just vegetables that the nation took to producing with gusto. Even in the city centres many returned to the ways of their ancestors and became successful smallholders, supplementing their paltry meat ration and the shops' limited availability with home-reared rabbit and chicken, and their own supply of fresh eggs. The immigrant from the countryside or overseas trying to move a menagerie into a slum dwelling would a decade earlier have been the butt of Charlie Chaplin's humour and had hitherto been as much of a class-ridden cliché as *Little Britain*'s Vicky Pollard's 'yeah but no but'. But in wartime, back-garden city farms were being endorsed right from the top, never mind the noise and dirt. In order to allow people to become effectively self-sustaining crofters in the suburbs and inner cities, local councils had to reverse previously draconian legislation designed to discourage exactly this kind of behaviour.

And these menageries had much to contribute to the nation's nutritional well-being. By 1943 about a quarter of the nation's eggs were coming from home coops – and this was the official figure: many were circumspect about declaring how many eggs they were actually collecting for fear of having their official rations cut, or having to give most of their own eggs away. Towards the end of the war the Domestic Poultry Keepers' Council had more than 1.25 million members keeping more than 12 million birds.[36] The government estimated that in just England and Wales rabbit fanciers were keeping 186,000 breeding does producing rabbit meat.[37] A few hardy souls experimented still further. Some turned to bee-keeping to bring more sweetness into their lives than the ration would allow, while others tried keeping a goat or even a Jersey cow to up their dairy intake. For all these livestock experimentalists, specialist publications such as *The Smallholder* and *Fur and Feather* proved invaluable.

Most famously of all, many turned to pig-rearing in a bid to bring home more bacon. Some joined one of the newly founded pig clubs, which, in exchange for an investment of money, pigswill, hard work or sometimes all of the above, gave each shareholder a cut of meat when the

time came to slaughter. In July 1944 the government estimated that there were at least 5,069 pig clubs, with 130,000 pigs producing 10,000 tons of pig meat annually.[38] These pigs were kept in gardens, on allotments, in at least one recorded case in a bath, and also more rarefied locales such as the (drained) swimming pool of the Ladies' Carlton Club in Pall Mall, and Hyde Park, where the local police station (police forces had some of the most active pig clubs) had built a sty from the timber of bombed-out homes, housing eight pigs bought for £1 apiece, fed on scraps from the local hotels, killed and then replaced with a new litter every six months. It was in fact in London that some of the most successful enterprises thrived. Pigs, maintained by a group of fire wardens, snuffled for acorns on Hampstead Heath, as they had done centuries before. The London borough of Tottenham, led by an enterprising alderman, became so famous for its pig clubs that the pigswill being collected on street corners everywhere was nicknamed 'Tottenham Pudding'.

The Dig for Victory campaign's lessons for today

She's eight now, but aged four my niece struggled to dissociate the golden arches of the world's best-known fast-food restaurant chain from a jolly song she'd been taught about an 'Old Macdonald' who had a farm. It was good, I suppose, that she had already grasped that everything served up at 'Old Macdonald's' had its origins, ultimately, on the land. Too few of us passive 'fuellies' stop, as we slam a ready meal into the oven or grab a pre-packaged salad to eat in our lunch hour, to think of the logistical challenges that food has overcome to get to us. If we visualised the unseen hands in farms, international transport hubs, kitchens, factory lines, on computer keyboards and in shops that had contributed to our ten-minute energy fix, we might question the cheapness of this food, eat our meal more slowly or actually want it to be a bit more memorable.

Today there is a compelling need for all of us to understand the logistically complex process by which food arrives on our plates because we need to try to simplify those chains of supply to waste less of the world's finite supplies of energy. The most obvious solution is to grow more of our own food, but that is not viable for most of us – at least not in the amounts that we need. We need others to feed us, but if we also need to preserve energy, we need to source the bulk of that food – as they did during the Second World War – from nearer to home.

We need, too, as they did in wartime, to be eating differently. The best thing we could do is to be eating food sourced seasonally and locally that has travelled only short distances through as few hands as possible to reach us. The next best thing we could do – as our grand- parents did – is to eat much less meat. And of the meat we eat, we should be thinking about how it was produced – checking if, for example, a piece of beef came from grass-reared or grain-reared stock. And we should be practising nose-to-tail eating, consuming not just traditional prime cuts but all cuts of meat.

It pains me to write this as a committed carnivore, who likes few things more than a slab of quality rump steak with béarnaise sauce on the side, but the facts speak for themselves. We eat 820 million chickens[39] in the United Kingdom every year, which works out at somewhere between thirteen and fourteen per person annually. And it's not for nothing that the French have long nicknamed us British *les rosbifs* but whereas a century ago the average Briton ate 25 kg of meat annually, today we each eat about 85 kg.[40] (Though we are hardly red in tooth and claw when compared to the Americans – they eat, on average, 124 kg of meat per head annually.[41]) Other developing – traditionally predominantly vegetarian – nations are catching up with us too. The United Nations Food and Agriculture Organisation (FAO) have warned that the world 'is in the grip of a "livestock revolution" . . . By 2030, the UN predicts, two thirds of world-wide meat and milk supplies will be consumed by developing nations, and by 2050, global consumption will have doubled.'[42]

And unfortunately, producing meat – any meat – is energy inefficient when compared to the production of grain or vegetables.

> Most animals we consume today are fed on grain rather than grass, with one third of the world's crop going to feed animals, not people. When you consider that it takes an estimated 11 times as much grain to feed a man if it passes through a cow first, that is hardly an efficient use of resources. It also takes a *staggering* thousand times more water to produce a kilo of beef than of wheat, which given that fresh water is in increasingly short supply worldwide, is not good news either. According to the UN, animal farming now accounts for a fifth of global greenhouse gas emissions, with forest clearances and methane emitted by cattle high on the list of contributors. Since climate change is a key driver of water shortages, our growing taste for meat is doubly damaging.[43]

It is also the meat that we deign to eat that is problematic. Some 160,000 male calves are slaughtered annually, their carcasses then sent to waste in Britain, while at least a further 100,000 are exported live in indifferent conditions, because we are squeamish about eating veal in this country.[44] Their sisters survive for milking. To supplement the 16,000 chickens we produce weekly in the United Kingdom we still import about 50,000 tons of chicken meat annually and export about the same amount. This is because we take other nations' chicken breasts, while the parts we would rather not know about spread their wings globally. Usually it turns out that the Chinese market takes the feet, the Caribbean the wings and Africa the legs. Buoyed perhaps by the fact that 'standard' chickens are so senselessly cheap (one labelled as British can be bought for £1.89 in Asda in January 2009), we throw away as rubbish huge amounts of chicken meat – about 5,500 birds daily in the United Kingdom, according to the government-supported rubbish watchdog WRAP. And the virtuous kitchen practices that would have been second nature to our grandmothers' generation – to roast a chicken, to then use leftover meat in two or three days' worth of meals, before boiling the carcass for stock – are alien to most contemporary Britons. When Hugh Fearnley-Whittingstall investigated the lot of 'standard' chickens for a Channel 4 television programme in January 2008, most of his interviewees ate only breast meat before disposing of the rest of a whole chicken.

Many of the currently most talked-about projects for increasing twenty-first-century food production hark back to the wartime Dig for Victory campaign by focusing on urban schemes. In June 2008 London's Royal Parks announced that they were to start growing crops in some flowerbeds as they had during the war.[45] Their decision was inspired in part by a park official's visit to Chicago where the city's ornamental parks are laid out with edible vegetables. In Middlesbrough in 2007, 2,000 residents volunteered to take part in a scheme to reclaim 280 fallow city sites for the planting of fruit and vegetables. The council was then able to serve 2,500 meals from produce grown locally. In Hackney, east London, Growing Communities runs three small semi-commercial gardens where it encourages locals to produce vegetables to sell at local farmers' markets and through an organic box scheme. While in south London Food Up Front, founded in 2007, provides £20 starter kits for local housing residents wishing to grow their own produce, with each kit including compost, seeds, containers and the promised support of a voluntary 'street rep' to pass on his or her own green-fingered wisdom. On an even more ambitious scale is a project being run by the environmental charity Sustain, which bills itself as an alliance for better food and farming. It has set up a Capital Growth project with plans to sow 6,000 acres in London to provide enough food for the estimated extra 14,000 meals that will be needed during the 2012 Olympics.[46]

These are all small-scale projects, which offer promise though not total sustenance. But Sustain's models are cities like Havana, Cuba, where the full body blow of the boycott of their powerful neighbour, the United States of America, was really felt after the loss of economic support from the Soviet Union, following the collapse of the Eastern Bloc. Eighty per cent of Cubans live in cities. The government set up community farms in these cities' suburbs and established market gardens in any free space within the cities themselves. Amateur farmers were given training, government-owned land was distributed and, importantly, the communist regime permitted produce to be sold on a free market. By 2003 more than 200,000 Cubans were employed as urban farmers and the country was approaching self-sufficiency in vegetables, though meat, grain and eggs were still in short supply.[47] Cuba's model of urban farming might have been familiar to their former Eastern Bloc allies. In the Soviet Union in the 1970s, when state agriculture failed, many Russian city dwellers began to cultivate land on the city's periphery as allotment-like plots and community gardens, or, if they were lucky enough to have one, to grow vegetables in their own back garden. Today, 'St Petersburg is the peri-urban farming capital of Europe, with 2½ million inhabitants engaged in agricultural activities.'[48]

And what of the chicken, rabbit and pig clubs that flourished in wartime? Well, one of the surprise sellers of recent years has been the 'eglu', a brightly coloured chicken coop designed in 2004 with city or suburban back gardens in mind by four students from the Royal College of Art. Eglus can be adapted for chickens, ducks and even guinea pigs, while there are rablus for rabbits. You can add a fox-proof run and buy organic hens. By the end of 2008 the company had sold more than 10,000 eglus. At least half a million British families are now estimated to keep hens.[49]

Urban pig-keeping is made more problematic today by exactly the type of legislation that was repealed in the war years. Some still dream of it, though, most impressively the fashionable Dutch architects MVRDV, who in 2001 drew up pig city, a plan for a seventy-six-storey city-centre high-rise populated by pigs, though administered by urban farmers.[50] The architects started with a calculation that if the Netherlands pork industry was to continue producing at its current rate, but convert to organic farming methods, those pigs would need to take over 75 per cent of the country's land mass. Their solution was to think tall, in a built but porcine and eco-friendly environment. The architects were half joking, but city-based Vertical Farming Projects, benefiting from on-site recycling, urban employment opportunities, offering zero food miles to city dwellers and largely protected from bad weather, do have their champions among academics, architects and town planners.[51]

It makes sense to try to source our food from our own land, but though it has the capacity to supply most of Britain's needs, the countryside is today as depressed as it was in the 1930s, with many farmers and agricultural workers feeling ignored, misunderstood and economically exploited, and struggling to keep their businesses afloat. As consumers, we have power. If we were to start taking more of an interest in what it is that farmers do and in how they do it, and if we bought produce from them as directly as possible, that would help their lot. If our government were to decide that Britain's agriculture was worth investing in – rather than just propping up – championing it or even changing it for the better, then that would help the countryside even more. I used to think the problem must be that the money wasn't there, but it seems that even in a major global economic crisis, vast amounts of money can be found to prop up the banking industry, despite its failings. We can't survive as a nation without financial security, but food security is one of the key issues of the twenty-first century too. To make sure of it we need to reconnect with our countryside, to ask what we can do for it and it for us.

Your own vegetables
all the year round . . .
if you
DIG FOR VICTORY NOW

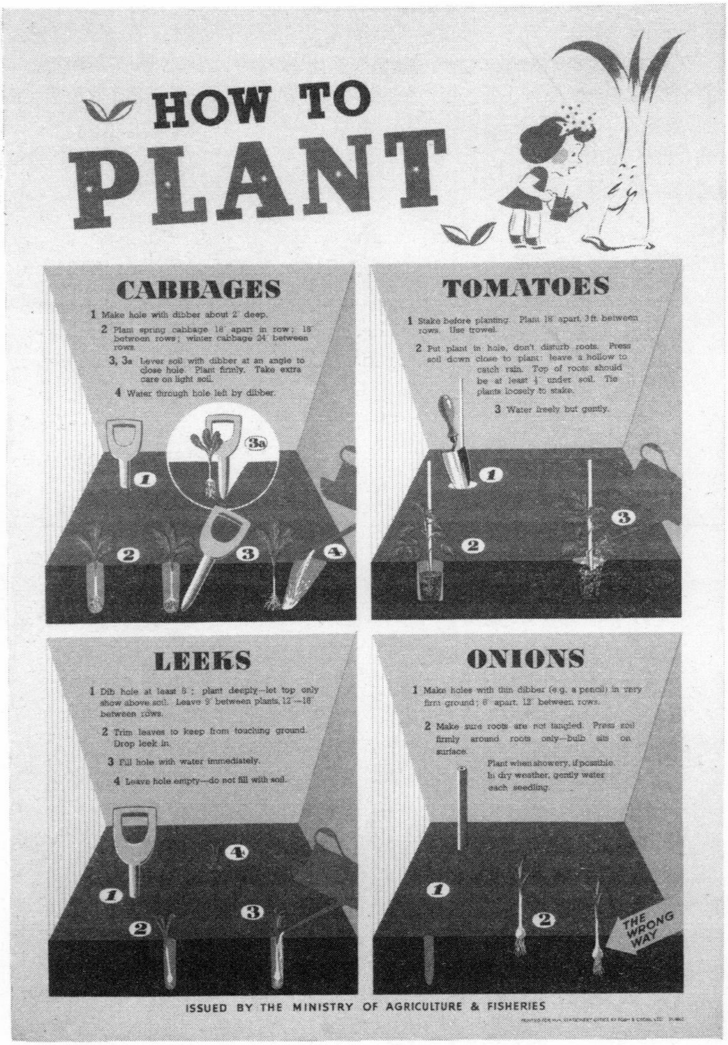
HOW TO PLANT
CABBAGES
1 Make hole with dibber about 2" deep.
2 Plant spring cabbage 18" apart in row; 18" between rows; winter cabbage 24" between rows.
3, 3a Lever soil with dibber at an angle to close hole. Plant firmly. Take extra care on light soil.
4 Water through hole left by dibber.
3a
1
2
3
4
TOMATOES
1 Stake before planting. Plant 18" apart, 3 ft. between rows. Use trowel.
2 Put plant in hole, don't disturb roots. Press soil down close to plant: leave a hollow to catch rain. Top of roots should be at least ½" under soil. Tie plants loosely to stake.
3 Water freely but gently.
1
2
3
LEEKS
1 Dib hole at least 8"; plant deeply—let top only show above soil. Leave 9" between plants, 12"—18" between rows.
2 Trim leaves to keep from touching ground. Drop leek in.
3 Fill hole with water immediately.
4 Leave hole empty—do not fill with soil.
4
1
3
2
ONIONS
1 Make holes with thin dibber (e.g. a pencil) in very firm ground; 6" apart, 12" between rows.
2 Make sure roots are not tangled. Press soil firmly around roots only—bulb sits on surface.
Plant when showery, if possible. In dry weather, gently water each seedling.
1
2
THE WRONG WAY
ISSUED BY THE MINISTRY OF AGRICULTURE & FISHERIES

Sucking Eggs: What your wartime granny's experience could teach you about buying, preparing and growing your own food

On the modern Kitchen Front

- Don't waste food. Plan ahead what you're going to buy and plan ahead what you're going to eat. Then don't buy more than you need, or cook more than you need if it can't then be frozen or recycled into another dish. Learn how to portion food and how to judge what people will realistically eat. Use recipes as a guide, if this is not yet instinctual. Avoid at all costs sending food to landfill – it would have been an anathema to your grandmother.
- Source your food locally. The ideal would be your own kitchen garden, but that is impossible for most of us. Still, the shorter the distance your food has had to travel, the less fuel is likely to have been expended in getting it to you. Buy British but, better still, buy food produced in your own locale.
- Buy local food in season. This is the simplest and most rewarding way to guarantee maximum taste with minimum fuel wastage. Go on, binge on asparagus in May and strawberries in high summer, then savour those tastes until the next year's crop comes in.
- Check labels or ask shopkeepers. Go home empty-handed rather than pay for food imported from overseas, if you know that similar food is indigenous to Britain and in season.
- Buy food in as naked a state as possible. The more cooking, seasoning, prettifying or packaging a piece of food has been subjected to, the more hands that piece of food is likely to have passed through, all prolonging its journey to you. It will therefore incur more food miles, while still more fuel may have been wasted on preservatives and fancy packaging. Oh, and you'll probably pay more – though the food will almost certainly not be as fresh.

- Don't martyr yourself. Your wartime granny was allowed a ration of imported staples such as sweets on points, sugar and tea. She could spend money on off-ration luxury goods. Choose which imported goods you can't live without and in what minimum quantity, e.g. wine, tea, coffee, spices, sugar, chocolate, bananas, citrus fruits etc. Work out the most ethical and fuel-efficient way to source them and relish still having them as part of your diet.
- If you eat a lot of meat, eat less of it. But also start experimenting with lesser-known cuts, so that you are practising nose-to-tail eating. Remember, certain cuts weren't rationed in wartime – offal, for example.
- Only eat fish from sustainable stocks and caught in British waters.
- In wartime they saved on cargo space by discouraging the import of liquids and foods kept in liquids. Meats were telescoped. It's worth thinking about today too.
- Know how to cook and teach your children how to cook.
- Know your nutrients. Know what foods provide which vitamins and minerals, what is carbohydrate, protein and fat, and how these should be apportioned to create a healthy, balanced meal. It doesn't mean you can't eat unhealthily sometimes.
- For all the reasons outlined above, avoid fast and packaged foods, unless they fulfil the above remits.

As a digger for victory

- If you live in a city or town, take time to visit the countryside and remind yourself of how its principal industry fuels your own industriousness. If you have children, take them with you and teach them about what's coming out of the ground, where milk, eggs, sausages and burgers come from. Take them berry picking or to an apple orchard. (If you can't face leaving the city, at least take them to a city farm.)

- Grow your own and if you have children get them to grow their own too. Even if it's just cress, or parsley, it's a start.
- If you have a balcony or outside space, dig for victory by growing herbs, salad, vegetables and fruit.
- If you have no outside space, offer to help out a friend who does. Turn guerilla gardener or apply for an allotment.
- If your outside space is big enough, become a smallholder, growing your own veg and rearing your own chickens, ducks or rabbits (and pigs, goats or cows too, if anyone will let you).

Sucking Eggs:
What our government could learn from the wartime government's experience of buying, promoting, preparing and growing food

- Offer more incentive to the neediest in the form of local competitions, reward schemes, subsidies, giveaways, advice and lessons.
- Promote all of the above, so that nobody is in any doubt about what they have a right to and where they can obtain it.
- Tighten rules about nutritional meals in all public-sector establishments and promote the healthiest eating options through subsidies.
- Force the food industry to produce healthier foods through using taxes, subsidies and tighter rules about how they promote food.
- Support the British farming industry with subsidies to grow healthier foods and the promotion of British produce over imported goods.

- Recognise, as the wartime Ministry of Food did, that it is a government's duty to enhance the nation's health through the food made available to the public, even if this involves sometimes standing up to the food conglomerates and supermarkets.

CHAPTER FOUR

THE BRITISH RESTAURANT AND CANTEEN:

How your wartime granny pioneered today's eating-out and drinking culture

'Is that the place,' asked Mr Thwaites, '. . . where you get black-market steaks and are charged five shillings for a small cocktail?'
'Well – I don't know about five shillings.'
'And where the cars are lined up ten deep outside on black-market petrol?'

Patrick Hamilton, *The Slaves of Solitude*[1]

At some point in the past decade we British stopped being embarrassed by our national cuisine and instead became quite bullish about it. Our chefs were getting Michelin stars. Our best restaurants were competing with European temples to gastronomy. Our television chefs were celebrities, instantly identified by first names only. And our produce? Well, if you set aside worries about BSE and salmonella, and scare stories of how fish farming methods were pumping hormones into our national waters, well, produce was second to none. Britain was booming and so was our restaurant scene. Indeed, a 2006 survey by the Office of National Statistics (ONS) showed that between 1992 and 2004 spending on food and drink consumed outside the home soared by 102 per cent. The ONS report suggested that a cultural shift was behind not just more people eating out, but also their enjoyment of a wider range of cuisines. Their survey also showed that for the first time – at least in the ONS's history – the British were spending more money on food consumed outside the home than within it.[2]

But what a difference three years can make. By January 2009 economic pundits were predicting a dramatic slowdown. An article in the *Guardian* heralded 'an about-turn in our eating habits as our increasingly indulgent dining lifestyle has been replaced with an era of austerity not seen since post-war rationing . . . Restaurants have seen an exodus of customers in the last two months as diners have turned to takeaways, supermarket promotional deals and fast-food chains.'[3]

Oddly enough it was the war that first introduced many people to the habit of eating outside the home. By 1941 an estimated 79 million meals were being eaten out weekly. By 1944 this figure had risen again to 170 million. Meals out accounted for between 8 and 9 per cent of the sugar, meat and fat consumed beyond the ration. The government sponsored its own chain of affordable fast-food restaurants. Work canteens, which in the 1930s had been rare – a hobby horse of a few altruistic factories and works owners – grew in number from 1,500 before the war to 18,486 in 1944. School meals properly established themselves in the wartime period, increasing from about 160,000 in the late 1930s to 1.6 million in 1945. Mobile canteens, emergency feeding stations and delivery schemes in rural areas all played their role in ensuring that the population did not go hungry for long.

Some aristocrats and Cabinet members dismissed their home cooks and moved for the duration into the Dorchester – believed, because of its concrete foundations, to be structurally the safest hotel in London. Working women such as secretaries now regularly lunched in one of the government-sponsored British Restaurants. Impoverished inner-city children could now enjoy a nutritious wholly subsidised school lunch.

The government had needed to provide such services because total war is totally disruptive. The 1939 census showed that more than 2.5 million people (roughly 5 per cent of the population) had moved homes within the first two months of the war. During the London blitz, between September 1940 and May 1941, 1.4 million or one in six Londoners were made homeless at some point. By as early as June 1942, across the population 20 million moves had been registered (of a population of 48 million). Even allowing for the fact that 'many of these movements represent removals of the same person at different times, it has nevertheless been estimated that by the end of 1941 the number of civilian adults residing elsewhere than in the [Parliamentary] constituency in which they were resident in 1939 was of the order of 5 millions, or roughly one sixth of the total electorate.'[4] These figures spoke only for the adult civilian population. Armed Forces mobilisation, evacuation from vulnerable areas and the transfer of industrial workers were estimated separately.

More than 40,000 British citizens arrived in the United Kingdom as refugees from overseas, while at least 120,000 foreign civilians sought safety here. But their numbers were insignificant when compared to the million-plus Allied, Dominion and colonial troops being billeted in Britain by the spring of 1944. By 1943 there were already in the United Kingdom 35,000 Free French, 25,000 Polish servicemen, 3,200 Czechs, 1,750 Norwegians, 2,000 servicemen from the Netherlands and about the same number from Belgium; 23,000 Canadian troops, too, had arrived in the United Kingdom. But the greatest impact came, of course, with the American entry into the war. In the run-up to the Second Front invasion there was an American force of approaching 1.5 million resident in Britain. In sparsely populated Suffolk alone there were 71,000 GIs, meaning that by 1944 every sixth person in the county was an American, 'and in Wiltshire the English probably only just outnumbered the GIs by two to one.'[5] Wartime Britain was by no means a grey monoculture: borscht, Russian salad and hamburgers, as well as tribute dishes such as Ohio Pudding and Roosevelt Scramble, featured in more adventurous establishments.

British Restaurants

Is it surprising to learn that the popular contemporary restaurant chains of today had their wartime equivalents? That the self-service system had been pioneered in wartime eateries and later copied by commercial operators? That the war had promoted the idea that restaurant meals were not just for the rich? Nowadays popular restaurants such as Wagamama, Canteen and Leon pride themselves on delivering filling meals, fast, in

Diners in a British Restaurant.

Opposite: British Restaurant in the opulent Fishmongers' Hall, City of London.

democratic canteen-like surroundings. So did the government-sponsored 'British Restaurants' of the 1940s.

Communal Feeding Centres first popped up in the autumn of 1940 during the London blitz to provide hot meals for those who had been bombed out of their houses or who could not access their cooking facilities. Many people found themselves stranded, far from home and hungry, and were glad of these not-for-profit self-service restaurants,

established by local authorities but supplied by the Ministry of Food. However, existing catering establishments saw them as unfair competition and their numbers never reached the 10,000 target that the government had at first hoped for.

Churchill is credited with changing the name from Communal Feeding Centres to British Restaurants. By September 1943 there were almost 2,200 British Restaurants nationwide, serving on average 600,000 meals daily. One could be found every half mile or so in the bombed-out East End. The greatest concentration remained in the capital where the Greater London Council found space for about 250 British Restaurants, most housed in places such as churches, schools and municipal halls; but a few in rather grander settings such as the Victoria and Albert Museum, the banqueting hall of the Fishmongers' Company and the Royal Veterinary College.

However lofty the ceilings, the intention was always democratic, reflected, some wags claimed, in the utilitarian nature of the brown meals. A Tory MP, William Darling, opined, 'One needs to be British to "take it" in a British Restaurant.'[6] But only a niggard would find cause to moan at the prices. A British Restaurant was open to anyone and affordable – a whole meal comprising a main course, two vegetables, bread and butter, then pudding, all washed down with a cup of tea could be bought for about a shilling. On average, 2d bought a bowl of soup, 8d a main dish with vegetables and 3d a pudding.

Surveys showed that 20 per cent of the overall population had eaten in a British Restaurant at least once, while 5 per cent did so regularly and most felt favourably towards them. The poorest uptake of their services was among housewives – one assumes they snatched lunch at home. As late as April 1947, 850 British Restaurants were still running but the government's withdrawal of financial support sealed their fate and they gradually closed down.

The people's pub

It was not, as might be thought, the Lieutenant who had introduced Miss Roach to the River Sun or to the habit of meeting and drinking in bars. The blitz in London, with its attendant misery, peril, chaos and informality, had already introduced Miss Roach to this habit. She had no longer any fear of entering public-houses, and would, if necessary, and provided she was known in the place, enter one unaccompanied. Here again the war, the sombre begetter of crowds everywhere, had succeeded in conjuring into being yet another small population entirely of its own to help fill and afflict the public places – a population of which Miss Roach was a member – of respectable middle-class girls and women, normally timid, home-going and home-staying, who had come to learn of the potency of this brief means of escape in the evening from war-thought and war-endeavour.

Patrick Hamilton, *The Slaves of Solitude*[7]

Patrick Hamilton's social satire *The Slaves of Solitude*, published in 1947, is one of the great fictional portrayals of day-to-day civilian life during the war. Its blue-stocking spinster heroine, Miss Roach, is bombed out of London and takes a room in a run-down boarding house in a Thames-side commuter village. You can almost smell the Woolton Pie as Hamilton describes in stewed-tea-stained detail the new experiences to which the war, for better or worse, has brought Miss Roach: drinking, even getting drunk, in public; taking refuge in public houses; contact with foreigners; eating communally; being taken out to dinner by American GIs. Hamilton makes a particular point of the buttoned-up Miss Roach's regular visits to her local pub, the River Sun, for a pink gin.

At the outset of war the Temperance Movement had lobbied vociferously to limit licensing hours and decrease drinks production. They had argued, not without some sense, that a blackout coupled with intemperance might lead to more crime. There was also something to their argument that it was wasteful to use precious imported wheat and barley to brew alcohol. In the First World War these ideas had had a sympathetic hearing from the teetotal Lloyd-George. But in 1939 the brewing industry fought back. 'The *Brewer's Journal* of October 1939 claimed that a barrel of beer had the equivalent value of the following: 10 lbs of ribs of beef, 8 lbs of shoulder of mutton, 4 lbs of cheese, 20 lbs of potatoes, 1 lb of rump steak, 3 lbs of rabbit, 3 lbs of plaice, 8 lbs of bread, 3 lbs of butter, 6 lbs of chicken and 19 eggs. "We would emphasise that a standard barrel of beer has the food value of the WHOLE of the above food," stressed the industry magazine. "We have had these figures checked by a chartered accountant."'[8] They also argued that beer, thanks to the antiseptic nature of hops, was the safest drink in the world and therefore vital lest water supplies be tampered with. And, finally, they pointed out that brewing's side product, yeast extract, was a vital source of vitamin B12.

The wartime coalition government – led, of course, by a keen imbiber, Churchill – seemed to believe that Britain Could Take It, but it would do so better after a pint. In May 1940 Lord Woolton said, 'If we are to keep up anything like approaching the normal life of the country, beer should continue to be in supply, even though it may be beer of a rather weaker variety than the connoisseurs would like. It is the business of the Government not only to maintain the life but the morale of the country.' To cheers he later told the House of Lords, 'There are many people who believe that a glass of beer is not doing anybody any harm.'[9]

In the First World War pubs were associated with anarchy; in the Second they came to represent the plucky nature of little Britain standing against the evil might of Germany. A celebrated photograph from the darkest days of the blitz shows a London publican behind his bar, still pulling pints for regulars, despite the rest of his establishment having been reduced to rubble. Another bombed-out hostelry pinned up a sign saying, 'OUR WINDOWS ARE GONE BUT OUR SPIRITS ARE EXCELLENT. COME IN AND TRY THEM.'[10] Those spirits may have been in limited supply, though. Pubs, bars and even home drinkers suffered from shortages. Many pubs reduced their hours of opening, while only the very best restaurants had cellars sufficiently well stocked to maintain their wine lists.

Before the war about three-quarters of the male population had frequented pubs, but many fewer women and hardly any of them middle-class. In the 1940s the new standing of pubs as dispensers of morale as well as alcohol brought a fresh acceptability. One woman, from the rural wilds of Essex, wrote to the *Monthly Bulletin* about her local, the Bull,

> It began when East End mothers and daughters were evacuated. They went into the public houses as a matter of course. Perhaps the pub was the only place where there was a bit of fun. They were followed by the younger women of the village. Our cook went to the Bull, to the horror of her parents. Indeed, many village parents were horrified. The wives and sweethearts of the RAF have followed their men stationed amongst us; and there is the Women's Land Army.
>
> The Bull was a quiet, sleepy (and rather unsuccessful) place in the old days. Now it's a regular village café – a bit noisy sometimes, but innocent enough – with dancing and a Channel Island refugee, a considerable performer, at the piano. Is this a bad thing, a sign of decadence? I don't think so. It means that the pub is changing its character, probably for the better. Women in the long run ensure a higher standard.[11]

The Blitz

Pubs were not the only novel experience. The war propelled most people down new avenues. Civilian men turned soldiers and young women were conscripted to replace men in the fields, the factories and the offices. Child evacuees from inner-city slums were billeted on country people. Bourgeois women, who had never before done a minute's housework, now volunteered to serve tea in mobile canteens. Servants left to be part of the war effort and their one-time employers had to learn how to keep house themselves. The war effort became like a giant sociological experiment, in which people from different walks of life lived and worked side by side as never before. Air raids pushed people together in circumstances of unsavoury proximity. Think of what it would be like to queue up at dusk each night to secure your sleeping spot in a London Underground station – as 177,000 elected to do at the height of the blitz – then pass the evening there, cheek by jowl with whole families, their food and entertainment, including their effluence? Or imagine being one of the thousands who boarded commuter trains from London at the end of each day to take up a regular night-time residency in Kent's Chislehurst caves, which by the end of the war had developed more mod cons than Hanna-Barbera ever thought to graft on to the post-modern *Flintstones*? The Chislehurst caves didn't just have entire suites of rooms underground, they even housed a cinema and performance spaces.

The richest had exclusive versions of these arrangements. Some of the top establishments, such as the Savoy, converted their basements into restaurant-come-air raid shelters, where clients could book a bed at the same time as they reserved a table. In the converted cubicles of what had been the Turkish Baths of the Dorchester Hotel were 'neat rows of cots, spaced about two feet apart, each one covered with a lovely fluffy eider-down. Its silks billowed and shone in the dim light in pale pinks and blues. Behind each cot hung the negligee, the dressing gown . . . The pillows on which the heads lay were large and full and white . . . There was a little sign pinned to one of the Turkish-bath curtains. It said, "Reserved for Lord Halifax."'[12]

Food delivery during bombing

How to continue feeding the public when mealtime, work and sleeping patterns were disrupted so regularly became a ministerial concern. Particularly since ration cards were often left in the rubble of homes. The Luftwaffe was no respecter of mealtimes. The air raid sirens might go off just as you were putting the finishing touches to your dinner, forcing you to make a decision between endangering yourself or sacrificing the meal you had eked out from the ration. Or you might find yourself spending the dinner hour stuck in an air raid shelter on the

One of the rail company's emergency canteens.

other side of town, prohibited from travelling home until the All Clear sounded.

On 7 September 1940 the Luftwaffe attacked the East End of London. They returned the next night and the next and the next. Their mission widened to rain terror, havoc and death on further parts of the capital – London was bombed for at least fifty-seven nights consecutively – and then on other cities. By the time the nightly bombing raids ceased on 10 May 1941, over 43,000 civilians had died – more than half of them in London. It was the poor and poorly built East End that bore the brunt of the blitz, precisely where the people had the least resources to cope with it. And this was of course part of the Nazis' policy – to bomb not just buildings but the British spirit into submission.

For the authorities on the ground, then, their mission became to feed the bombed-outs' morale as well as their hunger. At the Ministry of Food, Woolton and his bureaucrats were full of bold ideas, the most novel and arguably gimmicky of which was the 'Food Train' launched on 14 November 1940, to serve those sheltering on the platforms of the Underground. It moved between stations serving food from seven to nine o'clock in the evening, and half past five to seven in the morning, and was partly funded by the office of the Lord Mayor of London. Voluntary organisations such as the Salvation Army and WVS staffed all-night field kitchens near city air raid shelters. Volunteers soon noticed, however, that women, elderly ones in particular, were unwilling to quit their homes and preferred to guard their remaining possessions amid the rubble.

In his memoirs Woolton claims that he was in his office one day, fretting about old ladies who refused to leave their bomb-damaged homes, at the very moment when Mr Kruger of the British War Relief Society of America presented himself for a meeting. Kruger explained that he had come to Woolton as the man best placed to see where need was and to offer his organisation's money. Woolton sketched out his dream of establishing 'a mobile convoy consisting of an ambulance service with trained people in charge, of food supplies, kitchens and everything that would produce the hot drinks and food that shocked people needed'. He continued that each unit should carry a 350-gallon water tank and be composed of two lorries each capable of carrying 6,000 meals; two kitchen lorries with soup tureens and fuel; three mobile canteens, and five motorcyclists, whose job would be to keep in contact with the local authorities. Mr Kruger liked the idea so much that he agreed to finance the lot on the spot.

Woolton's next meeting happened to be with King George VI at Buckingham Palace.

> I told him of this plan and said '. . . but I want to call them "Queen's Messengers" because the women who will take charge of these convoys will indeed be messengers of mercy.' The King at once jumped up and said, 'Come and ask her.' Together we told Her Majesty of the idea . . . The Queen with much modesty said, 'But why do you want to call them Queen's Messengers? What will I have done?' Then, greatly daring, I said, 'But Your Majesty, don't you know what you mean to all of us in

> this country? It isn't only your high position that matters: it is the fact that the vast majority of people think of you as a person who would speak the kindly word, and, if it fell within your power, would take the cup of hot soup to the needy person.' Whereupon Her Majesty put up her hands and said to me, 'Oh my Lord, do you think I mean that; it is what I have tried so hard to be.' It was indeed a very moving insight into the mind of a great lady. And so they were called Queen's Messengers. The moment I got back to my office a private secretary rang up from the Palace to say that Her Majesty insisted that she should finance one of the convoys, and so I told my American friends that they could not pay for the entire outfit: they would have to share it with the Queen – and that increased their zeal.[13]

At the time of its launch in March 1941 the complete fleet was 144 vehicles, all but eight provided by the British War Relief Society of America. Presenting them, the Queen said: 'It is my hope that they will have a double value: they will not only provide what is sorely needed, but they will do what is no less vital – they will bring it on the instant and bridge the gap between destruction and swift reorganisation. The message which I would entrust to these convoys will not be one of encouragement, for courage is never lacking in the people of this country. It will rather be one of true sympathy and loving kindness.'[14]

At first the convoys were 'manned' by members of Lady Reading's WVS, but later other charitable organisations such as the Quakers and the YMCA ran convoys. The first Queen's Messenger convoy went into action during the initial heavy bombardment of Coventry and fed 12,000 people over three days. It was dangerous work because although the convoys did not get going until immediately after the All Clear had gone, they could still fall victim to bad roads, collapsing buildings, fires, stray bombers and unexploded bombs. Some died doing their duty, but for most it was exhilaratingly rewarding work.

Rosalind Desch recorded her activities as a driver for a mobile canteen administered by the Wimbledon YMCA, founded in March 1940. As well as dispensing tea, their canteen sold basic snacks and toiletries,

Preparing food for canteens: North Staffordshire, wartime Food Preparation Centre.

and in the quiet hours ran a knitting circle, which donated 'comforts' to the barrage balloon airmen. One entry for 1940 reads:

FRIDAY AUGUST 16

AFTER THE LOCAL BLITZ

A very bad night for Wimbledon District . . . when we arrived at the YMCA . . . we were told that a mobile canteen was to be sent to take free tea and buns to the demolition and rescue squads, also to the homeless people. I was fortunate enough to be one of those to drive the van. No sooner had we parked the car in one of the streets than numbers of very tired and worried men surrounded the car and were greatly refreshed by cups of tea and buns. At each place we went to we were greeted by the same words, 'We are so pleased to see you; we've been on this job since

8 o'clock last night and we've had nothing to drink for hours, can you come again tomorrow as we'll still be on the job . . .' Of course we would go tomorrow, and the next day, and any other day when we were wanted. And so it has continued ever since. Whenever the services of the mobile canteen are needed to serve the soldiers, airmen, demolition and rescue squads of the bombed out people, there is a van ready and waiting.[15]

Canteens

The canteen is no passing fad of a Minister, no temporary bribe to labour. It has come to stay . . . Ground gained will not be yielded. Money put into the canteen will never be wasted but will pay interest in peace as in war. Canteens are a part of a great forward sweep to restore the human factor to its true position as the factor in industrial production. They are as essential to industry as the machine itself in an age of machines.

Canteens at Work[16]

Wartime workers doing hard physical labour in heavy industry felt that the average ration was inadequate. The solution was to increase the number of canteens, ensuring that many workers were guaranteed a free energy-giving meal to supplement their RB1 allowance. Employers of more than 250 staff were legally obliged to organise canteens. Thus the war saw a significant rise in the provision of workplace restaurants. In rural areas, cheese and pies were delivered in the fields for agricultural workers.

Of course, one of the reasons the government was so keen to promote nutrition in the workplace was its need to increase productivity. With a canteen on site, workers left their stations for less time, while labourers, women and children alike benefited from subsidised food.

The government needed more coal. Before the war many miners had returned home for lunch. Increased production targets and longer shifts now made it desirable to keep them on site. Woolton met with the Miners' Federation and claimed: 'And so we established the provision for miners, who had been accustomed to eating very large amounts of meat, to supplement their rations by having a good meal at the canteen . . . and in some cases made an advance in the standard of life of the miners that was almost equal to the advances that were made when pithead baths were established.'[17] In fact, coal production never increased to the level needed and fuel shortages plagued successive governments.

Among the publication allowed by the Ministry of Information during the war years – despite paper shortages – were a number of guides aimed at those running canteens in industry, schools, pre-school and post-school clubs. One such book argues:

> Started originally by a few daring factory owners as an altruistic experiment, 'welfare' – and canteens – turned out to be good business . . . Many of the problems of industry – not only output, but absenteeism and health, accidents, labour turnover and contentment – were found to be related to breaking the long spell of work with a mid-shift refresher . . . With the advent of war and the call to the nation for every ounce of production, factory canteens are playing a more vital role than ever. Output has to be maintained and *increased* despite every drawback of longer transport, billeting, and unsettled meals and the strain of air raids and overtime. In the opinion of a leading welfare expert, the canteen has become *second only to wages as a draw*.[18]

The debates over luxury eating out

The Passionate Profiteer to his Love

Come feed with me and be my love,
And pleasures of the table prove,
Where Prunier and The Ivy yield,
Choice dainties of the stream and field

On caviar my love shall graze,
And plump on salmon mayonnaise,
And browse at Scott's beside thy swain,
On Lobster Newburg with champagne.

Come share at the Savoy with me,
The menu of austerity.[19]

Sagittarius (pseudonym of Olga Katzin)

For those who could afford it eating out became a means of dodging austerity, especially if they had sacrificed their cook to the war effort.

At first restaurants were not rationed at all, but were instead permitted to buy in only as much food as they had sold pre-war. This gave them a monopoly on the best supplies – if the clientele were prepared to pay eye-watering prices there was no reason why luxury products, including salmon, game and shellfish, which were too rare to be rationed, had to come off the menu. The wartime diaries of Harold Nicolson and Sir Henry 'Chips' Channon are replete with good dinners. Channon's entry for 22 September 1940 reads: '. . . to luncheon at the Ritz which has become fantastically fashionable; all the great, the gay, the Government; we knew 95% of everyone there. But Ritzes always thrive in wartime as we are all cookless.'[20] '. . . to the Dorchester' he chronicles on 5 November 1940:

> Half London seemed to be there . . . I gave Bob Boothby a big champagne cocktail in the private bar, which now looks, seems and smells like the Ritz bar in Paris, rue Cambon. Our bill must have been immense for we had four magnums of champagne. London lives well: I've never seen more lavishness, more money spent, or more food consumed than tonight, and the dance floor was packed. There must have been a thousand people . . . We left the modern wartime Babylon, and got quickly into Harold's air force car. The contrast between the light and gaiety within, and the blackout and the roaring guns outside was terrific: but I was more than a little drunk.[21]

As Woolton later recalled,

> The question was repeatedly raised as to whether hotel and other restaurants should not be closed down during wartime on the grounds that they constituted 'luxury feeding'. This was not right; people needed some relaxation . . . I did however appeal constantly – and particularly to the catering trade – not only to avoid waste, but to avoid the appearance of waste. At a caterers lunch, on one occasion I said to my audience, 'If you knew the amount of time, trouble, and anxiety that some of us have gone through to secure the bread supply, you would know my feelings when I see a waiter, clearing a table, take a roll of bread that has not been eaten and put it in an ash-tray.'[22]

By 1941 the idea that toffs were living the life of Riley shucking oysters in St James's had led to such class tension that the government commissioned a series of polls. Home Intelligence duly reported 'ill-feeling about the advantage of the rich over the poor in the matter of "feeding out"'. In October 1941, 55 per cent of those surveyed favoured introducing coupons for rationed foods eaten in restaurants. By March 1942, a Gallup poll showed that now 76 per cent favoured the 'promise of a ruling restricting the cost of restaurant meals', due to puritanical feelings that 'luxury feeding of all kinds should be controlled'.[23]

Worried about public morale, the Ministry of Food responded in 1942 not by introducing coupons – which they felt, rightly, would be

Business as usual in a smart carvery in London's West End.

impracticable – but by limiting the price of a restaurant meal to 5s, with only one main course per person. In practice this meant that a meal at the Ritz became more affordable to the aspirant middle classes. But the smart establishments had their means of keeping out the riff-raff: tips, taxes, myriad supplements, extortionate prices for alcohol and Byzantine booking systems. And the new legislation did little to curb the resentment that there was a select band of people at the top of society – many of whom happened to be government luminaries and cronies – who did what would today be the equivalent of eating at Nobu daily.

Conclusion

The good news, then, for gourmands is that even in austerity Britain the need to relax, and for people to find food while on the move, can be recognised. During the war, restaurants, hotels and cafés were allowed to continue trading, with a minimum of rationing interference. Mass catering establishments that could provide cheap, healthy fare were promoted as a means of boosting productivity and improving the nation's nutrition. A woman could enter establishments where once her presence might have been frowned upon, with or without a male chaperone. With her wartime wages she could even pick up the tab. But before saying a resounding 'Cheers, Gran', it is worth thinking of the thrifty, even green, virtues she would have applied, or had to comply with, while eating and drinking out in wartime Britain.

Going out to eat and drink

- Patronise establishments that shout up their green credentials.
- Select what is fresh and in season. This is not only the most ethical way to gourmandise, but also the most adventurous and the most enjoyable. Some of the fanciest foods – game, oysters, certain types of fish, mushrooms, pretty much all fruit and vegetables – are at their best for a few weeks only at particular points in the culinary calendar.
- Select items that have not crossed the globe for you. This does not mean eliminating far-flung cuisine or fusion cooking, as many of the spices and seasonings used in cooking are not flown in; but avoid fresh produce that is sourced overseas.
- Select items that have not crossed Britain for you. Local is best.
- Experiment in restaurants. If you are intimidated about trying out new foods or tricky methods at home – fiddly game birds, bony fish, mysterious-looking vegetables – get a professional chef to cook them for you first.
- Practise nose-to-tail eating. Rearing animals for their meat is an expensive business. Don't turn up your nose at any of it. A restaurant is the best place to try out lesser-known cuts of meat, fish from sustainable sources and offals that you might be nervous of tackling for the first time at home.
- Bulk out on vegetables. Your wartime granny would have eaten far less meat and fish than you do – even if she'd moved into the Dorchester.
- Don't over-order.
- Waste not, want not. The restaurant won't be allowed to recycle your leftovers because of Health and Safety Regulations.
- Ask for takeaways that are not overpackaged. The classic fish-and-chips newspaper wrapping is not only superior to a polystyrene box or a plastic tray, but easier to dispose of.

A freshly prepared sandwich from a lunch bar will come in less packaging than a pre-made one.

- Drink tap water, not bottled.
- Drink British beverages, locally sourced if possible. Remember that in wartime foreign beverages were hard to come by.
- Apply the same rules to eating out when you are overseas or on holiday.

PART TWO

THE AESTHETICS OF AUSTERITY

CHAPTER FIVE

MAKE DO AND MEND: *Wartime fashion*

It's economy time, but that doesn't mean that you need look shabby and down at the heels.

Ursula Bloom, *Woman's Own*, 1940

Are you a new recessionista shopper? With all this talk of credit crunch times there's a tendency to think tumbleweed will be blowing around Topshop and we'll all be wearing 'safe' black trousers and court shoes for the next five years. But according to our survey . . . that's not the case.

***Grazia*, November 2008**

By the end of the Second World War barely a shop on London's Oxford Street had survived unscathed. Some war wounds were just blown-out windows but other stores, such as the DH Evans flagship branch (now House of Fraser), had to wait until after the conflict to be rebuilt. Among the worst casualties was John Lewis, which in September 1940 had been hit directly by an oil bomb. It took firemen a day and a half to extinguish the flames, yet within three weeks what remained navigable of the store had reopened and in the meantime enterprising floor managers had been selling undamaged stock direct to customers on the street. The store's in-house magazine sounded a defiantly Churchillian note: 'We shall defend our Partnership with the utmost energy. What matters if we are bombed out of John Lewis? We shall fight on at Peter Jones.'[1]

Oxford Street, it seems, can still take it. In April 2007 the British media enjoyed reporting on a 'Primark riot' that broke out during an inaugural day's trading at the bargain basement fashion emporium's new flagship 70,000 sq. ft store. Crowds of women, keen to snatch a prize buy, had gathered outside the store from the early hours, their fashion hunger fuelled by Internet rumours of further discounts in the already almost unfeasibly cheap store. At 9.45 a.m. the shop's staff were forced to open up early due to the press of the queue outside. In the ensuing rush to grab bargains, fights and scuffles broke out. A security guard and manager were injured.

Queuing overnight was not new, of course. But waiting in line for the Harrods sale was once a tradition upheld by doughty bicycle-clipped women who bought their Christmas cards in January while being a lady of fashion was naturally aligned with decorum and elegance. By the early 2000s, however, there was a new lure: celebrity and aspirations to a designer lifestyle. The sales of stock designed or endorsed by Kate Moss and Celia Birtwell at Topshop; Stella McCartney and Karl Lagerfeld at H&M; Giles Deacon at New Look and Roland Mouret at Gap all led to handbags-at-dawn stand-offs. Even an anti-consumerist item, Anya Hindmarch's limited edition 'I Am Not a Plastic Bag' sold at Sainsbury's no less, had women queuing for hours. A wartime mantra was 'If you see a queue – join it'. Our grandmothers formed an orderly line outside shops in the desperate hope that some hard to come by item (nylons; shoes; fish; lemons) might still be being sold by the time they reached the head of it. They queued because it was worth it. In the early noughties we queued because we'd swallowed – hook, line and sinker – the notion that we're worth it. Many of us fell for the idea that it wasn't just a product we were purchasing when we bought a Kate Moss waistcoat in Topshop, but actually a scintilla of her glamour and a taste of her celebrity lifestyle.

This idea that we're worth it has been a pernicious one. Our opportunities to shop have never been greater. More females are in paid employment and women's pay – though by no means always equal – is nearer that of their male colleagues. Women's spending power has increased by a staggering 50 per cent in the last fifty years.[2] Domestic appliances mean that stay-at-home mothers are no longer shackled to their kitchen sinks. But with spare time and spending power come irresponsibility. Every weekday lunch hour, every evening after work and every Saturday and Sunday, thousands of women have been spending more than they are actually worth on high streets around the land. Where our grandmothers invested in National Savings for the country's good, we were – until the credit crunch really started to bite – persuaded that debt was good for the nation's financial security; that spending money we didn't actually have was almost a patriotic gesture. In early 2009 the government, by lowering VAT, once again tried to encourage us to throw caution to the wind and to go shopping for the sake of the nation's economy.

The average British woman spends more than eight years of her life shopping. In 2006 GE Money (interestingly, the company behind many of Britain's high-interest store cards) carried out a survey. The 3,000 women polled had, on average, spent just under 95 hours a year on food shopping, but almost twice that amount – 169 hours – seeking out new clothes, shoes and accessories.[3] Most of the women who responded to another 2006 survey (Alliance & Leicester) admitted both that they had no funds left over at the end of the month for savings and that they habitually bought items of clothing they did not need.[4] Another report (August 2007, market analyst Verdict) showed that the average British woman bought twice as many items of clothing as she did in 1995.[5] The results of this profligacy can be seen, not just in credit card debts and overstuffed wardrobes, but in the depressing fact that in the five years from 2003 to 2008 councils saw a 23 per cent increase in the throwing away of textiles. In November 2008 the House of Commons Environment, Food and Rural Affairs Committee visited a dump in Croydon, south London, where staff had labelled the problem 'the Primark effect'. The chair of the committee, a Conservative MP, explained, 'It is presenting real challenges, because these materials are not easily recyclable. In other words, it was a case of landfill or burning them . . . The whole notion of throwaway fashions needs to be re-examined. People may want something that is fashionable, but they should also be thinking about whether what they are buying will last.'[6]

Primark, which had recently announced a 17 per cent increase in profits to £233 million for the year ending in September 2008, told newspapers that it would continue with its successful formula of offering consumers 'good-value' clothes. Good value means knock-down prices and Primark is not the only retailer selling high fashion cheaply. From the mid 1990s the ardent UK shopper benefited from a 10 per cent drop in prices, driven by the entry into the rag trade of supermarket stores such as Tesco and Asda, and the fashion makeover of shops at the cheapest end of the high street such as New Look. It was not only prices that plummeted when we threw a couple of almost incomprehensibly cheap cashmere sweaters into our supermarket trolleys, but common sense. In previous generations even well-to-do women, even those who could afford couture in Paris, had bought with specific needs and occasions in mind, or because some item would prove invaluable in pulling together different elements of their wardrobe. From some point in the late 1990s, however, great numbers of us started buying for no better reason than that the stuff was there to be bought. Ramshackle excuses about 'silly prices', 'virtually giving it away' and 'it seemed cheeky not to' never quite tallied with the fact that when it was all totted up a hell of a lot of money was being squandered on tat that might at best be worn a handful of times. A worrying number of us weren't buying out of need or with purpose, but out of desire.

In the late 1990s George Davies, the designer guru who first reanimated Marks & Spencer with Per Una and then introduced unfeasibly cheap but good-looking clothes to the supermarket with George for Asda, told a journalist, 'You see, men are different from women when they are shopping for clothes. Men like logic. They like order. Women, on the other hand, are like scavengers when they hit the high street. Honestly, they are like wild fans at a football match sometimes. When women find a store selling desirable goods at the right price they will go in and wreck it. And the more it is wrecked, the more they will be drawn to it . . . and then they'll wreck it even more.'[7]

When I asked my mother, no slouch herself when it comes to shopping splurges, about her own mother she said, 'She always looked extremely smart.' My mother was born in September 1941, three months after the introduction of clothes rationing; her younger sister, Maureen, was also a wartime baby. For my grandmother, the young, left-wing, working-class but fashion-conscious wife of a Lanarkshire steelworker at Motherwell's famous Ravenscraig plant, it must have been no mean feat to keep herself and her two young daughters smartly turned out through those make-do austerity years. To be as smart as you could muster in the 1940s was seen by the government as key to public morale. If my grandmother were around now I doubt if she would be impressed by the cheery cheap excess of today's high-street fashion emporiums where clothes, sometimes manufactured in horrible conditions by underpaid women and even children mostly in the Third World, are sold at disposable prices. Or, at the other extreme, what would a woman who had dressed two young daughters in Utility wear make of our modern obsession with brands, celebrities and clothes? She was a proud woman who took pains to clothe her family as best she could afford, but she was also enough of a leftie to have appreciated some of the more levelling aspects of wartime austerity. Everyone was going without, or if they weren't they had enough sense not to show off about it.

Clothes rationing: the political context

Fashion . . . is out of fashion . . .
Harper's Bazaar

Il faut SKIMP pour être chic
Vogue

The introduction of clothes rationing on 1 June 1941 came without much warning.

The Whitsun break should have felt like a well-earned respite from the war. The previous year's Bank Holiday Monday had been cancelled at the last minute due to the British Expeditionary Force being stranded at Dunkirk. Soon afterwards the Luftwaffe had begun nightly bombing. However, by May 1941 not only did the blitz appear to be over, but many parts of the country were bathed in beautiful sunshine. Then, on the Sunday morning the women of Britain awoke to news that would darken their Bank Holiday spirits: clothes were to be put on the ration book. The government had deliberately timed its announcement to coincide with the holiday weekend in order to give retailers the chance to mark up goods and give women a couple of non-shopping days to get over the shock. There was also the wish to hide the fact that they had not yet produced clothing ration books.

It was not the first time the wartime coalition government had taken an interest in fashion. On 7 July 1940 it had issued advice to women to conserve wood by adopting flatter heels. At the Board of Trade its president, Oliver Lyttelton, had been keen to introduce clothes rationing. He had the support of his department and the Cabinet. Churchill, however, resisted him at every juncture, both because he believed clothes rationing would be bad for public morale and also because, as a Conservative, he was pro-business and pro-consumerism. He accused Lyttelton, an ex-Etonian, former Guards officer and City businessman who had entered Parliament only at Churchill's own behest, of wanting to see the British people 'in rags and tatters on the bureaucratic orders of a new minister'.[8] Lyttelton responded that the public was keen for sacrifice, providing, as food rationing had already shown, it was consistent with fair shares for all. Churchill shouted him down: 'Who are you to tell me what the public want? Why I only picked you out of some bucket shop in the City a few weeks ago!'[9]

It was Sir John Anderson, Lord President of the Council, who next mentioned the scheme to the Prime Minister. 'Can't you see I'm busy?' cried Churchill. 'Do what you like, but please don't worry me now.' Anderson had shrewdly chosen his moment: Churchill was utterly preoccupied with the hunt for the German battleship *Bismarck*. The Prime Minister had let down his guard, and clothes rationing was pushed through. By Tuesday, 27 May, by which time the *Bismarck* had been sunk, it was too late for him to revert to his dogged objections.

Proof that the introduction of clothes rationing was a rush job came with the comical instruction that for the time being the public should

Cover of a Make-do and Mend booklet.

exchange margarine coupons for clothing ones. 'Wake up, dear, you're in marg!' was how the wife of one dress buyer for a West End store welcomed her snoozing husband into the day.[10] Most of the wartime diarists reported the news with the same kind of jolly acceptance.

It was another curb on the people's lifestyle, but an expected one. Seventy per cent of the respondents to a Mass Observation survey said they supported the scheme. The comfortably wealthy Clara Milburn, having acknowledged it was a 'well-kept secret', wrote in her diary, 'Of course one did not walk Twink [her dog] today in silk stockings and best suit'.[11] She devoted more words in her entry for the day to the evacuation of British troops from Crete. The Mass Observation diarist Nella Last was also far more preoccupied with the withdrawal from Crete in her diary report for that day. But she had already been practising the virtues that would become a necessity through the long years of clothes rationing. 'Mrs Atkinson said, "summer has come – you *do* look nice!" – and we started to assess my rig-out. Broad-brimmed summer hat, four years old; sleeveless linen frock (three times remodelled), five years; white linen mesh fish-net gloves, three summers; woven braid sandals – lost in the mists of time – certainly seven years old; and navy flannel "swagger" coat belonging to a two-year-old suit.'[12]

The traditional English gentleman, meanwhile, was already well set up with the hard-wearing, best-quality clothes that his tailor had made to last a lifetime – or two. Chips Channon wrote jauntily, 'The big news this morning is clothes rationing. Oliver Lyttelton is only going to allow us 66 coupons per annum. A suit takes 26. Luckily I have 40 or more. Socks will be the shortage. Apart from these, if I am not bombed, I have enough clothes to last me for years . . .'[13]

Elizabeth Hudson was of the demographic – women in their twenties – who were least supportive of the clothes rationing policy, but even she sounded a note of stalwart acceptance in a letter home to her family in South Africa. She heralded the can-do attitude that would be the hallmark of a generation of Make Do and Menders:

> I don't think it will make much difference really because most people

> can't afford much now anyway and there's a very good excuse for being shabby. It's patriotic. But all the same I wish I'd been able to buy the shoes I need before. They take 5 coupons [soon they were to take seven] now and as there are only 66 all together for a year one can't buy more than one pair, we'll need more coupons for the winter. Wilfred suggests buying a sheet (unrationed) to make frocks and underclothes. It's a jolly good idea. A fine linen one could be dyed any colour. He was highly delighted that the notice: 'Sanitary towels are unrationed' should appear in *The Times* and says he is going to have his winter suit made entirely of STs and will patent the idea. To save paper they are using up the margarine coupons and I think it's going to be incredibly comic to proffer two margarine coupons and receive in exchange a pair of stockings. What a world![14]

Her husband's merriment about sanitary towels would probably not have amused the civil servants charged with formulating the scheme. What turned out to be the most difficult thing for the Board of Trade to get right was not the principle behind the policy of rationing clothes – as Lyttelton and Anderson had rightly insisted, the public were primed for sacrifice – but exactly what and how much should be put on coupons. As with food rationing, it was the items that the government could guarantee supply of that were put on rationing, not luxuries. In the main, civil servants were male and most struggled with the notion of what a basic annual wardrobe was. Allegedly, one of the people trying to decide what items to put on rationing was a rich Whitehall mandarin who confessed that he had forty suits (perhaps he was Chips Channon). Insiders who were seen as having a down-to-earth approach were brought in to advise. One such was the redoubtable Lady Reading, who asked civil servants searching questions about women's underwear. How many points should be given to bras as opposed to knickers, or a petticoat over stockings? It may have been through her valuations that sanitary towels got a mention at all. In the end it was decided that each person should be allocated enough coupons to represent two-thirds of the clothing the average person had bought in peacetime.

The scheme was announced in the morning's Sunday newspapers and in the BBC's bulletins. Once the news had had a chance to sink in, Lyttelton made a broadcast urging the nation to show steel through shabbiness and patriotism through lack of polish. 'In war the term "battle-stained" is an honourable one. We must learn as civilians to be seen in clothes that are not so smart, because we are bearing . . . yet another share in the war. When you feel tired of your old clothes remember that by making them do you are contributing some part of an aeroplane, a gun, or a tank.'[15]

Churchill had spent the previous week in a rage that he had been tricked into giving clothes rationing the go-ahead. But after the public appeared to accept the new restrictions he was magnanimous enough to acknowledge he had been wrong. The following week he marked Lyttelton out for praise, greeting him: 'Here's Oliver, who rejects the Prime Minister's view on public opinion about clothes rationing and turns out to be right . . . We will have an extra glass of champagne to celebrate.'[16]

Why clothes rationing was necessary

Were clothes rationing to be introduced today, its priorities might be to curb personal debt, to encourage ethical production or to reduce waste and thus our wardrobe's carbon footprint, which in December 2006 the UK government-supported Carbon Trust estimated accounted for almost 11 per cent (59 million tons) of the UK's 648 million ton carbon footprint. The thinking in 1941 was also tied into energy use – to curb imports, to save on shipping, and to put factory spaces, raw materials and the clothes industry's 450,000 workers towards the war effort. A lesser factor was, however, that gaps were already beginning to appear on the clothes rails. Supplies of cotton and wool were, as early as 1941, 20 per cent below that of pre-war levels. While the general cost of living had shot up by 39 per cent since the outbreak of war, the cost of clothes had gone up even further, by 69 per cent: the government had well-founded fears that if rumours of coming shortages were to take hold, those who could afford to would go on a panic-buying spree, stripping the remaining stocks and leaving nothing for the poor.

The clothes rationing allowance

The clothes rationing coupon scheme was based on a points principle scheme already in place in Germany. Everyone was to receive sixty-six coupons, the first twenty-six in margarine coupons from the food ration book. The civil servants had come up with a points value for every item of clothing, based on amounts of fabric, materials and labour, not cost. So, in fulfilment of the idea of fair shares for all, a Lancashire factory girl might find herself with the same coupon allowance as the 1938 season's most sparkling debutante, though the aristocrat doubtless already had a cupboard full of dresses of superior quality.

The most extravagant single points spend for both sexes were for a lined winter woollen coat or raincoat (eighteen points for a man; fourteen for a woman). A man's suit – depending on the lining – would set him back twenty-six to twenty-nine points; a light coat, jacket or blazer, thirteen; trousers,eight. A traditionally minded Scotsman had the advantage of his kilt being valued at fewer points (six) than a pair of trousers. Should a man have any remaining coupons, he might choose to spend them on making himself presentable in the bedroom with a pair of pyjamas and dressing gown (eight points each).

Both men and women were encouraged to mix and match selections of 'overlapping' and 'matched' clothes rather as is advised by those fashion magazine articles that demonstrate how to pack concisely and chicly for a long weekend. A woman might buy two suits and two pairs of shoes to form the basis for a summer and a winter wardrobe. Her remaining points would add to these outfits. A cotton dress, a blouse and a pair of knickers might be the items to refresh her summer wardrobe. In winter she might choose a jumper, skirt and two pairs of stockings. More efficient still was to buy fabric or wool unmade-up. Though rationed by the yard, you got more for your coupons and money this way: a yard of wool thirty-six

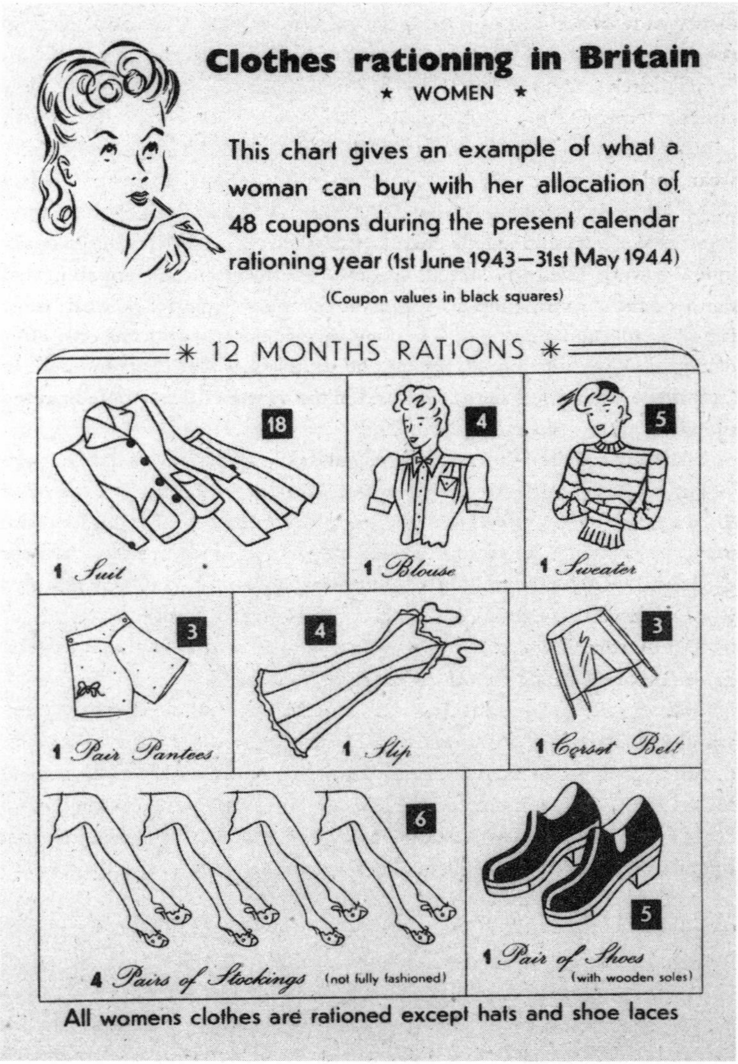
Clothes rationing in Britain
★ WOMEN ★
This chart gives an example of what a woman can buy with her allocation of 48 coupons during the present calendar rationing year (1st June 1943—31st May 1944)
(Coupon values in black squares)
✳ 12 MONTHS RATIONS ✳
18
1 Suit
4
1 Blouse
5
1 Sweater
3
1 Pair Pantees
4
1 Slip
3
1 Corset Belt
6
4 Pairs of Stockings (not fully fashioned)
5
1 Pair of Shoes (with wooden soles)
All womens clothes are rationed except hats and shoe laces

inches wide (three coupons); a similar measure of cotton or other material (two coupons) and two ounces of knitting wool (two coupons).

Children got extra coupons in acknowledgement of the fact that their clothes demanded less material, but were soon grown out of. A pregnant woman was given first fifty and later sixty extra coupons to buy maternity wear and a layette for her new-born. Those in the uniformed civilian forces were on rationing too, obliged to surrender coupons to their superior for a fresh uniform once a year. At first, those working in heavy industry were given an extra allowance, but after it became apparent that many of these extra coupons were not being spent on work wear, most factories adopted a policy where they gave replacement items only after damaged boilersuits, boots, aprons and smocks had been surrendered. In factories, coupons left over at the end of the year were distributed among the workforce as a sort of staff bonus.

Of course there were cruel oversights. Land girls did not have enough wellington boots, despite labouring outside in all weathers. The editor of *Farmers Weekly* wrote several campaigning editorials: 'If a Land Girl is not protected from drenching rain and the quagmire underfoot sooner or later she has to leave her work – at least until she dries out. She becomes, in a word, a casualty. What sort of an Army is it that makes casualties of her own?'[17] A sore point was that other Services, including the Royal Air Force, received rubber boots as standard issue.

Among others who felt the lack of sufficient coupons were mothers who had lost sons and wanted to buy mourning, doctors, dentists and, most audaciously, in August 1943 a mayor-elect of Blackpool who asked for an extra 328 coupons for himself and 178 for his wife so that they could fulfil their roles with suitable swagger. Their request, like those that might actually elicit some sympathy, was turned down.

Shopping on the ration

When I tried to stick to a wartime clothes allowance, I realised that for the past twenty-five years I had shopped for clothes with a recklessly wanton acquisitiveness that bore little or no relation to need or funds available. But it is one thing to put oneself on a restrictive regime for a year and quite another to look at strict control as a potential lifelong or at least decades-long habit. Forcing myself not to buy idly from a clothes rail but really to think about what I actually needed has made me more sympathetic to the slightly hysterical way many wartime women shopped when rationing was first introduced. Once they had their coupons many set out on shopping sprees determined to use up their allocation on the best stocks available. A member of the staff at Peter Jones was to remember, 'Our first reaction to rationing was that women were mad!'[18] And as evidence of this, one shopper at John Lewis, having used up all her margarine coupons, hopefully offered up those for sugar, bacon and cheese.[19] Arguably, she was wise to do so, since the following year the ration was reduced by a whopping eighteen points (the equivalent, lest we forget, of a lined woollen winter coat for a man, or a lined woollen coat plus two pairs of stockings for a woman) to forty-eight points per adult. In 1943 it was reduced still further to 40 points, but then returned in 1944 to 48 points. Though the coupon allowance was to fluctuate throughout the rationing period between 1941 and 1949, forty-eight points per adult was to remain the average.

The Board of Trade produced a 101-paragraph point-by-point explanation, 'Clothing Coupon Quiz: Answers to Questions on the Rationing of Clothing, Footwear, Cloth and Knitting Yarn'. Under the heading 'How the Rationing Scheme Works', it read:

1. There is enough for all if we share and share alike. Rationing is the way to get fair shares. *Fair shares* – when workers are producing guns, aeroplanes and bombs instead of frocks, suits and shoes. *Fair shares* – when ships must run the gauntlet with munitions and food

> rather than with wool and cotton. *Fair shares* – when movements of a population outrun local supplies. It is *your* scheme – to defend as a consumer and as a citizen. All honest people realise that trying to beat the ration is the same as trying to cheat the nation.

Despite the Board of Trade's hectoring insistence that seeking out more than one's fair share of the clothing ration was unpatriotic, it soon became apparent that the public felt more complacent about fiddling clothes than food rationing. After all, nobody was going to starve through these actions. So when relatives died their clothing ration books often never made it back to the authorities. Instead, the coupons were divided, as any legacy might be, among the grieving relatives. There were shops, too, that would let favoured clients pay a premium instead of giving over a coupon. The very poor, unaccustomed to having new clothes anyway, sold off many of their coupons, despite the legal threat that 'On summary conviction for the contravening of the Consumer Rationing Orders, a person may be imprisoned for 3 months or fined up to £100, or both. On conviction on indictment the penalty is up to two years' imprisonment or a fine not exceeding £500, or both.'[20] And the exchange of coupons on the Black Market became very lucrative, even forgeries being sold on at heavily inflated prices.

But most of the fiddling was close to home. Second-hand clothes were off the ration. So a rich relation might pass on quality seconds to a poorer family member, but then receive some of their coupons in exchange. Or if there was a wedding in the family everyone might pool their coupons in order to help towards a trousseau – no new bride wanted to be in threadbare patched pyjamas on her wedding night – or even a bridal dress (though, with good reason, long white frocks went out of fashion in the war, with many women making the practical decision to marry in uniform or a smart coat and skirt instead).

With food coupons, it made sense for most people to hand over their ration books to the person who did their household's shopping, usually the wife or mother, or if they were in digs the landlady. With clothes coupons it was easier to hold on to one's own supply; but many men had long since

poor people selling ration

given up buying clothes for themselves and thus surrendered their coupons to their wives, often to their disadvantage. Whereas, at the dinner table, a wife was likely to stint herself in order to give her husband a solid meal, it was he who was most likely to be short-changed in the allocation of clothes coupons. Many was the man who discovered that his allocation had contributed to a wife's summer frock, bought a son a pair of shoes or been given as a wedding present. At the end of the first year of clothes coupons most people had three left, but many had used all theirs up. Hugh Dalton, now responsible for rationing as the head of the Board of Trade, made a cack-handed attempt to endear himself to the public by boasting that he still had his full quota. His PR plan backfired, as housewives throughout the land took such claims as evidence that it was easier for the ruling classes – who already had wardrobes crammed with bespoke items of good, hard-wearing quality – than for those whose clothes were not built to last but somehow had to endure.

Wartime shortages

Some items were in short supply and could not be acquired even if you had coupons to spare. Sheer stockings were the most famous example, with young British women, popular lore has it, throwing themselves at American GIs in the hope of getting their hands on a pair of nylons, while others resorted to painting their legs with special dye and home-made concoctions such as tea. One girl coloured her legs with gravy browning, eliciting a wolf whistle and the cry of 'Hello, Oxo legs'.[21] Older ladies who preferred structured underwear, and those whose embonpoints needed upholstering, similarly could not buy everything they wanted even if they had the coupons. Corsets were hard to come by because they used whalebone. 'Smoothing' directoire pants inflicted their slimming torture via rubber, which after the fall of Singapore was virtually impossible for manufacturers to source. Rubber and steel shortages also made it extremely difficult to find suspender belts, garters, wellington boots ('very precious,' according to a government pamphlet, 'so only **wear them to keep out the wet**, and see that the children keep their gumboots for really wet days and never let them wear them for any other purpose',[22] plimsolls and Start-Rite sandals for children. The government cajoled mothers: 'WHY NOT EXCHANGE CHILDREN'S OUT-GROWN SHOES: In countless cupboards throughout the country, children's shoes are lying idle, not because they are outworn, but because they are out-grown. Perhaps the local school, welfare clinic, or some local women's organisation may already be running a children's shoe exchange – or be planning to run one. It's worth finding out anyhow.'[23]

In fact, shoes were a problem for everyone, not just children, as the government, which made them the subject of the pamphlet 'Heat plays HAVOC with Shoe Leather' recognised, saying 'Your boots and shoes have got to last you far longer than they ever did before, as leather and rubber are vitally needed for the Fighting Services.'[24] Those needing a new pair in a regular size were forced to plan their shopping trip with military precision. Lines would often form outside shoe stores hours before opening time. Chits would be issued on occasion to make sure nobody tried to jump the queue. Goods would sell out of the most common sizes within the first couple of hours of opening. That cheap standby, plimsolls (defined by the ration as 'a heelless shoe of any colour with canvas upper vulcanised to a rubber sole and includes shoes of this description which are sold as tennis shoes'[25]) were not being produced. No surprise, then, that some retailers tried to revive interest in that European peasant staple, clogs, and such adaptations as cork heels and 'woodies'. An article in *The Lady* magazine offered advice on how to adapt yourself to wooden heels (now having a revival in recession-bound Britain): 'If you find yourself walking a bit duck-footed in the first few days, concentrate on placing your toes in a pigeon-toed position and you'll find your muscles will soon co-operate and you'll be walking the right way once more. If you get them wet, dry them on trees away from direct heat so the wood will not crack, or the leather uppers dry out.'[26]

Specific restrictions

In May 1942 the government ordered that henceforth all men's jackets must be single-breasted, with a maximum of three pockets and only three buttons, with no buttons on the cuff. They also limited the manufacture of socks, banned elastic waistbands and limited trousers to a width of nineteen inches. These were the first of a series of Civilian Clothing (Restrictions) Orders and were accepted meekly. But the outlawing of turn-ups proved more than some men could stomach. The tailoring trade objected, so too did MPs expressing 'the serious dissatisfaction . . . to business and professional men'. Some got around the ban by pretending to have 'frayed' bottoms turned up, or deliberately getting a tailor to cut their trousers too long in order that they then required turn-ups. Nonetheless, in March 1943 there was a nationwide deputation to Hugh Dalton to beg for the reinstating of turn-ups. Dalton stood firm, presumably in his nineteen inch wide Utility-style trousers, first claiming that 'the prohibition of turn-ups to men's trousers was saving millions of square feet of cloth a year' and then responding sarcastically to questions at a hostile press conference: 'There can be no equality of sacrifice in this war. Some must lose lives and limbs; other only the turn-ups of their trousers.'[27]

Women had their crosses to bear too, or rather lack of stitch-crosses, for embroidery was banned from 1942 – even, it was specified, on underwear – along with fur and leather trimmings. Restrictions were imposed also on the number of pockets, buttons, tucks and pleats, while the law laid down a maximum length for belts, collars, depths of hems, seams and sleeves.

Sharing

Second-hand

Harrods is reputed to be opening a second-hand department!

Elizabeth Hudson in a letter home to South Africa, 8 June 1941[28]

The thrift store was a wartime invention. Internet swapping and recycling sites such as Freecycle and eBay are all twenty-first-century versions of lowtech 1940s sharing schemes, often administered by the WVS and the WI. Nella Last co-managed Barrow-in-Furness's Red Cross shop from 1941, taking in and making goods that were then sold to fund medical relief and parcels for prisoners of war. Oxfam, founded in 1942 to bring relief to the hungry, opened its first permanent second-hand shop in 1948, a year before clothes rationing ended in Britain and at a point when the nation was at its most threadbare.

With so many restrictions in place it made sense to stretch the principles of fair shares for all by literally sharing clothes through passing them on, swapping them, giving them to charity or buying and selling second-hand goods. The poor had traditionally been expected to be grateful for packages of clothes given by employers, richer relatives or the church. And in most households hand-me-downs for the younger children had been the norm. During the war it seemed negligent to have fashion mistakes hanging forlorn in your wardrobe. Nella Last gave her cleaning lady a pink blouse for Christmas; it was new but Nella thought it too young for herself and that she might never wear it. Local newspapers such as the *Manchester Evening News* carried notices placed by women who had excess clothes to sell, including a regular advertisement for 'The New Poor – a Dress Agency run by gentlewomen in the interests of gentlewomen'. Today, a leafy neighbourhood might boast an establishment selling 'nearly new designer seconds' from women who can afford to buy a new wardrobe every season, donated for the benefit of those who aspire to wear designer labels but can't justify the expense.

Make Do and Mend: The Board of Trade's propaganda masterstroke

In April 2008, Argos reported that sales of its cheapest model of sewing machine had risen by 50 per cent between 2006 and 2007.[29] The now defunct Woolworths had experienced a similar boom, with a 258 per cent rise in all sewing-machine sales. Correspondingly, there has been an upsurge in the numbers of novice needle-workers signing up for dress-making and crafts classes. Analysts say this boom is fuelled as much by a desire to save the planet by sourcing and renewing clothes more ethically as by a desire to save money or dress more individualistically. At the time these statistics were reported Richard Webster, the sewing-machines buyer at Argos, spoke to the *Independent* newspaper of a 'backlash against the throw-away society . . . a modern take on the "make do and mend" attitude of previous generations'.[30]

Today, Make Do and Mend is used as a shorthand description for frugal living. In the 1940s it was the catchword of the Board of Trade's chivvying government propaganda, which – though its primary purpose was to stop the public buying new clothes or household materials – would now be recognised as also extolling the virtues of the environmentalists' three Rs of Reducing, Reusing and Recycling. It was with great skill and energy that austerity was 'sold' to the war-weary British public. Make Do and Mend became both a rallying cry and a way of life. The campaign's coup was not to trivialise the role of housewives. The war had battlefronts at sea, in the skies overhead and overseas in four continents, where men were fighting. But the wives and mothers left behind to bring up families were placed at the centre of the civilian war effort, defined as the Home Front. If an Englishman's home was his castle then, in his absence, it was his wife's duty to defend it. She was urged to do so without surrendering her femininity, however coarsening the times. Her principal duty was to wage war on waste. Other tasks for the domestic commanding officer included keeping up the strength and appearances of her charges, so that they could best play their part in holding the line. The Make Do and Mend

Propoganda from the Board of Trade's Make Do and Mend campaign.

campaign placed women firmly within the domestic sphere, but eschewed the ideas of luxury and leisure that had been propagated by the advertising, design and entertainment industries in the 1930s through aspirational design and futuristic time-saving contraptions. Instead, the campaign emphasised old-fashioned virtues. Its heroine was not a self-indulgent creature in satin pyjamas lounging with manicured nails and a Veronica Lake peekaboo hairdo, but a headscarf- and housecoat-wearing, hard-working, frugally minded and above all practical domestic goddess of small things, winning battles at home on a daily basis through her virtuoso practice of good housekeeping.

It might seem extraordinary that a male-dominated government department was so preoccupied with housework, but the wartime Board of Trade's civil servants made even darning holes in socks their business. They produced more than a dozen Make Do and Mend pamphlets, several wall charts and scores of advertisements. All employed the rhetoric of battle, addressing the housewife as a soldier fighting a just collective war, where waste was in alliance with the enemy.

> ENGLAND EXPECTS ECONOMY OF CLOTHES, ECONOMY OF COUPONS BUT AN ABUNDANCE OF WELL DRESSED WOMEN. Although the rationing of clothes is a wartime necessity, there is no need for a woman to lose that cheerful confidence which comes from the knowledge that she is well dressed.[31]

The first Make Do and Mend pamphlet, produced in conjunction with the Ministry of Health and fronted by a perplexed-looking naked infant, was 'Getting Ready for Baby'. 'Babies don't need nearly as many clothes as people used to think', was its initial tip. Later pamphlets offered advice on prolonging footwear, household linen, rayon and knits. Suggestions for combating moths and instructions on darning, cleaning, knitting and reinforcing are as useful today as they were in the 1940s, including the advice, 'Don't carry a handbag under the arm of a coat or dress' (I now realise this is why so many of my jumpers and jackets need to be patched there). 'What Mothers Can Do To Save Buying New' – fronted by an impressed-looking boy and girl leaning forward to admire their mother's needlework – offered easy-to-follow sewing lessons. 'Simple HOUSEHOLD REPAIRS and How to Handle Them' suggested, 'Why not be your own "handy man" now that skilled labour has so many wartime calls upon it?' and taught women how to unblock sinks, repair leaky pans and replace handles. 'Children's Underwear Buying and Repair Hints "Keep them tidy underneath", says Mrs Sew-and-Sew' finished a series that, though its tone might seem arcane now, is full of information that is totally relevant today.

The Ministry of Food had Potato Pete and Dr Carrot to cajole the public into eating their vegetables; the Board of Trade had Mrs Sew-and-Sew – a stuffed doll with a pincushion head, a thread reel body and clothes peg legs – who, as her name suggests, was a bossy know-it-all. In wall charts, advertisements and leaflets, Mrs Sew-and-Sew never tired of thrifty suggestions on: How to Patch Shirts, Overalls, Elbows, Trousers, Sheets and Blankets, Darns and Tears, or How to Reinforce for Extra Wear. She had Guides to Woollies, Deft Darns and an ABC of Making Buttonholes.

MAKE-DO AND MEND
ADVICE CENTRE
Bring your problems here – says Mrs. Sew-and-Sew

She offered diagrams for Easy to Make Slippers for the Whole Family and Magpie Blouses (made of whatever bits of fabric you could lay your hands on). She entreated housewives to Never Send a Hole to the Wash. She even turned action heroine, to prove that when the going gets tough the resourceful get going: Nylon News from Mrs Sew-and-Sew showed her parachuting in to drop off her pearls of wisdom, read optimistically as, 'The nylon appearing in the shops at the moment is parachute nylon, so don't expect all the advantages next year's nylon will offer.'

Make Do and Mend classes

Of course, at the outbreak of war not every woman in Britain was an accomplished seamstress and those who needed to brush up their haberdashery skills, or longed for the camaraderie of fellow sewing soldiers to urge them to take up their needles as arms, were urged to pop into their Citizens Advice Bureau and ask about their nearest Make Do and Mend class. The WVS, the WI, local technological colleges, Evening Institutes and other such organisations all ran workshops at which women could be advised on coupon-saving wizardry. These classes received substantial support through advertisements with headings such as: 'Look what Mummy's done with my old overcoat: eight coupons saved: Any boy would be proud to wear a snug Battle Blouse like this'.

TWO INTO ONE SAVED 7 COUPONS:

An old stain that wouldn't come out and a cigarette burn had spoiled the look of a dark crepe dress brought to a Make-Do and Mend Class the other day. Its owner had a printed dress that was too small for her. She wanted the simplest way of combining them. The small sketches show how she did it – and she saves another two coupons by making a pair of knickers out of the leftover printed material.[32]

Beauty as duty: The fashion industry in wartime

Not many clothes around this autumn, I know, but there's no earthly reason why you shouldn't give your old ones that 'flip' which makes them look new and gives you the feeling of appearing at your best. It is your duty to make yourself look your best.

Ursula Bloom, *Woman's Own*, October 1940

In 2008, the editor of American *Vogue*, Anna Wintour, was seen in the same Caroline Herrera dress three times, albeit in three different countries. Was she signalling a fashion shift towards thrift or had she just been caught out by the paparazzi? Handbag.com's ten top tips from May 2008 included buying from second-hand shops like eBay, doing 'swapsies' with friends and even practising 'Make Do and Mend'. Spending less, the article argued, was no excuse for letting oneself go; indeed, 'Think Like a Princess' by dressing in 'classic investment pieces' and by remembering that beauty is a duty.

Plus ça change in fashion-land perhaps, yet I believe there is more to it than that. In times of austerity the fashion industry has to work harder. If you have decided you cannot afford to buy new clothes then is there any point in treating yourself to the latest edition of an expensive fashion monthly? Well, yes, the magazine's fashionistas would argue, if within its pages there are tips on how to update your existing wardrobe inexpensively and articles on 'investment pieces'. For the December 2008 issue of American *Vogue*, designer Phillip Lim showed a Christmas party frock he called the 'Recessionista', a floor-length ruffled silk affair, priced at £405 – an eye-watering sum for most, but a bargain for his core clientele.

The fashion press must always be one step ahead in distilling the mood of the times and then selling it back to an audience hungry for guidance. In the war years the expectation might have been for the fashion industry to voice dissent at the constraints the Board of Trade imposed on it, or at least to express weariness with wartime shortages. After all, rampant consumerism was its *raison d'être*. Instead, it not only co-operated with, but endorsed, what were effectively anti-consumerist controls. Turn-ups aside, the whole industry from *Vogue* magazine to Harrods, and even including the makers of goods made unavailable due to wartime constraints, fell into line. A newspaper advertisement for the Harvey Nichols sale encouraged women to visit its haberdashery department with the rallying cry: '**A sewing machine can be almost as much a weapon for Victory as a Spade.** Salute the sewing machine as an aid to Victory!' An Auxiliary Territorial Service (ATS) recruitment poster showed an elegant woman in coat and skirt, hat, jewellery and bright make-up, but stamped across it was OUT OF FASHION. 'Are you living a selfish life, thinking selfish thoughts, spreading complacency and thoughtlessness? If so you are dangerously out of fashion. You lack imagination. Russian women in slacks and smocks are fighting in the trenches. German women in ersatz overalls work side by side with men to make the barges with which they hope to invade Britain . . .'[33]

The advertising industry fed the public's expectations of optimism and carefree days to come. Thus an advertisement for Vida Elastic read: 'Every day brings Vida nearer: VIDA – the super elastic – went in to the war with the first drafts. Ever since, and in a hundred and one ways – it has been easing the lot and saving the lives of our soldiers. That's why you haven't been able to buy VIDA. But each day brings us nearer to Peace – and when the Joy Bells ring again, the famous 3-yard card will return to the shops.' *House and Garden* embraced the new simplicity, writing of how '. . . curbed in many directions, and unable to indulge in an orgy of pockets and pleats, they [women] are discovering a new beauty in austere lines and the drama of unexpected colour combinations'. *Picture Post* would have agreed. In an article from August 1942 it wrote, 'If you turn up the fashion magazines of 1939, you'll see how styles have simplified; how shoes, hats, fabrics, have turned from pretty to practical; how extravagances have disappeared altogether.' Thus the *Daily Telegraph* sold patterns under the headline 'Wartime Fashion', putting forward the 'in-or-outdoor suit' as 'Fashion's answer to the Clothes rationing problems'. *Country Life* entered the fray, writing, 'To be out at elbows was once a mark of amiable eccentricity, now it will be that of patriotism.'

At the practical end of the women's publications market was *Housewife* magazine. So popular were its haberdashery tips that the Board of Trade reproduced them in its own 3d booklet. Recognising the magazine's power, Hugh Dalton wrote the booklet's foreword:

> Clothes rationing . . . has saved much-needed shipping space, man-power and materials, and so assisted our war effort. The Board of Trade Make Do and Mend campaign is intended to help you to get the last possible ounce of wear out of your clothes and household things . . . No doubt there are as many ways of patching and darning as there are of cooking potatoes. Even if we ran to several large volumes, we could not say all there is to say about storing, cleaning, pressing, destroying moths, mending and renovating clothes and household linen . . . But the hints here will, I hope, prove useful. They have all been tested and approved by the Board of Trade Make Do and Mend Advisory Panel, a body of practical people, mostly women, for whose help in preparing this booklet I am most grateful.[34]

Hugh Dalton's words proved prophetic. Everything was recycled, from captured parachute silk into wedding dresses and underwear, to blackout blinds into dresses and skirts. One family made elegant dresses of lilac silk by bleaching the purple fabric salvaged from a bombed-out undertaker's. Others made warm winter coats from surplus army, RAF and naval blankets. What had been a winter woollen coat might later serve as a dress, then a skirt, then some shorts for a child until, finally, the remaining bits became patches or dusters.

Some standards were relaxed. The Church of England declared that it would be permissible for women to attend church bareheaded – although hats were off the ration they were hard to come by. Elsewhere a headscarf became an acceptable alternative. Headscarves were sensibly worn in factories. Clothes that had previously been frowned upon, especially trousers for women, gradually became more acceptable though many still struggled with shorts being worn in public. Nella Last expressed some dismay at the increasing appearance of slacks on the streets of Barrow-in-Furness, Lancashire, writing on Saturday, 14 March 1944, describing

'. . . queer hybrid creatures pushing prams and wearing pants, a woman's coat and either a pixie-hood or a beret – all seemed to make the streets so untidy in the bright sunshine. I could not help feeling that women are seizing the excuse of there being a war on to give full rein to the sloppy, lazy streak in their make-up. When the raids were on, anything could be understood or forgiven – but WHY NOW?'[35] An article in *The Lady* in May 1943 sounded an equally prissy note: 'Undoubtedly slacks are here to stay and they feel comfortable and look very well when worn for the right sort of activity. Gardening, for instance, or fire-watching, or going for a country walk, but sloppy and unsuitable in towns and never for fat women, or with high heels, or brightly-coloured, or by mothers pushing prams, or long, floppy hair.' All of which makes you hope that for the writer's sake she didn't live long enough to see hippies.

Utility fashion: the government turns fashion designer

Before the war there were 30,000 factories producing civilian clothes, but of these all but 1,500 turned to manufacturing for the war effort and shortages of clothes became severe. The Board of Trade's solution was both inspired and the greatest success of Hugh Dalton's leadership there: the government decided to produce its own fashion line. It borrowed – from the Army or their wartime civilian jobs – the best-known British and British-based designers of the day: Digby Morton, who had already designed the WVS uniforms; Norman Hartnell, the Queen's favourite designer; Edward Molyneux, an Irishman who in pre-war Paris had been a leading international couturier; Hardy Amies, who had been at Worth in Paris but was now in the Intelligence Corps; and Victor Stiebel, who had found wartime work in the Camouflage Corps. Each was asked to come up with four designs – for a coat, a suit, an afternoon dress and a cotton overall dress – that would look good without costing the earth and would also comply with regulations in terms of fabric and embellishments.

Models in Utility fashions.

When the Board of Trade first told Edward Molyneux and Hardy Amies of their scheme they laughed: 'We have been making Utility clothes for years.'[36] Molyneux, who after the fall of Paris had reached safety in Britain only by means of a lucky ride on a coal boat from Bordeaux, had long since established a style that was unfussy, the emphasis being on the cut rather than the embellishment. When Amies quizzed him about his puritan lines, his response was 'plainness is all'. Utility clothes had no greater champion than Winston Churchill, who set an example by wearing his one-piece 'siren suit' even to meet with President Roosevelt at the White House, though he also enjoyed sporting this attire in Downing Street. Chips Channon's diary records: 'It seems that Winston wearing an Air Force cap received the Halifaxes in particularly curious clothes and seemed rather put-out by Halifax's surprise; pointing out his strange garb he said "Clemmie bought me these rompers!"'[37]

In the past, being elegant and chic had been the preserve of the moneyed classes. Now pared-down simplicity, lean lines and smartness created by a top couturier was to be generally available. Ann Seymour in *Woman and Beauty* and Alison Settle in *Woman and Home* were agreed that the name Utility was 'awful', but both endorsed the scheme. *Vogue* wrote, 'All women have the equal chance to buy beautifully designed clothes suitable for their lives and income. It is a revolutionary scheme and a heartening thought. It is, in fact, an outstanding example of applied democracy.'[38]

The first Utility scheme designs were shown to the fashion press in September 1942. They received immediate support. 'Suburban wives and factory girls will soon be able to wear clothes designed and styled by the Queen's dressmaker,' the *Daily Mail* reported and the *News Chronicle* suggested that while the society lady might go direct to the designer and pay 30 guineas, the factory girl could buy the same design off the peg in poorer fabrics for 30 shillings. (Just as today we might fancy a Marc Jacobs design on the catwalk, but wait for New Look to rip it off on the high street.) Once the designers had come up with their template models, they were available for copying and adapting – within the Civil Regulations rules – by the fashion industry, at a cost of 7s 6d for a blouse and 10s 6d for a dress. Differentiations in the quality of fabric and workmanship made higher prices inevitable, but the Board of Trade's ceilings meant the average price was: suit 92s 10d; coat 83s 7d; rayon dress 53s 7d; cotton dress 17s 10d; blouse 21s 5d. All bore the Utility logo: two modernist-looking circles missing a c-like segment, plus the number 41. The style veered, by necessity, towards the severe and military, with most skirts cut straight to the knee and jackets nipped in.

In 1943 the Utility scheme took up 50 per cent of all cloth manufactured in the UK, as well as controlling that cloth's quality and price. Such a government-sponsored universal programme was, of course, the butt of many jokes, such as: 'Heard about the utility woman? She's single-breasted.' Utility goods were exempt from purchase tax and their prices could be kept lower through encouraging long production runs. Demand for fabric to make uniforms meant that by the end of the war, 85 per cent of clothes and cloths manufactured bore the Utility logo. As the fashion historian Colin McDowell writes in *Forties Fashion and the New Look*, 'It was the nearest thing to a civilian uniform for women in the history of dress.'[39] About four-fifths of the clothes made during the war and in its aftermath came under the aegis of Utility.

By 1944, however, sourcing even Utility goods had become tough. People complained of 'finding it increasingly difficult to keep themselves even respectable'.[40] When Christian Dior's wide-skirted swirling New Look came in, the government entreated people not to have their heads turned – but by then women had become frustrated by shortages and fed up with being dictated to, and they embraced the wickedly extravagant use of materials in the long, full dresses with the enthusiasm of the half-starved.

So what could the fashion-conscious consumer of contemporary credit-crunch Britain learn from her wartime predecessor? Well, bags of stuff. By trying to ration and rationalise her purchases she would save herself money, while also helping the environment by reducing her carbon footprint. She would have to be more resourceful with her existing wardrobe and to take better care of her clothes through repairs and revamps. Where it became clear that even with remodelling a piece of clothing was never going to be worn again by her she would take another leaf out of her wartime granny's book and make sure it went to a loving home elsewhere, by putting it up on a website such as eBay, by passing it on to a friend or by taking it into a charity or second-hand shop. With the time on their hands saved from going shopping, the more neat-fingered might decide to take up dressmaking or knitting, which in the long term could save them money, while also ensuring that their clothes were one-off individual pieces produced in non-sweatshop conditions. In a similar vein buying less, though not necessarily spending less, might leave more time and money to source clothes ethically, by spending more on individual Fair Trade-guaranteed or UK-manufactured goods.

Sucking Eggs:
Top tips about wardrobe housewifery to learn from your wartime granny

- **Ration and rationalise**. Take time to go through your wardrobe to see what you have, what you have forgotten you have, what could be brought up to date and what could be passed on. Then set yourself a points budget and/or a cash ration. Make a list of what items you actually need and buy only them.
- **Never binge shop. Never purchase idly or unthinkingly**.
- **Make do and mend through wardrobe maintenance: carefully clean, repair and refashion clothes so they can serve for years and not just a single season.** Even the most cack-handed can sew on a button or secure a hem, but if you're no seamstress yourself, take your clothes into a good local dry-cleaner with an in-house tailor. Money spent there will restore a whole wardrobe for less than buying a few items at the bargain end of the high street. By spending £120 on cleaning, repairs and alterations in September 2007 I got through the next winter and spring with only one replacement purchase and two new items.
- **Never throw away** something that might have a life elsewhere. If an item is not in good enough condition to be sold or passed on second-hand, then the textiles could still be recycled into another garment, children's clothing, a piece of household furnishing or at least rags.
- **Swapping.** There are dedicated online sites and services such as Freecycle, where you can advertise unwanted possessions; you can organise a swapping evening with friends; there are even swapping club nights.
- **Second-hand shop** on the Internet at sites such as eBay, on the high street and at warehouses, designer sales and charity

shops, where careful rummaging can unearth gems. It's worth noting that the leafier areas tend to have the more upmarket goods.

- **Source from ethical lines**, UK ones where possible, so products have travelled a shorter distance.
- **Make ethically sound but good investments**. It's not necessarily about price, but buying clothes that will last longer, be easy to recycle when you are done with them and that have been produced in a way that has a minimum environmental impact.
- **It's a cliché, but accessorise** – even something as simple as a pair of coloured tights can update an outfit cheaply and efficiently.

CHAPTER SIX

BEST FACE FORWARD: *Beauty and keeping up appearances*

We hardly need the latest report from the Mintel market researchers on beauty trends to tell us we are entering an era of 'austerity chic'. It's all too obvious that when cash is in short supply, frivolities such as cosmetics find themselves at the bottom of the list of life's necessities. Yet few women are prepared to ditch their make-up bags and brave the world bare-faced.

Alice Hart-Davis, *Daily Telegraph*, November 2008[1]

The slightest hint of a drooping spirit yields a point to the enemy. Never must careless grooming reflect a 'don't care' attitude . . . we must never forget that good looks and good morale are the closest of good companions. Put your best face forward.

Yardley wartime advertising campaign

In the 1920s the American economist George Taylor suggested that in periods of boom women wore their skirts shorter in order to show off their silk stockings, whereas in periods of bust skirts were worn longer to hide holey hosiery. His theory holds true of the 'flapper' 1920s, the micro-minis of the Swinging Sixties and the ra-ra and puffball skirt styles of the 1980s, though it doesn't fit in with the wide-styled skirts of the late 1950s when, according to Harold Macmillan, we'd 'never had it so good'. So might the 'leading lipstick indicator' be a better guide of how women spend their money when the good times falter? Apparently a coinage of Leonard Lauder, the chairman of the Estée Lauder group, the 'lipstick index' attempts to explain why in times of economic hardship sales of lipsticks and glosses tend to go up.[2] Recent surveys indicate that his theory might hold true: one sample of 1,000 women, published in October 2008 by feelunique.com, found that women were more likely to curb their spending on food than on the make-up and cosmetics they regarded as 'every-day essentials'.[3]

None of this would come as a surprise to a 1940s woman, who was encouraged to invest time, thought and energy into keeping up appearances, even when it was a struggle to do so. There were few women whose clothes did not bear Home Front battle stains, and those who could no longer rely on what they wore to semaphore the right message had to fall back on enhancing the gifts nature had given them. It had long been a sartorial truism that it was that bit easier to get away with last season's skirt length, an ancient blouse or a scuffed pair of shoes if, from the neckline up, you were putting your best face forward and looking *soignée*. Well-cut hair allowed you to dress how you pleased; while for the high-maintenance woman groomed brows and curled eyelashes were essential.

In the fashion rhetoric of the day painted lips, waved hair, powdered cheekbones and a jaunty hat were proof that the nation's women were keeping calm and carrying on, that femininity still had its place in a world torn apart by men's wars. For the Mass Observation diarist Nella Last, putting on her lipstick was a way of bolstering herself against the bad news on the radio. In June 1940, at the point when Paris had fallen and the Italians had just joined the war against Britain, she wrote of a depressing day, 'I slipped a gay flowered dress on, an old one but I love it for its bright colours. I put rouge and lipstick on – I needed them for I looked a haggard sight.'[4] Nella, who was forty-nine at the outbreak of war, was 'fashion-forward' to rely as she did on lipstick. On 19 May 1940 she expressed surprise at having become a woman 'who uses too bright lipstick and on dim days makes the corners turn up when lips will not keep smiling. Mrs Waite [a much older WVS colleague] used to be horrified at my "painted mouth", till one day she said thoughtfully, "It would not be a bad idea if we all bought a lipstick and got little Last to show us how to paint a smile." Since then she has never made "sick-making" noises when she has seen me with my lipstick.'[5] Though a civilian, Nella was part of a wartime trend to embrace warpaint. Many lipsticks, such as Elizabeth Arden's Montezuma Red, a cult best-seller lipstick, were designed specifically for women in uniform.

Nella Last

Recognising the importance of cosmetics to women's morale, the government never put them on the ration books, but fewer were produced. Perfume gradually disappeared from the shelves; its exotic ingredients were too hard to source. The production of make-up suffered from lack of oil to make it emollient. Other core ingredients that were diverted towards the war effort were castor oil, petroleum, alcohol, talcum power, glycerine and many fats. And it was not just the raw materials that were corralled into the war effort, but also many of the big brands' factories and their workforces. A firm had to prioritise producing sunscreen and camouflage creams for soldiers and sailors fighting in the Middle and Far East before they could get back to their former day job of churning out lipsticks. By 1942 the number of cosmetics available had fallen to less than a quarter of their 1938 levels. Many women had only two lipsticks to see them through the entire conflict.

Elizabeth Hudson, in a letter to her family in South Africa, wrote, 'There is a rumour that soap is going to be rationed next so Daisy went out and bought tons of it yesterday. I think cosmetics will be too and am trying to get a lipstick or two. They are not easy to find . . . No stockings, shabby clothes and no make-up. Women will soon be looking as battered as London does.'[6]

In fact, British women showed the spirit of the blitz in not letting the shortages of cosmetics defeat them. 'The backbone of morale is smartness' rallied an editorial in *Harper's Bazaar*. Women in the Armed Forces were never forbidden to wear make-up, but rather were encouraged to do so as something that might lift the spirits of both the wearer and the beholder. Think of Deborah Kerr's efficient but attractive ATS driver in *The Life and Death of Colonel Blimp*, with her dramatically crimped eyelashes and slash of scarlet lipstick. She could have bought that look, supplies permitting, in the NAAFI (Navy, Army and Air Force Institutes). Some female munitions workers were granted precious extra supplies of face powder.

Just as fashion firms had decided to continue advertising themselves even when their products were largely unavailable in the domestic market, cosmetics firms continued to make their presence felt in magazines, extolling an argument that allied beauty not just with duty, but also with

bravery. Their bold advertising effectively sold the idea that it was unpatriotic to not make an effort. A Yardley advertisement, portraying a woman in uniform under the headline 'No surrender', urged its customers, 'We must achieve masculine efficiency without hardness . . . Never must we consider careful grooming a Quisling gesture.'[7] Tangee, one of the most popular wartime brands, even went so far as to define femininity as an essentially Allied attribute: 'No lipstick, ours, or anyone else's, will win the war. But it symbolises one of the reasons we are fighting . . . the precious right of women to be feminine and lovely under any circumstances.'[8] For Elizabeth Arden, too, beauty – like business – must go on: 'the wise woman, in a period of strain and crisis, will keep up her regular night and morning routine of Cleansing, Toning and Nourishing – with Elizabeth Arden's famous Essential Preparations . . .'[9]

Woman's Journal told readers: 'If you have to stay in khaki, don't despair – there is a new lovely make-up for you, especially created for this rather trying colour. Its name is "Burnt Sugar". It is a warm glowing shade that goes beautifully.'[10] Peggy Sage marketed shades of nail varnish that would not jar with uniform: 'a discreet . . . subtle range of pale polish shades . . . but when women are in mufti – and what an exciting flavour that dull word has now that women have stolen it from men! – they gaily take their finger-tips out of uniform and turn to Peggy Sage's more burning colours. FEZ, a dark clear red, vibrant and exciting, is an especial favourite . . .'[11]

No product had quite the wartime USP of leg make-up, however. Who would have thought that the contemporary woman who strips to the buff to be sprayed or painted with St Tropez tanning lotion is a direct descendant of those wartime women? For many women in the 1940s one of the most persistently upsetting aspects of clothes rationing was the shortage of stockings. Aware of their discomfort, the cosmetics companies used some of their precious resources to create leg make-up that might, to the idle or short-sighted observer, convey an illusion of silk stockings. These are products assigned to the history bin, but at the time they fulfilled an urgent need. Cyclax's Stockingless Cream or Elizabeth Arden's Fin 200 both claimed to be rain- and mud-resistant. A drawn-on line down the back of the leg to represent seamed stockings – apparently more of a media invention than a reality – was an optional extra.

Women's magazines' role in promoting beauty as duty

Women's magazines enjoyed a good war. The Ministry of Information encouraged them to lift morale on the Home Front. Such publications toed the government line by giving readers tips on household economy, but they also promoted courage and beauty under fire. It was the most practically minded magazines, such as *Woman's Own*, that scored the greatest successes. *Woman's Own* doubled its readership before the war's end. On 10 November 1940, its star writer Ursula Bloom advised her readers how not to let the small matter of the Luftwaffe trying to bomb them out of their beds lay waste to their beauty routine.

Beauty Tips for Air Raids

> First invest in a warm dressing gown with large pockets to keep your air raid beauty make-up in. Some little refreshers for cleansing of any surplus grease (they'll cost 6d), a tube of powder cream which in an instant takes off all the shine and leaves you matt and composed (6d again), a handkerchief-puff well-filled with powder, and a tiny mirror. If you're fussy, have a lipstick, but it isn't necessary. In the second pocket, put a small comb, a bottle of smelling salts, a flask with something in it to keep cold out and your favourite tablets to quieten the nerves. You may need them. Add some cotton wool to ram in your ears if the world gets too noisy. There are special 'silencers' which you can use . . . and they shut out all that very demoralising din which is one of the most unpleasant parts of an air raid.[12]

It was the aristocratic *Vogue* and *Harper's Bazaar* that had to adapt the furthest to reflect the spirit of the times. Their bread-and-butter features had before the onset of war been reports of European couturier shows and who had worn what to Lady Mendl's last spectacular ball at Versailles. Now, Paris was under Nazi rule and the magazines had to address the fact that the lives of their target readers had changed dramatically. In the 1930s a lady's maid had made it significantly easier for a high maintenance aristocrat to be a dedicated follower of fashion. Her maid drew her bath, arranged her hair, applied her make-up, anointed her, dressed her and looked after her clothes when they were not being worn. Even the bourgeois wife of a professional man might have had as part of her household someone who performed at least some of these duties.

With war, however, many domestic servants found themselves looking for different work – either voluntarily, because there was an opportunity to do something more useful, or because households were being shut down and retaining only skeletal staffs. Now, instead of planning debutante balls, many landed ladies were accommodating evacuees. Yet with or without a maid there was still an expectation of looking one's best under the circumstances. *Vogue* urged readers to not let themselves go: 'Your face is probably not what it was. But don't despair. If you can't have treatments . . . clean it scrupulously, grease it regularly; use a patter, a moulder or even a spoon to work the cream well in . . . your hands probably tell a tale of hard work, coarse soap, lack of fats, inexperienced manicurists and cheap varnish . . .'[13] The Hon. Mrs James Rodney, writing in *Harper's Bazaar* in 1940, was keen to remind readers that even if they were now without servants and 'working those acres ourselves in the newly acquired converted country houses', the mark of a lady was still her smooth, soft, unblemished hands: '. . . it is a point of pride with the war worker to keep not only herself in as perfect physical condition as she can, but her hands as beautiful as possible . . . the care of the hands of the working woman in wartime is, if anything, more important than ever . . .'[14]

And keeping one's head

If I were to be transported to 1942 I think I would adapt quickly to food and clothes rationing. I am already an efficient housekeeper. What I would find most galling, after the well-watered luxury of twenty-first-century Britain, would be the lack of soap, which was rationed from February 1942. Equally, shampoo was in low supply. I would hate going about my business with the persistent itch and sweaty sheen of a greasy scalp and dirty hair. In the Second World War, when even make-up was hard to find, women still had their tresses to be proud of. But look carefully at pictures of civilians from that period and you will notice how greasy and dandruff-ridden much of the hair was.

Role models were changing in the twentieth century. For years, aristocrats had been the leaders of fashion. Yet who today can name a hairstyle particularly associated with Lady Diana Cooper, the most celebrated British beauty of the 1930s? The aristocrats' influence was waning, and the gleam and glamour of Hollywood was in the ascendancy. Most of us can easily picture Rita Hayworth's rich red locks drifting over a bias-cut satin evening dress. Hollywood's signature looks were more about luxury than well-positioned hairpins. In Home Front cinemas women could be heard sighing with longing at each shake of an actress's well-coiffed head. When Veronica Lake's undeniably sultry 'peekaboo' hairstyle was revealed in 1943 it was too much even for the US government, who pleaded with the actress to opt instead for a sensible hairdo more in keeping with the tenor of the times. There was a genuine fear that female factory workers imitating her cascading style might get their locks caught up in the machinery.

In the 1930s many women had abnegated responsibility for their hair, relying instead on a weekly visit to the hairdresser for a shampoo and set. The looks at the time were high maintenance. In their local salon women found whole new ranges of products that included dyes, permanent-wave lotions, fixers and conditioners, all of which manipulated their now shorter hairstyles into hitherto unimagined forms. Then war arrived and the products were hard to come by. Soon women were being asked to bring their own towels to salons. There, they would often find that what products remained had been watered down or replaced with ersatz home-made solutions.

Is the current trend for shorter hairstyles a response to the credit crunch? In August 1942 an article in *Picture Post* voiced the dilemma of so many who aspired to be fashionable but needed also to be practical and who felt that the glorious locks up on the big screen were now almost an insult to their own day-to-day experience. 'Why does that shoulder mane seem so out of date? Because it would look messy hanging on a uniform collar. What's wrong with those exquisite tapered nails? They couldn't do a hand's turn without breaking. The woman who could change instantly into uniform or munitions overall and look charming, *soignée* and right, is the smart woman of today.'[15]

Despite their own balding pates, wartime politicians and civil servants took a sympathetic interest in women's hairstyling. They kept hats off the ration in recognition that an attractive hat was a booster. A jaunty piece of headgear, albeit a home-renovated one, became one of the few ways a woman could inject some individuality into a well-worn Utility wardrobe. When core hat materials such as straw and felt became hard to come by, a woman could take up her knitting needles to make a beret, tam-o'-shanter or could crochet a beanie (all again fashionable today). Or she could instead try one of the medieval-inspired snoods and pixie-hoods Schiaparelli had pioneered in the 1930s, or one of their exotic relatives such as a turban.

For female factory workers and land girls toiling in the fields a headscarf was the safest way to ensure that your hair did not become a potentially hazardous interference with your work. 'Be in the fashion – cover your hair' was how one Soviet-style propaganda poster showed five different ways with a scarf, turban or safety cap. A headscarf also had the advantage, for those at some days' distance from their hairwashing night or trip to the salon, of covering up lank-looking tresses. And the print could be part of the war effort, too. Jacqmar's scarves and fabrics featured slogan prints, such as Dig for Victory, the British Isles and a red, white and

COVER YOUR HAIR
FOR SAFETY
YOUR RUSSIAN
SISTER DOES!
Issued by the Ministry of Labour and National Service and produced by the Royal Society for the Prevention of Accidents,
Terminal House, 52, Grosvenor Gardens, London, S.W.1.

blue flag-festooned victory pattern. Mostly designed by Arnold Lever and printed in rayon, because of silk shortages, Jacqmar prints were stunning and much imitated. Today they can fetch £500.

It would have been inappropriate for some women to wear a headscarf to work, however, and nobody wanted to sport one to a Friday night hop. A fashionable 'updo', if the grips could be found, was the piled-on-top pompadour, while the simple pageboy offered the most hassle-free solution. The government endorsed shorter, or more upswept styles, such as the Victory Roll which involved the hair being wound tightly around the head, while the front section was rolled on high. In order to help achieve the look, women often resorted to the hair being pinned round a piece of old stocking material. The Liberty Cut was a much shorter version, easier to curl and maintain. Embracing their new didactic role, magazines were quick to steer women away from the glamorous allure of the long looks peddled by Hollywood.

> Shorter hair means fewer hairdresser's bills, cleaner and healthier scalps. It means...goodbye to the Greta Garbo raggle-taggle locks to the shoulder. They never did make you look your best. There is today a new cut called 'The Liberty Cut'. It fits the crown and makes the hair much easier to manage so that you can set it yourself far more. Don't be afraid to show your ears. Ears are coming back into fashion, and personally, I think they look charming.[16]

Hair and cosmetics Make Do and Mend

When, in the mid 1970s, the late Anita Roddick founded the Body Shop with its ambition to recycle containers, to use products that had not been tested on animals and to take ingredients from the natural world, it was hailed as ahead of its time. But it was also about thirty-five years behind the times. Wartime women showed incredible resourcefulness and entrepreneurial savvy when it came to sourcing beauty products, eking out and packaging cosmetics and

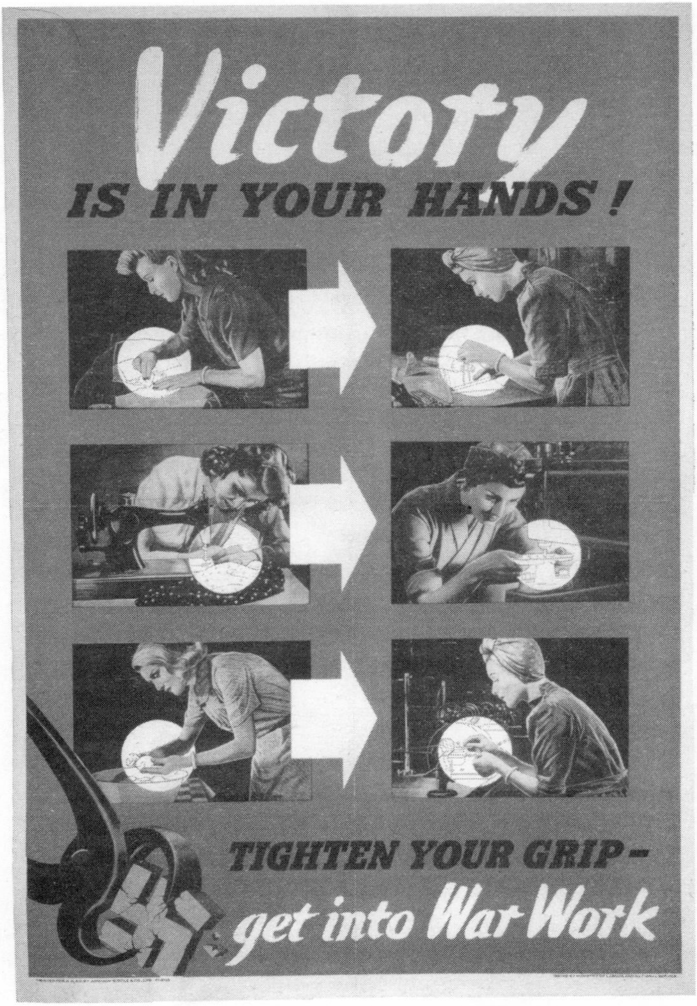

Before and After: war workers are encouraged to tie up their hair in headscarves for safety.

soap, shampoo and face cream. And like the generations before and since them, they used old wives' wisdom to take from nature's larder.

Today we live in thrall to organic and natural brands, such as Aveda, Eve Lom, Origins, Dr Hauschka and Ren, many of which have the roots of their success in the same traditional herbal ingredients. Looking around my bathroom shelves I have chamomile shampoo; a conditioner of rosemary and mint; four different bubble baths or shower gels claiming calendula, wild rose, extract of horse chestnut and wild alpine flowers as their core ingredient; a jojoba oil scrub, also with peppermint, lemon and rosemary; rose cream and baby oil infused with aloe vera.

Our wartime counterparts may not have had a Space NK or a well-stocked department store's beauty floor to lighten their purses in their lunch hours. They were, however, pioneers of natural products and beauty without cruelty, thanks to the success they had making their own cosmetics or eking out what they had. Local chemists, too, in what was then both a throwback to the days of the Victorian apothecary and a forerunner to Roddick's Body Shop, invented their own products with minimally branded packaging. Put 'home-made beauty treatments' into an Internet search engine and see how many of the larder ingredients they used – fruits, vegetables, eggs, vinegars, fruit and nut oils – are still being touted today.

Sucking Eggs: What your wartime granny knew about make-do beauty products

HAIR PRODUCTS

- **To shampoo**: women who kept hens had the benefit of being able to mix an egg with what shampoo was available to create a cleansing lather. The less fortunate experimented with what soap they could find, mixed with products such as vinegar.
- **To combat hair grease**: they combed corn flour through hair.
- **To fight build-up and add shine**: diluted cider vinegar was used.
- **To highlight**: blondes used the age-old infusion of chamomile flowers; brunettes tried one of crushed rosemary; coppery-toned redheads a dilution of boiled-up carrots and some plucky, plummier-toned women one of boiled beetroot. A lemon rinse, another tried and tested standby, particularly for blondes, was recommended but hard to come by.
- **A setting lotion**: many women sacrificed their sugar ration to mix with water to keep curls in place.

BEAUTY TREATMENTS

With products like vanishing creams having vanished, women had to find cleansers, moisturisers and masks where they could.

- **To cleanse or moisturise**: mixtures of olive oil (from the chemist) and beeswax; the paper from packets of margarine or lard, or even leftover fat from meat such as mutton. All helped remove dirt and increase the suppleness of war-weary faces and hands.
- **As a face mask**: Fuller's Earth spread on the face made a popular treatment. The rejuvenating properties of potatoes, cucumbers and carrots were also tested.

- **For lip and cheek colour**: ends of lipstick melted down, perhaps in an eggcup stood in hot water, then mixed with a few drops of almond oil could afterwards be poured back into the lipstick container, or used as rouge. Beetroot juice could stain cheeks and lips. In the latter case, following the beetroot juice with a lick of Vaseline created an ersatz lip gloss.
- **For eye make-up**: soot and burnt cork were pressed into action as eyeliner, shadow and mascara, as was shoe polish, though that was soon itself in short supply.
- **For deodorant**: a dusting of bicarbonate of soda was said to dry up minor perspiration and help counteract any smells.

PART THREE

WAR ON WASTE

CHAPTER SEVEN

THE GREAT SAUCEPAN OFFENSIVE: *Our grandparents' forgotten victory in the war on waste*

Housewives of Lewisham! The war on waste has started, and you are the shock troops.
Mayor of Lewisham, 1942[1]

If we are to get food prices down, we must also do more to deal with unnecessary demand, such as by all of us doing more to cut our food waste which is costing the average household in Britain around £8 per week.
Gordon Brown, 2008[2]

Here is a shocking thought: my local council collects a smaller percentage of household rubbish for reuse today than its wartime equivalent did during the darkest hours of the London blitz.

My council's website holds frequently updated pages dedicated to its plans to reduce CO_2 emissions. They explain what the council's rubbish service will collect and how the waste is then recycled, and they outline forward-looking schemes such as workshops for new mothers to promote reusable nappies. But a visit to the council's archives reveals there is nothing ground-breaking in these green policies. If Dr Who's Tardis were to transport me back sixty-five years to my street during the Second World War, on the same corner where moulded plastic recycling bins now stand I would find a momentous civic effort to impose order on waste in the shape of the wartime metal equivalent to our wheely bins. These salvage bins fulfilled a far wider remit than their counterparts do today, in even the most eco-conscious areas. Many collected, separately, paper, aluminium, rubber, wool, rags, bones, garden waste for composting and food waste to feed to local pigs. There was no need for bottle banks because it was commonplace to return bottles to the shop or milkman. Nor was there a need for textile recycling points – most housewives, spurred on by shortages in the shops and the limitations imposed by clothes rationing, were skilled at finding ways of breathing new life into their families' outfits, until they were fit only for the rag man. Where their ingenuity failed them, there were Make Do and Mend classes, and exchange centres run by organisations such as the WVS and the WI.

No other wartime initiative captured the public's imagination with quite such enthusiasm as the campaign to salvage. It became a national obsession that empowered mothers and children alike. Between November 1939 and May 1944, Britain's local authorities collected nearly 6 million tons of salvage.[3] By 1943 more than half of the country's already greatly reduced supply of paper and board was being recycled and thus billed as 'home-grown'. Along with this 3 million tons of paper, 130,000 tons of rubber had been recovered. Meanwhile, kitchen waste was being donated at a rate of 31,000 tons per month (which the propagandists announced was sufficient to feed 210,000 pigs), while 110,000 tons of scrap metal – as iron railings throughout the land were ripped from the earth – continued to be collected weekly.[4]

During the blitz an observer reported the devotion to this task, even among the battle-weary:

> War strain has been particularly felt by mothers living in bombed districts, but this has not prevented them from attending to such matters as cleaning and drying bones for the salvage collector, ransacking the house for scraps of paper, metal and rubber, nor from making the daily journey down the road with the food scraps for the kitchen waste bin.[5]

As the campaign to salvage progressed, the methods of collecting rubbish became more complicated – just as they are today. Many of today's councils have moved to fortnightly collections in what could be seen as a rather counter-intuitive attempt to coerce residents into more recycling.

Their Second World War equivalents preferred carrot to stick. The wartime councils stood to benefit financially from rates reductions and from selling off the scrap they collected, so services tended to increase, rather than decrease. Weekly rubbish collections were often supplemented by daily visits from street-cleaning dustmen or, after the mass mobilisation of the male workforce, dustwomen, while these in turn were sometimes aided by Salvage Wardens, usually members of the WVS, making door-to-door collections for anything from any old iron to string or pigswill. These local Salvage Wardens, identified by a brown badge bearing a white S, would often delegate to teams of young street volunteers drawn from the ranks of the Brownies, Boy Scouts, Girl Guides and, as the war progressed, even youngsters from the Children's Salvage Group (known as Cogs), who bore army rankings that reflected how much recycling they had individually brought in. A child who had brought in two books in the National Book Drive would be made a 'private' and given a white badge to wear; one who had brought in dozens of volumes might be promoted to 'general'. Some groups had an adult leader but others operated independently. In one COG division in Honour Oak the youngest member was three and the oldest fourteen. Housewives did their share, too. They took it in turn to be responsible for the cleanliness of specific bins. The most malodorous receptacles, such as the scraps bins, were positioned outside different houses on a turn-by-turn, week-by-week basis.

During the war, central and local government efforts to recycle were highly organised. Why, then, in the following six decades, did the overwhelming majority of us forget the wartime lessons that now hold such contemporary resonances – Reduce, Reuse, Recycle? In December 2006 Sir David Attenborough told the House of Commons Rural Affairs Committee for Climate Change,

> I grew up during the war and during the war it was a common view that wasting food was wrong, and it was not that you thought you were going to defeat Hitler by eating up a little bit of gristly meat but that it was wrong to waste. People felt that widely and universally.[6]

The spectres of recession and global warming have galvanised many of us into born-again salvagers, yet still campaigners for Friends of the Earth claim that 'if everyone in the world was as wasteful as we are in the UK we would need eight worlds to keep going'.[7] According to the most recent figures from DEFRA (Department for Environment, Food and Rural Affairs), each person in the United Kingdom produces on average 511 kg of waste each year.[8] And for every ton of household waste we produce, commercial, industrial and construction businesses produce another six tons.[9] Perhaps the worst aspect of this is the extent to which so much of this waste actually represents squandered money, time and sense, especially when it comes to our food culture. You wouldn't pay for three bagfuls of groceries at your local supermarket, then dump one of those bags in the car park. Yet that is the equivalent of what so many of us do. The 2008 audit by the government rubbish watchdog WRAP revealed that almost a third of all food we buy annually in Britain (amounting to 6.7 million tons, at a cost of £10 billion and rising), and specifically 40 per cent of all fruit and vegetables, is thrown away untouched. Indeed, the report specified that each day we throw away 4.4 million apples, 1.6 million bananas, 1.3 million pots of yoghurt, 660,000 eggs, 5,500 chickens, 300,000 packs of crisps and 440,000 ready meals. Many of these are apparently still in date. Food represents the largest percentage (around 35 per cent) of household waste in this country. Local authorities spend £1 billion annually disposing of food waste in landfill, which then produces methane. Better meal planning, food shopping, cooking, portioning, fridge and larder vigilance, and then better composting, WRAP argues, could reduce our carbon emissions by 18 million tons a year – the equivalent of taking one in five cars off the road.[10]

There are other shameful examples of wastefulness. Every day we carelessly accumulate articles that, with a little forethought, we would realise we do not require. Many of us buy more clothes than we need or even use. Few of us think, when upgrading household furnishings, of the most environmentally friendly way to recycle the items that have been replaced. The bulk of us upgrade appliances – from mobile phones to computers and television sets – without researching what life these objects might have beyond our own homes. And some of the rubbish we accumulate, such as plastic bags, is not only a wholly unnecessary pest, but also potentially damaging to our environment. DEFRA estimates that 17 billion plastic bags are handed out every week to British shoppers, with the 88 per cent of us who use them taking between three and four per shop. On average, we each receive 300 every year. There are, of course, many worse forms of rubbish but a discarded plastic bag, be it on the beach where plastic bags represent 2 per cent of the rubbish found on our coastline, or blowing around an urban street, is an eyesore that can take years to break down, damaging animal and marine life as it does so.[11] Other countries have taken firm action. In 2002 Ireland's introduction of a 15p 'plastax' on carrier bags led to a 90 per cent reduction in use. Despite well-publicised campaigns such as the sale of Anya Hindmarch's celebrity-wielded 'I Am Not a Plastic Bag' bags, or individual towns such as Modbury in Devon declaring themselves plastic-bag-free zones, Britain has been slower to act.[12] The March 2008 budget did propose, however, that shops should start charging for bags.[13]

By the later years of the Second World War most British customers had to do without gift wrapping and packaging. Most housewives were already accustomed to taking their own shopping baskets to the shops. Having led the way in wartime, today we trail behind other European countries on such environmental issues. Rhetoric across the political spectrum may have acquired a greener hue, but according to Friends of the Earth as a country we are still recycling only around a quarter of our household rubbish, a figure that compares badly with the record of land-locked Austria on 64 per cent, Switzerland, Germany and the Netherlands on around 60 per cent and the Flanders region of Belgium, where citizens recycle 70 per cent of what goes out of their households.[14] Our figures are improving year on year and our government's target is that at least 45 per cent of household waste should be recycled by 2015.

Even our recycling practices can seem mired in toxicity. There has been widespread concern that the collection of commingled rubbish for recycling, practised by many UK councils, reduces quality, rendering some of that rubbish non-reusable.[15] Another thorny issue is the 12 to 14 million tons of waste that, it is claimed, Britain exports annually to developing countries.[16] While it is illegal by European directive to export rubbish for landfill, to export it for recycling passes muster. In 2008 ITV carried out an investigation into what they alleged was illegal dumping in Tamil Nadu, India, of rubbish from four separate UK local councils. Similar allegations have been made about the rapidly industrialising southern Chinese province of Guandong. There, whole towns have made a speciality out of recycling richer nations' waste. To do this the province has paid an environmental price seen in its clogged-up waterways, polluted skies and a rise in respiratory disease. For its dirt-poor economic migrant workers, however, the short-term financial gains far outweigh the hazards. The province is also where many of the plastic bags handed out daily to British shoppers are manufactured. In 2006 Britain imported £12.6 billion worth of manufactured goods from China. Some of those cargo ships returned home with 1.9 million tons of our rubbish for recycling. Since the ships were travelling anyway, it was cheaper for us to do this than to dump the waste in a UK landfill site or to recycle it here. 'If you can easily dump waste overseas then there is no motive for having a waste reduction programme at home,' said Kevin May of Greenpeace's Beijing office at the time. 'The argument that developing nations need recycled resources from wealthy nations is only partly true. The environmental costs are too high. Just look at the filthy water and polluted air of China. If we can stop the waste trade, I am sure it will lead to more sustainable development around the world.'[17]

Of course, any archaeologist or historian can tell you that how to dispose of rubbish has been a conundrum for as long as there have been urban dwellings. But the predominant factor in pre-industrial times was that most household and agricultural waste was biodegradable, while everyday items were reused and repaired until there was no use left in them. There is evidence that the Chinese were composting as early as 2000 BC, and in pre-Victorian cities the euphemistically named 'night soil' was for centuries sold on to local market gardeners as fertiliser.

Battle-torn Britain's war on waste

> The war is driving Hitler back
> And here's one way to win it
> Just give your salvage men the sack
> And see there's plenty in it.
>
> *Picture Post* advertisement, 1942

The drive to donate salvage was first launched by the Chamberlain government in 1939, but few seem to have noticed. It was Lord Woolton who, making his mark at the Ministry of Food, really brought it to the public's attention in April 1940 with a well-received speech denouncing food waste.

> I took the example of tea and asked them to make it a war-time rule that it was 'one spoonful for each person . . . and *none* for the pot!' I knew it would not get home if I asked them 'not to waste bread', so I told them that if everybody wasted a slice of bread a day, it would take 30 shiploads of wheat a year to make up the shortage.[18]

Meanwhile, at the Ministry of Supply the 1940 Limitation of Supplies Order banned the manufacturing of 'inessential' goods and limited the production of many others by between 33 and 75 per cent. Today's green watchwords – Reduce, Reuse, Recycle – became a necessary way of life in a society where even a new hot-water bottle needed a doctor's prescription. Within days factories that had previously made prams or bicycle pumps were making armaments. But the government needed raw materials to make these armaments and, unable to import all that it required, was forced to ask its citizens to ransack their homes for goods that could be broken down and recycled into weapons of war.

It was in July 1940, with the launch of the 'Great Saucepan Offensive', that the campaign to salvage metal for the war effort took off, almost literally. Lord Beaverbrook's rallying cry was 'Women of Britain, give us your aluminium . . . We will turn your pots and pans into Spitfires and Hurricanes.'[19] But it was Lady Reading who captured the public's imagination with her plea for 'any old iron'. At 1 p.m. on Wednesday, 10 July 1940 she was invited to Broadcasting House to make an appeal to the nation's housewives.

> . . . The Minister of Aircraft Production is asking the women of Great Britain for everything made of aluminium, everything that they can possibly give to be made into aeroplanes – Spitfires, Hurricanes, Blenheims, and Wellingtons. Now you're going to be able to have a chance of doing something positive that will be of direct and vital help to our airmen, and of doing it at once . . . I am asking for the things which you are using every day, anything and everything, new and old, sound and broken, everything that's made of aluminium . . . Cooking utensils of all kinds; bodies and tubes of vacuum cleaners, coat hangers, shoe trees, bathroom fittings, soap boxes, ornaments and even thimbles may be of aluminium. If you are doubtful, give our aeroplanes the benefit of the doubt and be generous . . . Very few of us can be heroines on the battle-front, but we can all have the tiny thrill of thinking as we hear the news of an epic battle in the air, 'Perhaps it was my saucepan that made a part of that Hurricane.'[20]

She had stressed in her speech that 'whoever gives at once gives twice as much', but she perhaps didn't expect her words to be taken quite as literally as they were. On leaving Broadcasting House only minutes later, she and her aide were surprised to witness droves of women bearing saucepans aloft, en route to salvage collecting points. The desire to give, the empowerment of being able to do something – anything, even – to contribute to the war effort was manic. Within hours, valuable three-tiered steamers, copper saucepan sets that had been wedding gifts, even kitchen goods bought specifically for the purpose of donating them were piling up at depots. Some, it was claimed, were still warm from the hob. The royal family donated a full set of kitchenware and a miniature set that had been given to the two princesses by the people of Wales. The War Office donated 500 tons of pans. But enough was enough: the offers from

"UP HOUSEWIVES AND AT 'EM!"
PUT OUT YOUR
PAPER · METAL · BONES
THEY MAKE PLANES, GUNS, TANKS, SHIPS & AMMUNITION

several First World War veterans to sacrifice their mobility to the war effort by donating their artificial aluminium limbs were politely rejected.

Collection depots, which had been started at local WVS centres or in small post offices, soon had to requisition other shops to accommodate their haul. Within the first two months of the campaign thousands of tons, enough in theory to make squadrons of fighter aeroplanes, were gratefully received. One old lady was reassured that every effort would be made to respect her request that her frying pan go towards a Spitfire (she believed it to have the edge on the Hurricane). A radio song from the period captured that same sense of pride in domestic sacrifice:

> My saucepans have all been surrendered,
> The teapot is gone from the hob,
> The colander's leaving the cabbage,
> For a very much different job.
> So now, when I hear on the wireless
> Of Hurricanes showing their mettle,
> I see, in a vision before me,
> A Dornier chased by the kettle.
>
> Wartime song

One woman working at WVS headquarters wrote to her mother on 11 July, only a day after the broadcast, 'These last two days have been hectic with aluminium . . . Already we have sent lorry loads down to the works . . . It poured in everywhere day and night and I have made my first war sacrifice and given up my lovely casserole that cost £1 in peacetime.'[21]

The propagandists' battle for salvage

Household aluminium, as it turned out, was just the beginning. Soon the rubbish recruiters were calling out for paper, cardboard, rubber, string, rags, old bones and food waste for pigswill. By 1943, government statistics claimed that each of the country's homes had provided about half a ton of salvage.[22] As the war progressed the public were asked to donate more and more. Some grumbled, but the guilt-inducing propaganda proved too powerful for most to ignore. 'Is this your house?' demanded one advertisement in 1943. 'Paper, metal tins, bones, string and other materials go into it every week. But how much comes out again as salvage? Is your house slacking?'[23] A copywriter's masterstroke was always to provide conversion tables explaining – much as the heartrending appeals for charitable donations do today – just where your gift would go and what it could achieve. 'Sufficient aluminium to build fifty Lancaster bombers is lost each year through aluminium milk bottle caps being thrown away,'[24] claimed one poster. Others explained how wool could be converted into uniforms and blankets; glycerine from bones into bombs; and cartridges and rags into maps and blankets.

THINK OF YOUR WASTE SALVAGE

THINK OF THE AMOUNT OF MUNITIONS WE NEED

And remember that

One newspaper makes three 25-pounder shell cups
One magazine the interior components of two mines
Six books one mortar shell carrier
One soap powder canister four aero engine caskets
Five medium size cartons one shell fuse assembly
60 large cigarette cartons one outer shell container
20 breakfast cereal cartons one case for three-pounder shells
six bills one washer for a shell
four assorted food cartons one box for aero cannon shells
one envelope one cartridge wad
twelve letters one box for rifle cartridges

So you see

We must GO TO IT!!

Ministry of Supply poster[25]

Rag

"ENEMY SHIP TORPEDOED with the help of Old Rags"

It sounds impossible doesn't it? But the charts that guide our submarine commanders are made from old rags. In addition, rags help to make maps for our bomber crews and tank crews, paper for medical supplies, wipers for cleaning machinery, battledress, blankets and other equipment, roofing felt for army huts, etc.

Give all the old rags you can find and spare for salvage at once. Rope, string and twine are also urgently needed. Keep rags clean and dry in a rag-bag ready for the salvage collector or rag-and-bone man when he calls.[26]

Paper, packaging and books

NATIONAL EMEGERGENCY NOTICE: That's right SAVE WASTE PAPER carefully

Waste paper isn't rubbish. It's precious. And it's doubly necessary now to salvage every scrap for the salvage collector. Munitions and spares to fight Japan need an average of nearly three times as much paper as for the war in Europe. Waste paper is used in the making of those munitions too. So remember – your waste paper is urgently needed – it's got a big job to do.

WASTE-PAPER is urgently needed for SALVAGE.

Ministry of Supply advertisement[27]

By 1943 it had become poor form not to reuse envelopes until there was no space left on which to write, and not to correspond on both sides of writing paper. Today, some claim self-righteously that they will not send Christmas or birthday cards for environmental reasons. In wartime there was no humbuggery about it – cards, other than those created imaginatively out of recycled newspaper, were considered an unnecessary extravagance. If shoppers wished to have their purchases wrapped they had to provide their own paper. Daily newspapers that had had as many as twenty-four pages in the 1930s, now had to cram their news into between four and eight pages, despite world-changing events to report. The Sunday newspapers, multi-sectioned behemoths today, rarely ran to over eight pages during the war. And though the stories were skilfully written and presented in their limited space, as time went on they were printed on stock that grew more and more to resemble blotting paper. In a world where print runs were restricted, even *Vogue* urged its readers to share copies. People gave away their treasures – love letters, albums and confidential records went into the same salvage sacks as old newspapers and magazines. It was not until 1944, with victory in sight, that the delicate subject of the national shortage of toilet paper was finally raised in the House of Commons.

AUSTERITY PICNIC – TO SAVE PAPER

Now that the spring days are coming and we'll all be trying to get as much fresh air and sunshine into our lungs as possible, many people will be eating out of doors. Please remember that sandwiches wrapped in grease-proof paper and a table napkin keep just as fresh as if they were wrapped in the peacetime layers of tissue – and you'll be saving lots of valuable paper towards the war effort.

Text of an advertisement issued by the Ministry of Supply[28]

In 2005 signatories representing 92 per cent of the UK's grocery market joined the Courtauld Commitment, an agreement that they would all work towards reducing food packaging. During the war the Ministry of Supply gave the food sector no choice but to radically slim down the packaging on those few goods allowed to stay in production. The grocery industry's advertising departments responded with alacrity, the canniest

NATIONAL BOOK RECOVERY & SALVAGE APPEAL
YOUR BOOKS ARE WANTED
FOR THE SERVICES • FOR BLITZED LIBRARIES • FOR SALVAGE

brands making a virtue of necessity. Orlox suet pudding suddenly arrived on the shelves wearing a sombre, tight-fitting package, emblazoned with the legend: 'This is an Orlox plain suet pudding in a wartime jacket.'[29] Amusingly, this was later changed to 'Utility jacket'. Gibbs toothpaste was advertised as 'Now in battledress refills'.[30]

Many goods, such as toiletries and soft drinks, were sold in refills to save materials – a practice that, sadly, has since died out as it is not aspirational to use refills. In wartime Britain it would have been considered wanton not to have recycled everything possible.

> **Take all empty tubes** shaving cream, tooth paste, ointment, paint, rubber solutions etc **to your chemist**. Do not put with other metal salvage, or the vital tin and lead will be lost in the smelting – **they are wanted for munitions**.
>
> Text of advertisement paid for by Euthymol toothpaste [31]

By 1943, with educational establishments complaining of too few textbooks to teach adequately and what paper there was being in a frail state due to having been pulped and reused again and again, the Ministry of Supply looked to private libraries to revitalise the national paper stock. In the first few months the campaign brought in 56 million books, more than one for every British citizen. Librarians were to check each title before it was sentenced to the thresher and 6 million books were considered too valuable for pulping; these were returned to those who had donated them or distributed to libraries whose stocks had been depleted by war damage. A further 5 million were sent to the Forces. The rest were sent off for recycling.[32] By 1945 the National Book Drive had brought in more than 100 million books.[33]

Iron railings

One of the most famous, if not infamous, casualties of the war on salvage were the Victorian iron railings that had previously guarded institutions, buildings of note, private square gardens and churchyards. The official figures trumpeted that when the national salvage drive was at its peak in 1943, 110,000 tons of scrap metal were being collected weekly. This remarkable figure was largely due to the wholesale uprooting of railings. They were often replaced with unsightly and precarious chicken wire. But their removal was popular in some parishes. 'Dare one hope', wrote a resident of London's Montpelier Square to *The Times* in April 1940, 'that the exigencies of war will at last rid London and other places of one of their major disfigurements – iron railings . . . If all useless railings could be freed forthwith into the Greater Reich it would considerably enhance our amenities.'[34] In September 1941 this correspondent's wish was granted by central government orders to all local authorities to survey and then remove unnecessary railings, with every landlord or tenant being given only a fortnight to appeal against their removal on artistic, historic or safety grounds. Dissenters from this initiative included Osbert Sitwell, who wrote to *The Times* from his Derbyshire estate to complain of 'the various acts of vandalism and sabotage' that had been committed in the name of the Ministry of Works.[35] The yield of metal was huge. Six months after the campaign of destruction was launched, 10,000 tons of metal were still being recovered from 100,000 houses each week. By September 1944, when the removal of railings ceased, the total weight of those demolished for scrap had reached a million tonnes. Many, however, lamented the scarring of the landscape and complained that some piles of scrap remained uncollected for years.

THE HOME FRONT HANDBOOK, APRIL 1945

SALVAGE COLLECTIONS

Material	*1940 tons*	*1944 tons*	*Total salvage collections 1939–44 tons*
Paper	257,797	273,173	1,584,159
Ferrous Metal	254,599	170,935	1,237,482
Non-ferrous Metal	11,630	4,527	38,566
Rags	16,210	19,420	160,827
Rubber	*None collected*	4,962	29,717
Bones	12,224	12,224	55,148
Kitchen Waste	435,845	435,845	1,381,034

IMPORTS OF FOOD AND ANIMAL FEEDING STUFFS TO THE UNITED KINGDOM

(to nearest thousand tons)

	1934–38 average	*1944 January–June*
Wheat and Flour	5,451	1,747
Rice, Other Grains and Pulses	1,524	60
Maize and Maize Meal	3,395	24
Other Animal Feeding Stuffs	1,719	12
Meat (including Bacon)	1,423	848
Canned Meat	63	107
Oilseeds, Oils and Fats	1,783	1,001
Sugar	2,168	497
Dairy Produce	889	289
Fruit and Vegetables	2,604	368
Beverages and Other Foods	1,007	441
TOTAL	22,026	5,394

IMPORTS OF DRY CARGO TO THE UNITED KINGDOM
(million tons)

	Food	*Raw materials*	*Finished goods, munitions etc*	*Total*
1934–38	22	26	7	55
1940	18.8	21.5	1	41.3
1941	14.7	15	0.8	30.5
1942	10.6	11.5	0.8	22.9
1943	11.5	12.8	2.2	26.4
1944, Jan. to June	5.4	6.1	1.3	12.8 [36]

The housewives' rewards for their wholehearted embrace of thrift were few and far between. The only holidays that were encouraged were farm breaks or visits to evacuated children, although in 1942, when Britain's military fortunes were at their lowest ebb and the essential workers exhausted from two years of working flat out, the government introduced a morale-boosting Stay-at-Home Holiday Scheme. This could be compared to the vogue among the British chattering classes in the summer of 2008 for eco-friendly 'staycations' (holidays in your own home to the layman). Among the suggested entertainments for stay-at-home holidaymakers was fundraising. Towns campaigned 'to buy their own Spitfire' (expensive at £5,000; in 1939 a large detached house in Twickenham could have been yours for £799). War Weapons Week raised £469 million between September 1940 and June 1941. Warships Week, between October 1941 and March 1942, raised £545.5 million (the £478 million raised in England and Wales alone being enough to cover the building cost of 5 battleships, 45 cruisers, 300 destroyers, 160 corvettes, 33 submarines, 4 aircraft carriers, 267 minesweepers, 124 motor torpedo boats, 170 depot ships, sloops, monitors etc.). Wings for Victory Week, between March and July 1943, raised £616 million. Salute the Soldier Week, as victory was in sight, between March and July 1944, raised £626 million.[37]

The success of these fundraisers was not down to patriotism alone.

After the hungry 1930s this was an era of high employment; although it was a time of thrift, it was not a time of poverty. With a far greater number of women working in paid jobs, many households had a higher income than ever before and neither the leisure nor the opportunity to spend much of it. To respond to the propagandist's heart-wringing pleas to win peace more quickly, by helping to pay for the country's air fleet or by investing in National Savings, had a self-serving logic.

The Children's Salvage Army

Children were among the country's most enthusiastic salvagers. A picture from the Imperial War Museum's collections is not untypical: it shows six primary-age schoolchildren from Blean School, Canterbury, with a chart setting out their summer fundraising efforts to 'Buy a War Weapon'. Their stated aim is to buy a light machine gun for £100 and a heavy machine gun for £350, adding, 'Lend your money to give our boys these tools.' Between April and June they had raised £231 15s 3d and they wanted to raise their £450 target by September.

Today gangs of adolescent boys are seen as purveyors of potential knife-wielding terror. In wartime gangs of knife-collecting youths may well have been encouraged – at least if the knives were being sent for salvage. Just as today green policies are seen as a youth vote winner, so during the war the campaign to salvage engaged young minds like no other. A 1941 correspondent to *The Times* pointed out: 'There are not many things that small boys can do [to help with the war effort], but this is one.'[38] Even Richmal Crompton's William had a go at salvaging with, characteristically, comically disastrous results. Most children, however, proved to be among the best salvage collectors, being enthusiastic, energetic and hard to refuse. For them it must also have been empowering to leave the house, work as a team and do something that gained public approbation.

The future of all *Blue Peter* collecting campaigns and charity telethons

Saucepans for Spitfires: schoolboys and their dogs collecting salvage at a wartime shelter in Nottinghamshire.

was surely sown in those war years. The Brownies paid for an aircraft and a lifeboat through collecting jam jars. As they worked, child recruits sang salvage songs, adapted from the popular anthems of the day, such as 'There'll always be a dustbin . . .'

The enthusiasm of the young is shown in *Welsh Schools Prize Winning Essays: Salvage as munitions of war, 1943*, a collection of polemics on the subject written by schoolchildren across Wales and presented to HRH Princess Elizabeth in 1943. In the opening essay nine-year-old Melba E. J. Thomas writes:

> And to you the children of this island I give a big and serious task, the task of going on hard with this great and bitter struggle for the honour of the country . . . I give you the task of dealing a blow to that vile

> coward without honour or mercy . . . This blow can be delivered by salvage of paper, metal, bones and iron. The more you salvage the more ships you are keeping for essential cargo. Salvage is necessary . . . This can be done singly or in a group. Rise now and become the leader. Organise the group of workers. You can become like busy work bees with you as the captain . . . Make two or three children responsible for a street.[39]

Local councils

Local councils today are often depicted as lazy and self-serving when it comes to rubbish collections. I am thinking of headlines such as 'Dustbins: Now We Face Fines and Taxes'[40] and scare stories of Orwellian measures like 'Pay-as-you-throw bin taxes will encourage cancer-causing bonfires'.[41] In autumn 2006 the *Mail on Sunday* even led a campaign against 'the Green Gauleiter' councils that refused to carry out weekly collections. The paper's campaign claimed not to be anti-recycling per se, but did stress the marked inconsistency between councils when it came to outlining what rubbish would be collected, where from, how, how regularly, in what sort of condition and from what type of receptacle. The goodwill and public spirit of council-tax-paying residents, the paper claimed, were being sapped by the near-tyranny of petty-minded small-town bureaucrats.

This campaign coincided with a visit to my parents where I witnessed my law-abiding seventy-something-year-old father's distress at trying to get to grips with stringent new rubbish-collecting rules. The exact interpretation of these diktats was the cause of much concern. 'And where does this go?' one parent would demand in a tone of shrill anxiety, shaking a plastic beaker. On rubbish day my father was in a blind panic. He explained his dilemma: if he took the rubbish, in all its separate, sorted, colour-coded containers, out too early the seagulls might scatter it, the rubbish men refuse it and the council might impose a fine. However, he did not want to miss the rubbish men and build up too much rubbish, for fear of them refusing it the next week and imposing a fine. In the end, he kept watch all morning for the rubbish men and hand-delivered his haul. 'Then it all begins again,' said my mother wearily from the kitchen counter, where she was searching for the correct receptacle for carrot peelings. And I thought: 'Taking your rubbish out shouldn't be made to feel this punitive. Why isn't their council selling this better? Why aren't they making this process clearer and easier, or perhaps even offering incentives to those households who recycle more? Why aren't they explaining what the benefits of recycling might be?'

Of course, my grandparents' generation benefited from an increase in collections and can-do propaganda. In the 1940s councils were able to sell off what they collected to increase their revenue and lower their rates. In December 1941 the London boroughs of Bermondsey and Bethnal Green challenged each other to a paper-collecting competition; Paddington ran a 'Mile of Keys' campaign to collect a million keys for metal salvage; while Tottenham was famous for its gargantuan quantities of pigswill.

METROPOLITAN BOROUGH OF LEWISHAM
SALVAGE CAMPAIGN
JAN 19TH to FEB 14TH 1942

A PERSONAL MESSAGE TO EVERY LEWISHAM HOUSEWIFE

The Mayor's Parlour
Town Hall, Lewisham

Dear Madam,

In the great **Salvage** effort which Lewisham is now making, I address this appeal particularly to you, because I know that such a drive must depend for the greater part of its success on the co-operation of the housewife.

In addition to food scraps for pig-feeding we want **all** your waste paper, rags, bones and old metal. All these are essential to munitions-making and Britain **must** have them. Remember, if you have a friend or relative in the forces, **your** contribution to Lewisham's Salvage Drive will be directly helping **him** in **our** fight.

With this in mind, apply this test to everything in your home. Ask yourself, is your need for it as great as Britain's? And if in doubt, turn it out, – for Salvage – for **munitions**!

Throughout Lewisham's own Salvage Drive, the Borough's regular collections will be supplemented by special collections by voluntary organisations. All these will be helping towards the one aim – to put Lewisham in the lead with salvage. Turn out all you can – we can take it! One final word. It helps a lot and saves sorting costs, if you put out the waste paper, rags, metal and bones in separate bundles or cartons. The food scraps, of course, go into the communal bin: there will be one on every street corner in the very near future, meanwhile will you please put out the food scraps in a tin or other container and we will collect it.

Housewives of Lewisham! The war on waste has started, and you are the shock troops. I give you my thanks now, with every confidence that they will be fully earned.

Yours faithfully,

Mayor of Lewisham

PS – You doubtless know of the London Boroughs' Prize Competition whereby the more Waste Paper, old Books, Cardboard and Cartons you salvage the greater the chance of helping Lewisham's local Charities. Please make your effort a record.

What we could learn from wartime salvagers today

For years after the war, piles of rusting iron, defunct machinery and even offal festered on the outskirts of towns and villages. Perhaps this discouraged people from properly managing their waste at times when increased consumer spending was leading to a steady increase in non-organic household rubbish, which then had to be disposed of in landfill sites.

The decades following the war gave birth to a politicised green movement that made waste a core campaigning issue – but it has taken years to gain centre stage. Eve Balfour founded the Soil Association in 1946 to advocate organic farming methods, but it was to be another half-century before it became part of mainstream debate. In 1970 Friends of the Earth launched itself in the United Kingdom, with the stunt of returning thousands of bottles to Schweppes. The first bottle banks did not appear in the UK for seven years after that. Increasing concerns about hazardous waste led first to European legislation, with environmental protection finally being included in the Treaty of Rome in 1986, then legislation in Britain. In 1990, the Conservative government produced 'This Common Inheritance', a white paper on the environment which led to the Environment Agency being established in 1995.

As I write in the spring of 2009, the three mainstream political parties are seeking to outdo one another in terms of their green credentials. Recycling has again become a popular vote winner and national recycling levels have increased from 7 per cent in 1997 to 27 per cent in 2007, with the country's greenest councils collecting almost 50 per cent.[42]

It seems that we were very quick to forget the successes and achievements of our recycling-savvy grandparents and have been painfully slow to realise that actually they were on to a good thing. Now, in our bid to be greener and to turn our country into a more resourceful and less environmentally damaging nation, surely we can draw on the lessons from that era? Haven't our grandparents provided us with a lot of the answers? Their triumphs show us the importance of propaganda and leadership from government, and also of the public being able to see the results of their efforts. Perhaps one of our current problems is that people feel doing their bit – whether by recycling paper or composting their food waste – doesn't actually make a difference, because the scale of the crisis is too large. But if we were encouraged by being shown what our endeavours can do and even rewarded for them, maybe things would change? Our local councils would do well to look back and consider the wisdom of increasing rubbish collections, rather than bringing in what are perceived as punitive policies. Government could do more to reward local authorities that increase recycling and decrease the amount of rubbish being sent to landfill. That reward could then be passed on to individual households with a reduction in council tax for those that recycle more and throw away the smallest amounts of non-biodegradable waste, and this scheme could even be extended to businesses. The nation's young people could have an empowering role in a nationwide effort to recycle more through local projects led by their primary and secondary schools. Perhaps former COGs, who now must be in their seventies, could show the way by teaching their grandchildren's generation recycling lessons from their own youth. Some towns, such as Middlesbrough with its 'Environmental city', are trying schemes where waste food composted on reclaimed derelict land can be used to grow vegetables for the canteens of local institutions such as schools.[43] Why not go one step further and revive the pig clubs too?

Sucking Eggs:
What your wartime granny could teach you about waging war on waste

IN THE KITCHEN:

- Plan your meals and your shopping trips.
- If buying fresh ingredients, make them seasonal and local. The shorter the journey they've had to your basket, the less energy they will have used already.
- Choose goods that come without packaging – or at least packaging that can be reused and recycled.
- Where possible, buy products (e.g. kitchen staples, toiletries) in bigger volumes – it's cheaper and in the long run uses less packaging.
- Plan meals that use up your most perishable goods first.
- Know how to portion food, but also know how to make new meals out of leftovers. Remember, some of the most delicious recipes – from gratins to stews and risottos – involve judicious kitchen recycling. Get ideas at the website www.lovefoodhatewaste.com.
- If you've cooked too much, freeze extra portions for future quick individual meals.
- Get a stockpot going weekly as a means to use up leftover odds and sods.
- Food that really has to be thrown away should be composted. Check your local council's website for offers on composting bins and collections of compost.

WITH YOUR BIN:

- Recycle and compost all that you can. Go to your local council's website to find out more about what schemes are available to you.
- If you are unhappy with your council's recycling provisions, tell them so.

- Set yourself rubbish reduction targets.
- Check at www.recycylenow.com how packaging might be reusable before discarding it.
- Recycle all your waste paper and cardboard.
- Make an effort to become as paperless as possible at home and work, by advertising your intolerance of junk mail and moving all your accounts online.
- If you have a baby, try the subsidised schemes run by your council that encourage use of non-disposable nappies.
- Don't bin textiles, appliances, batteries or anything that may have a life beyond you without first checking other options such as swapxchange sites, charity collection points, altering at a dressmaker's, gifting something to a friend or taking it into a council-run salvage point.

OUTSIDE THE HOME:

- Don't accept even more plastic bags. Always take extra bags or a basket with you.
- During a coffee or meal break from work, try to eat in instead of buying the kind of elaborately packaged takeaway fast food that ends up overfilling bins. Or else bring in your own food in a reusable container.
- If you're going to buy a paper or magazine for your commute, either pass it on to another passenger when you're done with it, or post it in a recycling bin.
- Walk that bit further to seek out a recycling bin – there are more and more of them.

CHAPTER EIGHT

THE BATTLE FOR FUEL

When we arrived at the palace the [King and Queen] took me to my rooms, explaining that I could only have a small fire in my sitting room and one in the outer waiting room, and saying they hoped I would not be too cold . . . The restrictions on heat and water were observed as carefully in the royal household as in any other home in England. There was a plainly marked black line in my bathtub above which I was not supposed to run the water.

Eleanor Roosevelt[1]

There is an episode in the cult 1980s comedy *Blackadder* in which a stag party organised by the wastrel hero, Edmund Blackadder, clashes with the surprise visit of a puritan aunt and uncle from whom he hopes to inherit a fortune. When Blackadder offers his aunt a chair she responds, '*Chairs? You have chairs in your house? Chairs are an invention of Satan! In our house Nathaniel sits on a spike!*' Blackadder asks, '*And yourself?*' And is answered, '*I sit on Nathaniel – two spikes would be an extravagance.*'

Being green can sometimes seem a bit 'two spikes would be an extravagance'. I am constantly trying to rethink my life and its environmental impact in terms of what I buy and eat, dress in and how I travel. But I am weak and confess that there have been occasions when I have overfilled a kettle, run a deep bath and flown on a scheduled airline. There are doubtless hemp-cycling-shorts-wearing paragons of the Green Movement, New Puritans, who would revile me. But then I can find their rhetoric ('two kids would be an extravagance', 'four wheels bad, two wheels good', 'we're all going to hell in a Tesco shopping trolley') a little wearying and actually immobilising to my good intentions.

Life would be more straightforward for many weaker vessels if the path of environmental righteousness were clearly signposted and maintained by effective government environmental policies, such as rebates and penalties. Our contemporary New Puritans, steadfast or hypocritical, sure or wavering, might look back on the 1940s as a golden age, when much of the wanton and selfish wastefulness that angers eco-warriors today was socially unacceptable. With petrol rationing it was a glorious time for cyclists. Those of us who sigh outside shopfronts over the amount of electricity being wasted at night to highlight their wares would have appreciated the blackout. Today's water monitors would surely approve of a time when even a hard-working princess-turned-mechanic was discouraged from bathing in more than five inches of water once a week only. And even the richest could not holiday abroad, or far from home, without being continually reminded there was a war on.

Government guidelines on curbing the use of fuel were extremely effective. In 1944 the country burnt 33 million tons of coal, which was 3 million less than in the previous year and three-quarters the amount it had sent up into the atmosphere immediately pre-war,[2] while expenditure on petrol per head was one-fiftieth of the pre-war average.[3] In the 1930s motoring had been a growth industry. By 1944 only 700,000 of the 2 million cars owned in Britain were still on the road – and these were operating only by special permission and on strict petrol rations.[4]

Modern warfare is not energy efficient. After the Japanese bombed Pearl Harbor and the Americans were drawn into the war, Admiral Nimitz, the US Commander-in-Chief of Pacific Naval Forces, commented that winning would be down to 'beans, bullets, and oil'. By the end of the conflict he had turned that round to saying, 'Now, it's oil, bullets and beans!' To keep Allied fighter planes airborne for just *one* day had required *fourteen* times as much gasoline as was shipped to Europe from the US during the whole of the First World War. A further *60,000* gallons of gasoline had been needed to keep just *one* armoured division on the road. With the oil that filled the tanks of just *one battleship, 500 US homes* could have been heated for a year. A *one-hour flight* on a Navy Hellcat expended the same amount of fuel as a car trip from Chicago to Los Angeles.[5]

The British statistics are just as sobering. In two raids, on the German

Bateman cartoon: poster for Ministry of Fuel and Power.

ports of Wilhelmshaven and Düsseldorf in November 1943 the Allied air forces used up *5 million gallons of fuel* in *twenty-four hours*. It took at least *2,000 gallons* of petrol for a Lancaster bomber – 7,000 of which were produced between 1942 and 1946 – to reach Germany's industrial heartland, though some missions expended up to *3,540 gallons*.[6] And it was not just keeping battleships afloat, fighter planes airborne and military juggernauts on course that expended petrol. War production in factories across the country also burnt up vast amounts of fuel.

Power in Britain came mostly from coal. However, at the outbreak of war many miners had grasped the opportunity to exchange one dangerous, back-breaking career for another. They joined up – soldiering at least had the advantage of mostly taking place above ground. Still more miners were called up, with the result that by 1941 there were 84,000 fewer miners than there had been in 1938. A further problem was that the miners still working in the pits tended to be men past the age of military conscription who, being frailer and older, were less productive. In 1941 the total coal output in tonnage was 206 million, 20 million less than it had been in 1938. Yet the calls for coal had never been greater.[7] The government did its best to reverse the exodus. They increased pay – miners leapt from fifty-fourth in the industrial pay league to twenty-third – and improved conditions. One knock-on effect of demand for more miners was that some of them found it easy to take time off with virtually no risk of facing the sack.[8] Hand in hand with coercion went a government Essential Work Order that released 30,000 ex-miners from the Forces back to their original trade.[9]

However, this all proved too little too late and in the end there seemed no choice but to make the people of Britain bear the brunt of fuel shortages. From 1942, being cold was to be part of one's patriotic duty.

Arguments for fuel rationing – now and then

If you remember your grandparents' house in the 1950s, 1960s, 1970s, or even 1980s as chilly, your memory serves you well. Our grandparents' solution for feeling a bit nippy of a weekend afternoon was to put on an extra layer of clothing, perhaps move around a bit more or maybe warm one shut-in room to sit in. Our solution is to crank up the thermostat and luxuriate year round, wearing only a T-shirt, in our fashionably (but often draftily) floorboarded and open-plan houses, in which our through doors stay open round the clock.

The average temperatures of our homes rose between 1991 and 2002 from 15.5 degrees to 19 degrees.[10] Homes consume 51 per cent of Britain's energy,[11] with 82 per cent of that figure going on space and water heating, a rise of 32 per cent since 1970.[12] The Energy Saving Trust, a government-supported body established in 1993 to advise on how to curb UK emissions, has estimated that UK homes waste £910 billion a year by leaving appliances on standby.[13] Despite these domestic extravagances the government's Communities and Local Government Department pronounced in December 2006 that by 2016 every home in Britain would be zero-carbon.[14] What exactly that means and how they plan to achieve that figure is not clear. With only seven years to go, you would think we would all have been leafleted by now. No, me neither.

It seems that however well-intentioned we are, we cannot by ourselves control our fuel squandering. Is it any wonder that many environmentalists argue it is time for an energy rationing scheme? One proposal is that there should be a global system with each country dividing its target usage between its population and its corporations. The basic tenet of wartime rationing – fair shares for all and a guaranteed but limited supply – applies. Special cases, such as cold-weather benefits for elderly people, could be calculated into the equation. Perhaps each of us would be issued with a debit card that would be credited seasonally, so we could spend our points as we saw fit. A paragon who lived in a passive house (a form of energy-efficient housing first pioneered in Germany in the late 1980s), commuted to work on a bicycle, had a raw vegan diet and never holidayed abroad, might find that he or she had spare energy units, which could then be given or sold to others. The government could turn a blind eye to such transactions, just as in wartime it did not intervene in the trade of clothing coupons swapped for second-hand outfits. In his book *Heat, How We Can Stop the Planet Burning* the environmental campaigner George Monbiot suggests calling the units of such a scheme 'icecaps',[15] to give a neat visual reminder of what is at stake.

In the early 1940s Sir William Beveridge, the people's economist, had worked out a scheme whereby fuel rations would be calculated on the number of rooms in your house, the number of people in your household and what part of the country you lived in – those in the north were to receive 30 per cent more than those in the south. Older people were to benefit from a supplementary ration – as they do now in the form of cold-weather payments. Just as clothes rationing had been introduced on margarine coupons, Beveridge proposed that until the country's fuel ration books had been prepared, clothes coupons would be exchanged for fuel units.

Hugh Dalton (the Minister of Economic Warfare, 1940–42), meanwhile, was keen not only to bring in fuel rationing but also to nationalise the mines in the hope this would encourage the miners to increase productivity. The wider public endorsed Dalton's plans because they supported the principles of fair shares for all. The Conservatives and the Tory press were, however, bitterly against. They were worried lest rationing electricity and coal discomfited their natural – and, of course, wealthier – constituents. (A fear that could have some resonance for today's politicians, who are nervous of introducing legislation that could open them to accusations of using green issues as a veil to introduce stealth taxes and limit civil liberties.) Dalton, though Eton-educated, was a Labour member of the wartime coalition government, and his opponents feared nationalisation, seeing it as a sign that the Labourites in the government were steering the country towards increasingly socialist policies. They were already concerned about the power the miners could wield as a mass and had no desire to make it easier for them to strike.

SAVE FUEL
IN THESE WAYS!
THE MINISTER OF FUEL AND POWER URGES EVERY HOUSEHOLD TO PRACTISE THESE ECONOMIES
ROOM HEATING 1. Postpone lighting coal fires till as late as possible in the season and then late in the day. 2. Heat only one room at a time. 3. Fit firebricks in the grate.
WATER HEATING 1. Use less hot water. 2. Do not use more than 5" of water in your bath. 3. Use solid fuel boilers only twice a week except in very cold weather.
COOKING 1. Turn the heat off or down as soon as possible. 2. Use the minimum amount of water for cooking vegetables and making tea.
Save Fuel for Battle
ISSUED BY THE MINISTRY OF FUEL AND POWER

In the end the Tory backbenchers, with Churchill's support, won the day. Instead of fuel rationing, a further 7,000 ex-miners were forced out of the Army and back underground. Churchill created a new Ministry of Fuel, Light and Power and appointed Major Gwilym Lloyd-George (second son of the former prime minister) as its minister. Local fuel offices were set up across the country. Major Lloyd-George had previously been a popular deputy to Woolton at the Ministry of Food, so he knew the value of propaganda in urging the public to curb their excesses for the common good. The people themselves could be trusted to be cautious in their use of fuel.

As had become almost a tradition, the government chose to launch the new austerity campaign on a Sunday – in this case 24 June 1942 – with a radio broadcast from Major Lloyd-George and full-page advertisements in all the Sunday papers. Their target was the housewife, who was exhorted to join the battle. Women were told to wage war on three fronts: space and water heating, which burnt up about three-quarters of domestic fuel; cooking, which accounted for about a sixth; and lighting, which used about a twentieth.

The first recommendation was for responsible citizens to go about their homes removing unnecessary light bulbs. Then they were told to shut off rooms they could do without. Instead of using a sitting-room, drawing-room or parlour, they were encouraged as their main living space to use the kitchen, it being the room that, because of the water storage heater and cooker, was most likely to remain warm without necessitating the lighting of a fire. Later, the kitchen was to be the focus of numerous guides on how to cook thriftily. On that first summer Sunday, however, the instruction was to not cook at all – but instead to subsist on summer salads.

Calculating fuel targets – now and then

Many of us today have little or no clue how much fuel we burn in our homes. The small print of our bills is so meaningless that it might as well be written in some ancient cuneiform. Some environmentalists go so far as to argue that the gas and electricity utility companies make things deliberately opaque by steering us towards friendly sounding tariffs deducted by direct debit. Some of us may be looking more carefully as the credit crunch bites, but most scrutinise energy bills only when we are bewildered by a sudden hike in prices.

I am, as I'm sure are most people, a fairly passive consumer of power. When I rented a small one-bedroom flat where the electricity was on a rechargeable smart card I was far more aware of the real cost of moments of forgetfulness such as leaving a mobile phone charger plugged in or a television on standby. Since moving in with my husband I've become less attentive. I pay him a direct debit. He then pays another to our energy supplier. I know where our meter is, but I'd need to mount a stepladder to read it. The location of meters is just one of the problems highlighted by a February 2008 Energy Savings Trust survey. It also reported that a third of its respondents found their gas or electricity bill 'not easy' to understand, while 82 per cent did not know what tariff they were on.[16]

Although their widespread introduction is now promised, Britain trails behind many other developed countries in the promotion of 'smart meters'. With this technology a little knowledge is a positive thing for both supplier and consumer. The supplier, furnished with a clearer idea of usage patterns, can cater more effectively to the customer. The consumer, equipped with a clear idea of where his energy is being consumed, and indeed wasted, can make his home more efficient. The Energy Savings Trust calculates that if every household in the UK had one and used just 5 per cent less fuel, we would collectively save £1.2 billion per annum and the equivalent of 7.4 million tons of CO_2 emissions.[17] In a survey where electrical cookers were fitted with smart meters, usage dropped by 15 per cent.[18]

Other countries are already benefiting from the technology. In Italy

Enel, the biggest energy supplier, spent five years and 2.1 billion Euros supplying their 27 million customers with smart meters. They now claim the technology is saving them 500 million Euros a year, thus the project should have paid for itself in just over four years. The Dutch government plans for every home in the Netherlands to be equipped with a smart meter by 2013. The state government of Ontario, Canada, hopes to have theirs in place by 2010.[19] In May 2009, the Labour goverment belatedly announced ambitions for smart meters to be rolled out across the UK and to be installed in every home by 2020. The costs should not be exorbitant – between £100 and £200 apiece.[20]

There was no smart metering during the Second World War. There was, however, smarter practice. Finding your meter incomprehensible was no longer tolerated as an excuse – not after the Ministry of Fuel had issued their first four-page leaflet in the Battle for Fuel, titled 'Here are your Battle Orders', which introduced itself with the rallying cry: 'Every citizen – particularly every housewife – is now in the front line in the vital Battle for Fuel.'[21] On its back page it offered instructions on how to read both gas and electricity meters, and how to calculate your household's annual fuel allowance.

Though the government made it clear that it was one's public duty to calculate an 'annual fuel target' and work out how to stick to it, most people found it as onerous a task as we do today when struggling to understand our fuel bills or fill out our tax returns.

The wartime feedback was uniformly grumpy, with many resentful that the government hadn't done the mind-numbing number-crunching for them. 'Lord Woolton never suggests a tea target or a sugar target but says what we can have,' wrote one wearied correspondent to *The Times*. The word 'target' aroused criticism too. One newspaper cartoon showed an old lady standing by her meter, declaring proudly, 'We've nearly reached our fuel target already.'[22]

At the same time as the government announced its Battle for Fuel it introduced further power-saving measures. Blackout regulations had already banned shops from lighting up window displays at night. Now some luxury electrical goods such as coffee percolators and hair-curling

THE BATTLE for FUEL
WE MUST ALL KEEP WITHIN OUR TARGET!!
WHAT YOU HAVE TO DO: Work out your Fuel Target in fuel units from the chart below. Check this against last year's consumption to see how and where you must cut down. Then divide your allowance of fuel units amongst the different kinds of fuel you use. Remember the Fuel Year has already started and there's colder weather ahead – so go carefully now.
YOUR PERSONAL ALLOWANCE
is 15 Fuel Units per year which equals 7½ cwts. of coal or a corresponding amount of other fuels. This applies to adults and children alike.
NUMBER OF ROOMS
NORTHERN
MIDLANDS
SOUTHERN
HOUSE ALLOWANCE IN FUEL UNITS
1 80 60 50
2 90 70 60
3 110 90 70
4 120 100 80
5 140 110 90
6 150 120 100
7 OR MORE 170 140 110
FUEL UNIT
1 FUEL UNIT EQUALS ½ Cwt. Coal or Coke
1 FUEL UNIT EQUALS 500 Cubic Feet of Gas
1 FUEL UNIT EQUALS 50 Units of Electricity
1 FUEL UNIT EQUALS 1 Gallon of Paraffin
HAVE A CURFEW FOR ALL COAL FIRES–
Never put on a new lump after 9 p.m . . . Never use a larger gas ring than necessary . . . Turn out unnecessary lights . . . Have your meals in the kitchen . . . Keep the boiler damped down . . . Sift cinders

tongs were taken out of production for an indefinite period, while others such as electric blankets and vacuum cleaners could henceforth only be bought with a special licence. This was as far, however, as legislation would go.

Campaigning in the wartime battle for fuel

WHY TO SAVE Coal is essential to our advancing forces. Your fuel savings in the home will help to keep them supplied.

WHAT TO SAVE Over two-thirds of the fuel most of us use in our homes is burnt as raw coal. Thus while we economize in the use of gas, coke, and electricity, which also comes from coal, *the biggest saving must be on raw coal.*

WHERE TO SAVE MOST Roughly half our fuel is used for room heating and one quarter for water heating, i.e. three-quarters for those two purposes alone. Therefore *we must cut down on room heating and water heating.*

WHEN TO SAVE Nearly half our fuel is used in the three coldest months, December, January and February, but do *remember that big savings can be made in the mild and less cold weather.*

HOW TO SAVE *Most households following the simple hints given in this folder can save at least 5 lbs of coal per day without much discomfort.* This does not sound very much, but see on the back of this folder what it means to our fighting men, and start in real earnest to economize *now.*

From the leaflet, 'Save Fuel for Battle',
issued by the Ministry of Fuel, Light and Power[23]

Major Lloyd-George appointed a fellow ex-officer as the Ministry of Fuel, Light and Power's director of publicity. Commander Stephen King-Hall had an established pre-war reputation as a political commentator. As a spin doctor he excelled. Even more blatantly than his fellow media manipulators at the Ministries of Food, Agriculture and the Board of Trade, he brought the language of war into his manifestos. In his Battle for Fuel communiqués he spoke as a general addressing his troops on the eve of yet another battle in which, despite small victories, there was no end in sight. His sergeant majors were the doughty housewives of Britain. His troops were the entire citizenry. He addressed them through all forms of media. On the radio 'Fuel Flashes' interrupted *Kitchen Front*. At the cinema short preview films offered instruction on such burning issues as how to poke a fire most effectively. In newspapers and magazines King-Hall would dress up a boringly worthy communiqué on the need for lagging your boiler with the exhortation: 'In the Battle for Fuel we must not neglect our defences.'[24] Indeed, jackets for boilers were often easier to come by than those for humans.

When he felt spirits were wilting on the domestic front, King-Hall tried rallying his home troops with news of inspirational sacrifices elsewhere. His sixth fuel communiqué told how 'an Order has been issued prohibiting the use of central heating in government offices, hotels and large blocks of flats until after October 31 . . . It is hoped by this prohibition to save sufficient fuel to manufacture 1,000 spitfires.'[25] This had the knock-on effect that some smaller businesses not engaged in war or other necessary work mothballed their operations. The heroine of Patrick Hamilton's *The Slaves of Solitude*, for example, becomes a home worker after her publishing firm decides to open the offices less to save on fuel. The government's advice was for neighbours to take it in turns to keep their home fires burning:

> Share your fires . . . One well-warmed room in one house is more sensible (and much more comfortable) than two rather chilly rooms in separate houses . . . So don't delay – get together with your friends and neighbours now and work out a scheme for sharing firesides this winter.

Insulation – now and then

In environmental terms many of our houses are disastrously leaky. Lacking adequate insulation, they are responsible for massive household emissions. The Energy Saving Trust claims each UK household creates around six tons of carbon dioxide a year. That figure is six times the weight of the rubbish the average household throws away annually and double the annual carbon emissions of an average car. Making each one of our homes more efficient, the trust argues, could save around two tons of carbon dioxide per household a year.[26] They claim further that if everyone in Britain with gas central heating installed a new condensing boiler our country's emissions would be cut by 13.7 million tons, at a saving of around £1.6 billion per year on our energy bills. The fuel saves would also create enough energy to heat over 3.7 million homes a year.[27]

A 2002 survey discovered that 10 per cent of British homes lacked any form of insulation. There are an estimated 17 million homes in Britain with cavity walls but only 6 million with insulation. We get away without making these improvements to our homes because our rules are far less stringent than in other countries: a house deemed up to standard in Norway and Sweden uses about a quarter of the energy of a house that would pass the building codes of England or Wales. Indeed, Sweden's building regulations were tougher in 1978 than ours are today, while Germany's laws against leaky houses are three times as strict as ours. In 2005 Chancellor Angela Merkel implemented a costly refurbishment plan to bring every house built in Germany before 1978 up to high energy standards. Meanwhile in Britain, when the then Homes Minister Yvette Cooper was asked to impose Energy Efficient Standards for the refurbishment of homes, she dismissed the idea as 'unnecessary gold plating'.[28] But it doesn't have to be gold plating to do the job; just some old-fashioned lagging would make a noticeable improvement. If everyone put an insulation jacket on their hot water tank we would cut CO_2 emission by 740,000 tons – enough to fill around 148,000 hot-air balloons.[29]

It is the homes of the poorest that are the worst insulated and therefore the most expensive to heat. Even in property developments marketed squarely at the rich, insulation guidelines are flouted daily. A regular scam is for builders to bring in the correct amount of insulation, but to leave it tied up in bales in the attic – not rolled out it is worthless. This had happened in almost half the properties visited in a 2004 survey by the Building Research Establishment, although all had received Energy Efficiency certification.[30] Yet loft insulation pays for itself quickly: if every home that could had 270 mm loft insulation we would save 3.8 million tons of CO_2, the same as the annual emissions of around 650,000 homes.[31] A passive house can retain an ambient temperature of 21.4 degrees through the harsh German winter without central heating.[32] Most of us who live in badly insulated houses simply crank up the heating when we feel cold. By investing in insulation we would in the long term save money and CO_2 emissions. Mineral insulation fibres can, for example, be injected between cavity walls. This has been proven to pay for itself in a reduction in heating bills within two to five years. Indeed, the Energy Trust works out that it would save 4.6 million tons of CO_2 emissions, enough to fill one million hot-air balloons.[33] However, 65 per cent of homeowners never bother to insulate properly. If the government were to give them an incentive to make environmental improvements – George Monbiot suggests a rebate on stamp duty – it might lead to a virtuous form of home improvement that also helped the environment. Experts suggest that if the government insisted on insulation being put under all new roofs and floors, it could cut the UK housing stock's energy usage by 40 per cent.[34]

'LAG' YOUR HOT WATER SYSTEM Examine your hot water system and wherever possible cover up hot water tanks and the hot water pipes nearby with old bits of felt, thicknesses of newspaper or corrugated paper. Use string or wire to lash these or similar materials round your tanks and pipes. The object of this is to save fuel by preventing the heat from radiating into the air. You will use much less fuel and your water will keep hot much longer.[35]

ROOM WARMING

ONE THERM OF GAS, with an average-sized gas fire (7 narrow or 3 wide radiants) full on, will give you seven hours' warmth.

Never light a fire unless really necessary. Put on warmer clothes instead.

Turn down the gas fire as soon as the room is warm enough, a small fire will keep it warm.

Turn out the fire if the room is to be left empty for any time.

Make one room your living-room and dining-room, and give up bedroom fires except in cases of illness.

If you use a gas poker to light solid fuel fires, take it out the moment the fire is alight.

Leaflet issued by the Southern Metropolitan Gas Company

The Ministry of Fuel's propaganda department had its own equivalent of Potato Pete and Mrs Sew-and-Sew. However, the slightly sinister sounding 'Fire watcher' never garnered the same degree of affection. Perhaps this was because his tips along the lines that one should 'not light a fire just for the sake of having a fire' were rather obvious. More significantly, the government missed its chance to introduce proper fuel rationing. By the winter of 1942 it was too late. Industrial and military demand had outstripped supply, and it was now impossible to guarantee fair shares for all.

'LAG'
to keep heat in!
LAGGING PIPES AND TANKS
KEEPS WATER HOT AND SAVES FUEL
Lagging a 25 gall. tank may save
as much as one ton of fuel a year.
Lagging gives more even clothes-airing
ISSUED BY THE MINISTRY OF FUEL AND POWER

It was the public who ended up having to go without. Many remember the cold as the most difficult and miserable aspect of the whole war. Families went out to gather firewood; they resorted to buying fuel off people whom they didn't entirely trust; they queued outside factories in the hope of some coal going spare; they had to throw sticks of old furniture on to the fire or to creep into the blackout to fell a tree. To try to get a decent blaze going on a winter evening, many experimented with the fuel potential of whatever they had to hand from newspapers to vegetable peelings. Those living in the countryside took inspiration from Irish peasant customs and experimented with peat and turf. In the cities people salvaged waste timber from bombed-out houses. A lump of coal became a luxury symbol in those straitened times: a wedding gift, or something for a new baby or literally a 'house-warming'.

Everyone was forced to follow the Ministry of Fuel's advice: many shut off parts of their homes, making the kitchen their domestic hub, perhaps even following one government scientist's advice that they should 'make it comfortable by bringing chairs from the parlour and having a screen or perhaps an old curtain on a clothes horse, to keep off draughts'.[36] Cinders were sifted for reuse; appliances were kept spotlessly clean to promote efficiency; fire bricks were advocated to keep the warmth in. Above all, the householders of Britain were instructed to be stoical. The Ministry of Fuel's 'Battle Orders: Eight Rules for Users of Combination Grates', recommended: 'Get together and combine against Hitler by making one grate serve two families. What hardship is this compared to Russian conditions?'[37]

The letters pages of the newspapers were full of eccentric tips on how to keep out the cold: wooden Japanese hand warmers; filling a sack with heated up cherry-stones; concentrating on only one sense by listening to the night-time radio in the dark; simply going to bed much earlier. But even turning in early must have been tough in the depths of midwinter. The histories of clothing rationing show that as the war progressed a surprising number of people dispensed with nightwear. I suspect that this did not reflect slipping moral or hygienic standards but that so many were clambering between the sheets in full outer wear. By 1943 not even the most obvious ways of heating yourself up at night without lighting a fire or flicking a switch were easily available: hot-water bottles were on prescription and blankets on special licence.

What your wartime granny knew about cooking efficiently

You are a good housewife. You pride yourself on being economical.
And you can say with truth that no food is ever wasted in YOUR kitchen.
But – and now search your conscience – can you say the same of fuel?
From the leaflet, 'Food and Fuel Planning'[38]

Golden Rules for Gas Cookers

Never light your oven to cook a single dish. With a little planning you can easily prepare an entire meal while the oven is hot, as well as a pudding or tart that can be eaten cold the next day.

Turn out the burners directly the food is done – it will keep hot in the oven for some time. Always clean your cooker regularly – burners clogged with grease are slow and extravagant. More than half the gas which is used in homes on the gas cooker, is used on the large ring. By using the small ring instead, there is a saving of over one fuel unit in ten, although the job takes longer.

Keep lids on saucepans to contain the heat. Cut down hot meals to a minimum.

From the Ministry of Fuel's leaflet, 'The Battle for Fuel: Here are your battle orders, Practical Hints for saving Fuel at Home'[39]

To coincide with the summertime launch of the Battle for Fuel the Energy Ministry issued a leaflet of recipes for 'Food without Fuel', many of which included uses for the meagre cheese ration. Leaflet No. 12 from the Ministry of Food, meanwhile, advocated *'A SALAD a day all the year round'*.

> During the past few years we have discovered how good a daily green salad can be. People who tell you that they feel much better now that they eat salads are not just food faddists. They are stating a fact that has been proven over and over again. We know now that many vegetables contain more vitamin C than some fruits and, in addition, mineral salts which are essential to health.
>
> Ministry of Food Leaflet No. 12[40]

Many men were used to having three or four hot meals cooked for them every day – from a traditional British breakfast to a substantial meal in the middle of the day, followed by a high tea or supper. Now the instruction to the housewife was that if she really had to cook, she must at least not use fuel wastefully: 'Every inch of the oven ought always to be loaded with as much cooking as possible – your neighbours' as well as your own.'

> Fuel is money. Every time you turn on a switch or light the gas, and every time you put a lump of coal on the fire you are spending money just as surely as when you hand it over the counter of a shop . . .
>
> Suppose, just for example, that we are thinking of switching on the electric oven to roast the joint. We know that the oven simply gallops away with our electricity-pennies. What else can be cooked while the oven's hot? Roast or baked potatoes – of course. Yorkshire puddings – if it is beef this week. A pie? Baked apples? Perhaps we could braise some onions, or celery, or parsnips?
>
> All the time the oven is on we should be thinking of those pennies we are spending – a penny every five minutes in some districts. When we remember them, we remember, too, that electric ovens stay really hot for a long time after they are switched off. So twenty minutes or a quarter of an hour before dinner time – just when we are beginning to think about laying the table and making the gravy – our fuel sense tells us to switch off the oven.
>
> And at the very end – if we have a really big fuel sense – we remember the washing-up. When we have taken out the meat, we put a bowl of water in the oven. There'll still be enough heat to warm it up while we carve and eat the dinner!

> Of course this is elementary fuel sense. You probably do it already. Probably your mother taught you. But many of us forget. We forget because we do not keep on telling ourselves that fuel is money.[41]

Ideally vegetables were not to be boiled, or even parboiled, but steamed. The advice was to seek out Chinese-style multi-tiered steamers and stack an entire meal on the one cooking ring. Those unable to source steamers – perhaps they had given away this formerly neglected piece of kitchen apparatus to salvage – were told to improvise 'with a colander fitted into a saucepan – and fish can be cooked between two plates on top.'[42]

Other types of one-pan cooking were all the rage in the Ministry of Food's kitchen workshops. Leaflet No. 35 gives seven recipes for 'one-pot' meals, all to be prepared within two hours. The first menu for sausage roll, gravy, carrots, chopped parsley and potatoes, to be followed by a steamed pudding with jam, makes ingeniously efficient use of only two old cocoa tins and one large saucepan. The sausage roll mixture and pudding mixture are put in the separate cocoa tins, then steamed in the saucepan for ninety minutes. After seventy-five minutes the vegetables are added to the same saucepan. When the vegetables are ready the vegetable water is used to make the gravy.[43]

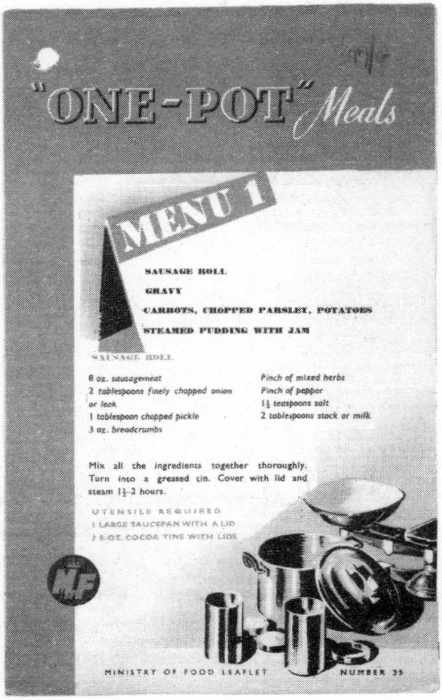

Hay boxes

For the zealous saver of fuel there was the hay box, a fuel-free method of keeping food warm for up to twelve hours that has recently enjoyed a resurgence of interest in ecological circles. On the site, www.selfsufficientish.com is the Australian Nev Sweeney's description of how he created one from an old coolbox and some discarded polystyrene. In the war the standard recommendation was to source a wooden crate. This would then be lined with straw or, if not available, newspaper – though in modern times, polystyrene, as Nev Sweeney has done, might have even better insulation.

The hay box is billed by its fans as an ideal way to keep dishes going, without expending fuel. It is suitable for long-cooking, slow-cooking items such as soups, stews and casseroles. During the war Mrs Ethel Sutton wrote to *The Times* extolling the virtues of her homemade hay box, which she described as,

> a strong wooden box . . . 23 inches by 17 inches by 17 inches, raised on feet, divided into two sections and tightly packed with 20 pounds of hay. Each section has a well in the hay to take a saucepan or casserole . . . Anything which requires long, slow cooking cooks to perfection in the box after being brought to boiling point on the gas-ring and keeps hot for at least eight hours. We do porridge, potatoes, prunes, stew etc. . . . On Friday we had one pound of leg of beef, price 10d, which was . . . cooked in the box all day . . . was beautifully tender and full of flavour and provided ample meat for five persons.[44]

My brothers and I would attest to the fact that it is sometimes great fun to apply Scout Camp practices to cooking at home. If my mother (a brilliant cook) was away for an evening when we were little my father (an awe-inspiringly inept chef) would prepare our meal of Territorial Army rations on a camping stove set up outside. Truth be told, this was probably because he did not know how to work the kitchen cooker. It was an enjoyable challenge though, much as successfully producing a meal with a hay box must be. As well as attracting interest from the most committed greenies, hay boxes have been used in the contemporary world by aid agencies investigating low-fuel cooking. It's a technology we could all be grateful for one day . . .

Lighting – now and then

ONE THERM OF GAS WILL LIGHT AN AVERAGE SIZED ROOM FOR 44 HOURS.

Never leave lights on unnecessarily

Keep the burners clean and dust-free

Metropolitan Gas Board leaflet

No street lights, shielded traffic and vehicle lights, darkened shopfronts and blacked-out windows. Even trains travelled in dimmed-down conditions. In environmental terms, however, wartime gloom, supervised by blackout wardens, was enlightened when compared to today's softly lit homes or strip-lit office blocks that twinkle into the night long after the last workers have departed for the evening.

Environmental campaigners are right to be riled by those who leave lights on unnecessarily or use incandescent lighting where energy-saving bulbs might do the job as well. Energy watchdogs tell us that if just one incandescent bulb per household were replaced with an energy-saving one, lasting around ten times longer, it would save enough CO_2 emissions to fill the Albert Hall 1,980 times. There would be a financial saving too: up to £60 on electricity in the bulb's lifetime.[45]

Such instructions were familiar to our wartime forebears. The good citizen's first tour of duty was to go round the home removing unnecessary light bulbs. People were told to make sure they were not using high-wattage bulbs where something dimmer would do: 'In passages and halls and for reading-lamps you seldom need a very bright light,' chastened the Fuel Sense Leaflet in one of its sixty-five easy tips.[46] People then, as we are now, were pressurised always to turn off lights when leaving a room. And there was also the wartime equivalent of standby: leaving a radio and its lights on when you were busy in another room. 'Two hours waste of your radio every day uses up half a hundredweight of coal a year at the power station,' chided the Fuel Sense Leaflet.[47]

Hitler and the Japs loved switched-on taps: The battle to save water – now and then

> Hot water so abundant for all domestic purposes in peace-time, must now be regarded as a definite luxury. Countless gallons of hot water can be thoughtlessly wasted unless you exercise care and economy every moment of the day. Use less water for **all purposes** and never wash under a running tap. Except when hot water is required for weekly bath it is more economical to heat small quantities in kettles. NEVER use MORE than 5 INCHES of water in a weekly bath.

From the leaflet, 'Save Fuel for Battle',
issued by the Ministry of Fuel, Light and Power[48]

Visualise, if you can, 150 litres of water. Perhaps see it as a grocery store's entire supply of those larger 1.5 litre Evian bottles, stacked five deep in a row of twenty. Imagine how you might carry all those bottles of water into your home. Or how many baths you might fill with the water (actually, only two decent-sized ones). Then think upon the fact that 150 litres of water (that is 100 of those bottles of Evian) is how much the average British person uses in a single day.

Compared to our forebears we are extraordinarily clean. Technology has brought in some improvements: a full modern dishwasher is more efficient than washing crockery by hand; a full washing machine is more efficient than a whole Monday spent doing the laundry by hand. But twenty minutes in a warm power shower daily, green campaigners warn us, is not environmentally sustainable. The rate at which we use water has risen by about 75 per cent since 1930 and continues to rise by 1 per cent a year.[49] Living in a sodden, rain-lashed island such as ours, it is sometimes easy to forget that water is our most precious resource. And so we squander it daily. Leaving taps running while we clean our teeth or wash our hands, prepare vegetables, do the dishes or wait for colder drinking water can waste as much as six litres per minute.[50] We flush toilets more than we should and, indeed, flush more down toilets than we should. Our mains water supplies and often our home plumbing are poorly maintained: a single dripping tap can waste as much as 5,500 litres of water annually, enough to fill a paddling pool weekly through the summer.[51] In short, the advice given by Waterwise, the UK's leading authority on water efficiency, is along much the same lines as that given during the Second World War.

For our 1940s forebears, too, the Ministry of Fuel, Light and Power's warnings against being extravagant with water must have felt like a fall-back to an earlier, less civilised era. Being able to get fresh water at the turn of a tap was, after all, a relatively modern achievement, as was clean drinking water. The ministry's mandarins took a particular interest in the nation's bathing habits. 'A big saving could be made by cutting down the depth of the bath water to five inches, marking the five-inch level with a spot of enamel'.[52] I've tried a bath of this size. It is the most egregious disappointment. You end up with a pathetically meagre amount of water that does not even cover your knees – as a concept it is as remote from the Cadbury Flake ideal of a luxuriant bath as the Outer Hebrides' Benbecula is from the Pacific's Bora-Bora. Worse still for wartime folk was that they were meant to go to the extravagant lengths of this five-inch bath a maximum of three times a week – and preferably only once. The rest of the time they were meant to perform their ablutions as best they could with a cloth and small basin of cold water.

Even in smart hotels the baths bore plimsoll lines and pinned to the wall would be a 'polite notice' that read: 'As part of your personal share in the Battle for Fuel you are asked NOT to exceed 5 inches of water in this bath . . . Make it a point of honour not to fill the bath above this level.'

In fact in what must have been a nadir, even in the inglorious history of the British hospitality industry, hotels were full of fuel-saving measures that added greatly to the discomfort of their lodgers. Under the guise of patriotism, rooms often went unheated and were poorly lit, while in the morning a 'fuel-saving breakfast', a cold Continental-style one (sometimes of spam), was served instead of a cooked 'English'.[53]

All along the line: Saving fuel on laundry day

The pressure on the housewife to save water and to think twice about heating water was felt especially on Mondays, the traditional British laundry day. The Ministry of Fuel issued a four-page information leaflet titled 'All Along the Line' that went into exhaustive details (never sprinkle rayons; always iron shantung garments bone dry) to optimise the British wash day's efficiency. Introducing its message, the leaflet declared:

> Directly or indirectly, Fuel enters almost daily into the domestic business of washing, drying, ironing and so forth, and since fuel must be saved 'all along the line' this pamphlet has been prepared to help housewives to save fuel whilst actually improving the results of their work . . . Do you know, it takes one quarter of the fuel used in the average home to make fuel hot.[54]

Gas makes munitions: The rewards of fuel efficiency

A war-weary woman wanting to splash out in an, oooh, twenty-inch bath or throw an extra log on the fire and be damned might be stopped in her tracks by the propaganda about what could be achieved through collective parsimony.

READ THESE AMAZING FIGURES

Do you know that one single family reducing fuel consumption by the equivalent in gas, coal or electricity of 5 lbs. of coal per day during the thirty weeks of colder weather could save enough fuel to produce:

2,000 more cartridges and bullets
2 more 25-pounder shells
3 more sten guns
10 more rifles

If every family did the same it would mean all the following:

1,000 More Heavy Bombers
1,250,000 More Rifles
5,000 More Spitfires
5,000,000 More 6 in. shells
5,000 More 6 in. Guns
500,000,000 More Cartridges
5,000 More Light Tanks[55]

Following a similar vein, the pamphlet, 'Gas Makes Munitions', claimed:

If everyone took a cup of tea less each day it would save enough gas in a month to make 75,000 250-lb armour-piercing BOMBS.

For every 1,000 of the millions of people enjoying the comfort of gas water-heating who take one less bath per week, enough gas will be saved to make 8,000 28-lb armour-piercing SHELLS.

For every 10,000 of the millions of people enjoying the comforts of gas-water-heating who will use one inch less hot water in the bath each week, enough gas will be saved to make 280 15-in SHELLS.

If you used your gas fire one hour less every day during the winter, you yourself would save enough gas to make 16 4.7-inch armour-piercing SHELLS.[56]

In a country in recession it might be helpful for consumers to be furnished with facts showing how savings on fuel and water could be converted into financial savings. A related campaign might project in simple terms how our squandering of fuel could advance global warming, cause the world to run out of oil and visit disasters on communities around the globe. Harnessing the interest of the young could be effective. Can we be persuaded to act – as our grandmothers did – not as individuals, but as a nation? Peer pressure is as great a motivator as any legislation.

Sucking Eggs: Your wartime granny's fuel efficiency know-how

TIPS FOR SAVING HEATING AT HOME

- Don't forget your defences. Keep heat in your house and cold outside as effectively as possible with the best lagging, windows, insulation and draught prevention.
- Understand your fuel meter and bill, so that you can fight for the most efficient service and tariff. A smart meter would help with this.
- Set fuel targets for yourself. Experiment with lowering the thermostat by degrees, heating your home for less time or only heating the rooms you are using, to effect fuel savings. While doing this, shut in heat by closing doors and close off the unheated rooms. Never heat an empty house unnecessarily or an empty room.
- Use the most efficient appliances and keep them clean.
- When chilly, put on more layers before the heating.
- Share your heat with others; or share theirs.

TIPS FOR SAVING FUEL WHILE COOKING

- Plan meals ahead.
- Where possible avoid cooking altogether, especially in the summer months.
- Never light the oven for a single dish. Fill it with meals that can be cooked in advance.

- On the hob, use the smallest ring for all but the biggest pans.
- Try tiered steamers – an entire meal can be cooked on one ring.
- Steam vegetables in small amounts of water in preference to boiling in excessive amounts.
- Cook vegetables and pasta al dente. Rice should be steam-cooked.
- If there is excess water, don't drain it down the sink. Reuse it in gravies, sauces and stocks.
- In general, keep the lids on pans.
- Remember the oven will remain usefully warm after it's turned off. Your meal could be kept hot or you could even use it to heat up water for washing up.
- Only grill quickly and in bulk. Don't make toast on the grill
- Experiment with a hay box.

TIPS FOR SAVING ENERGY ON LIGHTING AND OTHER APPLIANCES

- Remove unnecessary bulbs.
- Always use fuel-efficient bulbs.
- Don't light rooms, or even areas of rooms, that are not in use.
- Never leave anything on standby.

TIPS ON SAVING WATER AND HEATING WATER LESS

- Use less water in your bath or shower. Even cold water needs fuel to pump it at the water works.
- Consider giving up a daily bath or shower habit, or at least washing hair less often.
- Never wash or wash up under a running tap or have one going unnecessarily.
- Never let taps drip.
- Never flush toilets unnecessarily. Use the hippie mantra, at least at home: 'If it's yellow, keep it mellow. If it's brown, flush it down.'

- Save all the washing-up to do in one batch (or, if you have a dishwasher, only run it when full).
- Less grease means less hot water. Scrape dishes and plates and wipe cutlery before washing up.
- Do all your laundry at once in a full washing machine, not in inefficient small batches.
- Don't run the tap to cool water, but keep it cool in the pantry/fridge.
- After washing vegetables, reuse the water in the garden or on houseplants.

CHAPTER NINE

IS YOUR JOURNEY REALLY NECESSARY?

There should be a general moral view that wasting energy is wrong. Everything we do goes on up there and stays up there for 100 years or so in terms of carbon dioxide, and the more it does, the hotter it is going to get, the less it does, the less hot it will get. Therefore, it does not matter whether it is a tiny bit or a big bit, but it is your general attitude to life . . . I sense that is already in the process. People do look at 4x4s in central London and curl a lip already. It is part of the conversation, that that is wasting energy. I am hopeful that there is a real change taking place in moral attitudes which is not to do with saving pennies here or there, it is just that it is morally wrong to waste energy because we are putting at hazard our own grandchildren.

Sir David Attenborough giving evidence to the House of Commons Rural Affairs Committee on Climate Change[1]

Imagine this. You arrive at Heathrow in good time to check in for a long-distance flight. You hand over your passport and booking reference. Then, before the flight attendant issues you with your boarding pass, she asks, 'Is your journey really necessary?'

Your answer would almost certainly have to be 'No'. Mini-breaks, ski trips, shopping excursions to New York, cooking holidays in Umbria, cultural breaks in Florence, walking trips in Mallorca, clubbing weekends in Ibiza, a hop to Inverness to climb or fish in the Highlands. Even an annual holiday worked towards for the last twelve months. For all the life-enhancing pleasures of these jaunts, none of them is *necessary*. However much we may moan to colleagues about 'really needing it', it is not vital for any of us to holiday abroad. Nor are many of the flights professionals take for work – to conferences, presentations and team-bonding enterprises. Great as the benefits might be – from face-time schmoozing and kicking back with colleagues – much of the actual hard work could now be done through video-conferencing software.

More difficult to refuse, in our globalised diasporised world, are flights associated with rites of passage. Can we begrudge someone a journey to an elderly ill parent's bedside? A holiday on the back of a sister's wedding in Australia? Attendance at an American parent's or grandparent's funeral? A return trip to New Zealand to meet a first niece or nephew? These journeys, as weighted with emotional baggage as any other sort, seem the most necessary. Yet during the Second World War they would have been ruled out.

Perhaps it is unfair to equate air travel then with now. In those days flying was comparatively new and barely used for leisure purposes. I make the comparison between then and now to argue that, with peak oil and rising fuel prices, we may need to self-ration the energy we use to get about, for fear that the government will otherwise make that decision for us. Part of that self-rationing could be a return to an age when people asked themselves if each journey was really necessary, and when efforts were made to ensure that the trips that had to be made were undertaken by the most fuel-efficient means. In such an environment a flight would become an occasional rather than a regular luxury.

In the UK, air travel is the fastest growing source of greenhouse gases. Despite a brief downturn in passenger numbers following the bombings of September 11, 2001, the numbers of passengers flying from UK airports between 1990 and 2004 rose by 120 per cent.[2] We all know what happened in that period, because I'm sure almost all of us at some point seized the opportunity to fly somewhere for next to nothing. The successful launch of no-frills airlines including easyJet and Ryanair, and the pressure they put on established airlines to lower their prices, seemed to bring the world closer. Continental mini-break weekends went from being the preserve of the rich and jet-setting to a pleasure to which millions could aspire. But that lifestyle comes at an environmental cost. Between 1990 and 2004 the energy consumption of aeroplanes flying from UK airports increased by 79 per cent, while their carbon dioxide emissions almost doubled from 20.1 million tons of CO_2 to 39.5 million tons,

IS YOUR JOURNEY REALLY NECESSARY?
TICKETS
IS YOUR JOURNEY REALLY NECESSARY?
BERT THOMAS
RAILWAY EXECUTIVE COMMITTEE

5.5 per cent of all the emissions this country produces. Air travel may account for only 2 per cent of the world's emissions, but that figure is going up all the time, especially in the developed and developing world.[3]

And this jet-setting doesn't stop with holidaymakers. An average British supermarket racks up air miles too, since so much of the fragile fresh produce we hunger for year round is flown to us. Strawberries from Mexico, blueberries from Chile, fresh-cut roses from Kenya, herbs from Israel, mangetout from Thailand and dwarf beans from Zambia. Shop unthinkingly and you carry the world – or some responsibility for its fate – in your basket. It is as if agricultural communities overseas exist to support a myth that British shoppers can get whatever they want whenever they want it at a minimum of cost and effort. Some have argued that there would be nothing to sustain those overseas communities if all First World shoppers retrained their palates to eat only locally and seasonally. But my research has thrown up no evidence that it is agricultural workers in the developing world who are the primary beneficiaries of our yearning for fruit and vegetables sourced from abroad year round. The poor remain poor while the middle and top man gets rich. (I am, for the record, a proponent of Fair Trade products that are transported to this country by fuel-efficient means.)

Fuel inefficiency, meanwhile, is also a factor in how most of us get to the shops. Sixty-two per cent of our shopping trips are made by car. In the countryside, where many have no alternative but to shop at an out-of-town supermarket, almost all food shopping trips are made by private car.[4]

At present the government's commitment is actually to continue to expand our airports and their traffic. The fear is that otherwise Britain will miss out on vital revenue and perhaps even lose its position as Europe's business capital. The government's stated aim is that our airports should plan to increase passenger traffic from about 200 million passengers in 2008 to allow for around 470 million by 2030. Attitudes to rail travel are also morally questionable. The public have in growing numbers been abandoning their cars to commute by train. Yet, instead of being rewarded for this, commuters face hikes in daily train fares. In spring 2009 rail fares went up by 11 per cent. This is apparently because the government wants rail users to pay for a decrease in the government's subsidy to the rail companies, which is currently raised through taxation.[5]

Air travel may be our fastest-growing cause of emissions, but it is still road traffic that pushes most carbon into the atmosphere. Private cars produce 10 per cent of the UK's carbon emissions.[6] In a more eco-friendly age, drives to the gym and supermarket, school runs and solitary commutes to work would not be rubber-stamped unless they could justify themselves as necessary journeys. The days of gridlocked city streets might become a distant memory as more of us took to our feet, cycled, used public transport – including dedicated school buses – or at least signed up to a car share scheme. Many of us might even give up on the daily commute altogether, choosing instead to work from home via the Internet or in an office hub nearer to home. That way, even if we were rationed or self-rationing, we would be able to save up more points of our precious travel ration to use towards a foreign holiday.

Wartime priorities

> The time has come for every person to search his conscience before making a railway journey. It is more than ever vital to ask yourself:
> **'Is my journey really necessary?'**[7]
>
> Wartime Railway Executive Committee poster
>
> Food, shells and fuels must come first.
> If your train is late or crowded – **do you mind?**[8]
>
> ibid.

The Second World War accelerated the jet age. There had been flyers in the First World War and there had been aeroplane journeys in the interwar period. It would have been a flight of fancy, however, for the average 1930s citizen to imagine himself boarding an aeroplane any time soon. Civilian air travel was then for world leaders and the more daring of the super-rich only.

At the outbreak of war, the government recognised immediately that it would have to preserve fuel by imposing domestic petrol rationing and rationalising the country's transport networks. It also realised that transporting military personnel would have to take priority over civilian passengers on the railways. So civilians embarking on any rail or road trip were asked: 'Is your journey really necessary?'

A greener government today might borrow from its wartime predecessors the idea of exerting moral pressure on the public to travel in the most fuel-efficient way, but there would be justified uproar if they replicated the misery of wartime conditions. Travel was neither banned nor rationed, but journeys became so tiresome that many vowed not to do it again until peacetime and normal services had resumed.

Wartime travel by rail

The government's priority was to save fuel for the war effort and to transfer troops and supplies. Civilian services were prone to severe disruptions as the network responded to more pressing military demands. Through the war 353,000 special services were put on to transfer troops.[9] These included the 260 commandeered to get the British Expeditionary Force to embark from Southampton in 1939, 200 to launch the men of the unsuccessful Norwegian expedition from Scottish ports in 1940[10] and, in preparation for the North African campaign, 440 troop trains, 680 freight trains and 15,000 wagons by ordinary goods service. For that campaign, in just one month 185,000 men, 20,000 vehicles and 22,000 tons of stores were carried by the railways to the ports for Africa.[11] None of these manoeuvres could hold a candle, however, to the logistical upheaval of the Allied Forces' preparation for the 1944 invasion of France and the launch of the Second Front. From 26 March 1944 to the completion of the initial D-Day moves, the railways somehow sourced 24,569 trains for special troops, ammunition and stores. Among their cargos were

7,000 vehicles, including tanks. In the same period a further 6,000 wagon-loads of supplies and equipment were transferred by ordinary goods trains. In one record-breaking week 3,636 special trains were put on, while the total for the three weeks was no fewer than 9,679 trains.[12] And it was not only men and weaponry that made up the military effort. In just one six-month period 1,700 freight trains moved 750,000 tons of rubble salvaged from bombed-out London sites to East Anglia to build bomber command's runways. The rubble from Birmingham's blitzed sites became recycled as runways for the American air force in Sussex and Kent. Those shell-shocked walls might not have been able to speak to the Luftwaffe but they did eventually exact a kind of revenge.[13]

The war had also been hugely disruptive to the civilian population. In December 1942 the Committee on Electoral Machinery in Great Britain reported on abnormal population movements.

> When the National Register was compiled at the end of 1939 over 2½ millions of people (5 per cent of the total population) had already left their homes during the first month of the war. Up to the end of June 1942 the total recorded changes of residence between local administrative areas numbered nearly 20 millions. Taking into account the fact that many of these movements represent removals of the same person at different times, it has nevertheless been estimated that by the end of 1941 the number of civilian adults residing elsewhere than in the (Parliamentary) constituency in which they were resident in 1939 was of the order of 5 millions, or roughly one-sixth of the electorate.

Additional to that estimation was the 'large-scale disturbance caused by the mobilisation of the Armed Forces, the movement due to evacuation from vulnerable areas, the transfer of industrial workers and immigration of British and foreign refugees from the theatres of war'.[14]

The war had scattered people around the country as never before: to go to battle; to return home from it; to reach evacuated workplaces or children; to reclaim homes from which they'd been evacuated; to catch a precious weekend with a loved one on leave; to get to work for the first time; to move from one job to another. Inevitably, that level of population movement greatly increased the public's dependence on the rail network.[15] Yet for the government these kinds of civilian needs, however poignant, were not a priority. The railways had lost 100,000 men in the 1939 call-up.[16] With an understaffed network barely coping with the military demand, transport policies were designed to deter the ordinary public from travelling. Following what was effectively a nationalisation of services on 1 September 1939, they withdrew deal fares such as cheap day returns and weekender tickets, unless it was provable that a journey was war-related. Those eligible for cheaper fares included Land Army workers being billeted to another posting; on-duty Home Guard troops; Civil Defence workers; shift factory war workers and volunteers travelling to farm camps. Parents visiting evacuated children were issued with only one cheap ticket every two months. Vacations, unless they were working farm holidays, were discouraged. Despite these price deterrents passenger demand increased by 60 per cent, even as the numbers of passenger trains and their mileage decreased by 30 per cent. In wartime, the average train's load was increased by 125 per cent.[17]

In the 1930s the rail companies had vied with each other to produce the most enticing posters selling their regions and the holiday activities available there – from rambling in the Lake District to the sun spots of 'the English Riviera' – now all rail propaganda was geared towards putting people off travelling anywhere. 'Stay at home. You may be stranded if you travel,' was one poster's bleak, bald statement.[18] In railway waiting rooms where once had hung colourful posters delighting in the bracing nature of Skegness or the genteel delights of Torquay, there now hung lists of seaside resorts that the public were banned from visiting due to wartime activity. The phrase 'Is your journey really necessary?', first asked of evacuated civil servants in December 1939 in a bid to stop them travelling home for Christmas, was soon being asked of everyone. The government decision was not to introduce travel rationing on a points principle, but instead to appeal to the civilian's sense of public duty by hammering home a message that to travel for leisure or pleasure was to derail the war effort.

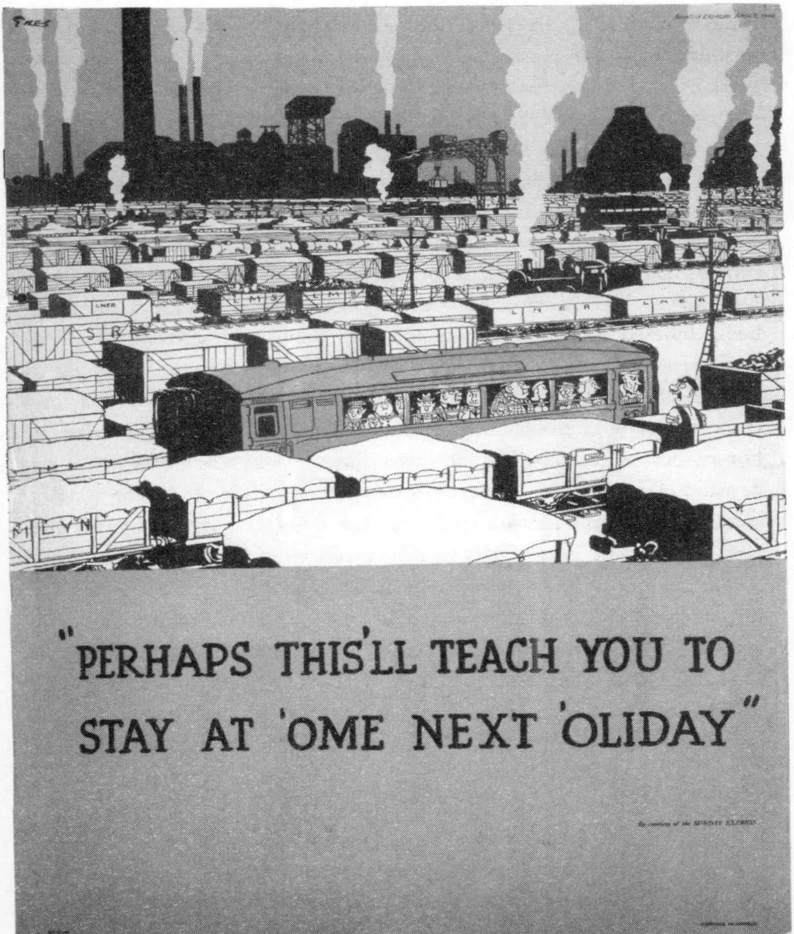

A wartime propaganda poster designed to deter rail travel for leisure or pleasure.

The oddities of wartime rail travel somehow make sense of the surrealism of post-war comedies such as *The Goon Show*. Several wartime price hikes were accompanied not by any amelioration in services but instead by a gradual deterioration. Neither extra trains nor extra carriages were put on in holiday periods. Finding a seat was a treat, rather than an expectation. Refreshments both on board and in stations, if available at all, could run out within minutes. It wasn't just food and drink that disappeared, either. From August 1942 people were being advised to bring their own crockery on all journeys. Most, however, knew better than to risk abandoning a hard-fought-for seat, or even standing space, on what was bound to be a fruitless mission to a buffet car. For overcrowding reasons there were strict restrictions on how much luggage you were allowed and even, in February 1942, an attempt to ban people travelling with flowers. (After noisy rebellion, not least from the appropriately named journalist Ursula Bloom, this restriction was overruled – an early flower power victory.) You might be lucky enough to grab a window seat, but at night standard blackout rules applied, while even in the daytime you could only hazard which stations you were passing through, since all the place names had been scratched out to comply with Civil Defence Regulations. A railway poster's official advice was 'If you can't see the name and can't hear the porter's voice – ask another traveller . . . If you know where you are by local signs and sounds please tell others in the carriage.'[19]

There was always the risk of being bombed. Moving trains and railway stations were a prime Luftwaffe target. Approximately 900 people, 400 of them railwaymen, were killed on rail property and a further 4,500 were injured.[20] As one Ministry of Information manual stated wearily, 'In the course of the war over 10,000 "incidents" have been reported on British railways and London Transport property as a result of air attacks. Ninety-two hits were made on one stretch of 2¼ miles of railway in South London in the eight months September 1940, to May 1941. Track repairs have been completed generally within twelve hours.'[21] The on-board instructions for what to do in an air raid were:

1. Do *not* attempt to leave the train if it stops away from a station, unless requested by the guard to do so. You are safer where you are.
2. Pull the blinds down, both by day and night, as a protection against flying glass.
3. If room is available, lie down on the floor.[22]

TRANSPORT OF FLOWERS BY RAIL

The Minister of War Transport hereby directs that on and from the 25th March, 1943:—

Flowers or plants shall not be accepted for conveyance or conveyed by rail except at such times and for such distances as the state of traffic will admit of their being conveyed consistently with the observance of the following conditions, and only at owners risk rates and conditions of carriage:—

(a) special or additional trains shall not be run for the purpose;

(b) the conveyance shall not interfere with the carriage of perishable foodstuffs and other essential traffic;

(c) accommodation for passengers shall not be reduced by reason of the conveyance.

These Directions shall not apply to:—

(i) flowers or plants for export for which a certificate of health for export has been granted by the Ministry of Agriculture and Fisheries or the Department of Agriculture for Scotland;

(ii) plants used for producing food crops;

(iii) hardy nursery stock not in soil or in pots.

In these Directions "flowers" shall include cut flowers and decorative foliage; "plants" shall include plants in pots, in soil or otherwise; and "hardy nursery stock" shall mean trees, shrubs and bushes with persistent hard woody stems, but not including herbaceous plants.

These Directions may be cited as "The Transport of Flowers Directions, 1943."

RAILWAY EXECUTIVE COMMITTEE

The last instruction was the source of much mirthless sarcasm, as often there was barely standing – let alone lying – space. Potential bombing raids also slowed services. By 1944 the average beleaguered train was travelling at less than two-thirds of its 1938 speed, while being weighed down by more than twice as many passengers. The blackout and any overhead activity further slowed journeys, as did the lower-grade fuel powering the service. Man shortages and round-the-clock demands on the network system meant there was no real upgrade or maintenance work done during the war. In time, British rolling stock had to be supplemented by some US locomotives (which was at least exciting for train spotters).[23]

London Transport

In the blitzed capital, London Transport dealt fairly efficiently with the maintenance of its 3,093 miles of routes and its provision of transport for some 10 million passengers daily. This despite periods of coming under sustained air attack and a decrease in staffing levels due to male staff leaving to join the Forces.

In the first period of heavy bombing some 170,000 people sought evening shelter in the Tube system. Initially the authorities discouraged the public from using Underground stations as bomb shelters. But after bowing to the inevitable, London Transport in conjunction with the Ministry of Home Security and the local authorities fitted '79 tube stations with bunk beds, special sanitary equipment and clinics, and 124 canteen points were established'. In January 1945, when London again came under attack from the terrifying V1 rockets and flying bombs, 25,000 returned to spending their nights underground.[24]

Travel by car – now and then

In contemporary Britain many who can drive choose to do so rather than taking public transport. In the countryside, such is the woeful inadequacy of our non-integrated public transport systems, people are left with little choice but to make journeys by car. Trains don't coincide with bus or ferry routes; services often seem geared more towards what works for the transport company workers than customers. In our grid-locked cities, even after paying for congestion charges, parking spaces and upkeep, many prefer to depend on their own cars rather than to risk the Underground or buses. For drivers there is the benefit of being in your own private, secure space with its own inbuilt storage system, and being able easily to adapt a new route in response to heavy traffic. Public transport passengers may find themselves delayed by weather, roadworks, congestion on designated routes, signal failures, services running late, or even suicides and security scares.

But the hour has now come for car drivers to ask themselves if using their cars as much as they do is really necessary. In our clogged-up cities, why should one person's selfish preference to drive to work in the solitary splendour of his or her own vehicle add to the commuting time of seventy people in one bus? Every day our cities reach gridlock. School runs? Drives to work? Using the car to get to the gym? Nipping into the supermarket? All these journeys should be doable by foot, public transport or by turning the problem on its head by, for example, getting the shopping delivered, or by using a regular journey as an opportunity for a workout – cycling to work, for example, or running home after walking the kids to school. Or where there really is no logical choice but to use a car, make the ethical decision to share that resource. Form a car pool with colleagues (collecting petrol and car maintenance money from them if yours is the only car and you are the only driver). Share a school run. There could soon come a time when, if we have not started self-rationing fuel, a higher authority will impose fuel rationing on us.

In *The Lion and the Unicorn* George Orwell wrote, 'The lady in the

Rolls-Royce car is more damaging to morale than a fleet of Goering's bombing planes.'[25] It was a lady in a Rolls-Royce car, caught stockpiling sugar, who in 1940 became the first person to be prosecuted for trying to flout food rationing. For the most part, though, even those who could afford flashy cars understood the principles of shared sacrifice that underpinned all the wartime government's austerity policies. The Second World War letters between the aristocratic Vita Sackville-West and her friend Virginia Woolf are full of discussion about whether they will be able to eke out enough petrol to visit one another's Home Counties homes.[26]

How would today's government encourage a sense of shared sacrifice? Can it shame the yummy mummy into leaving her 4x4 Chelsea tractor parked outside her home? Can it make her feel it is morally reprehensible to run such a big car? Can it reinforce that moral disgust by making it financially punitive to run a car for journeys that could be made by more community-friendly means? Can it assert its authority through purchase taxes, road taxes, increased congestion, parking charges and raised petrol prices? First it has to make the alternative environmentally friendly options more appealing. It is an acknowledged problem in this country that cars dropping off children at school clog up roads, so why not have school run buses picking up from designated points? As apparently every school in that most gas-guzzling of countries, America, does. Or why, when children join a school, are their parents not informed of other families who live nearby, so that they can at least investigate sharing a school run between two to three households? The latter plan could also be feasible for work commutes: an office Intranet site could team up drivers with others commuting by road from the same area. Thus one car on the road could potentially replace four.

Car sharing was certainly encouraged during the Second World War, when extra petrol rations were made available to the 20,000 people who displayed a notice on their windscreens signalling their participation in the 'Help Your Neighbour' car share commuting and lift scheme. Meanwhile, a 'Take You Home' scheme involved ferrying servicemen from railway stations to their homes. The WVS signed up their drivers only after they had answered the question: 'Do you mind a child being sick in the back of

WALK SHORT DISTANCES
says Shanks' Pony
AND LEAVE ROOM FOR THOSE WHO HAVE LONGER JOURNEYS

your car?' In the crisis of summer 1940, when Britain expected invasion, more than 25,000 vehicles were signed up for active service – 14,000 on standby as ambulances and 15,000 to carry sitting wounded. With the entire public transport system oversubscribed, hitchhiking was encouraged for both sexes. To be in sole occupancy of a vehicle was seen as an act of great selfishness. In rural areas an unexpected lift from a passing driver could ease the working day of a land girl or Timber Corps volunteers. In the city, where buses were nearly always packed full, a lift might give a working mother time to collect her rations, her children or her sanity after a back-breaking factory shift.[27, 28]

Andrew Lane's *Austerity Motoring 1939–1950* records: 'There was something special about August Bank Holiday, 1939. It seemed that all the cars in Britain, two million of them, were on the roads.'[29] Presumably they all stopped off for a drink in the last chance saloon too. Europe was on the brink of war again and everybody knew it. Who could blame them for one final frolic in the late summer sun, when soon the men would be off fighting and the pleasures of Sunday motoring set aside? The lot of British car drivers during the subsequent period of austerity is the stuff of every eco-warrior's dream and Jeremy Clarkson's nightmares. Cars at the time were a luxury: with only one in every ten British families having one. However, that still meant 2 million were on Britain's roads at the outbreak of war. By October 1940 that figure had gone down to 1.4 million. And by January 1944 the number had halved again – only 700,000 – still on the road. The rest had been sold off or were up on bricks in private garages.[30] No new cars were being built for the British market. Indeed, from July

1940 it became illegal to buy a new car without a special licence. The car-manufacturing industry moved from civilian to war production. Gradually the determination of those who had hoped to motor on started to run on empty: petrol price increases, fuel rationing, the cost of maintaining a car; the difficulty in buying a new one (even post-war, the mantra for British car manufacturers was export or die) and the scarcity of replacement parts for a broken car – all problems that became more acute after the fall of Singapore in early 1942 – meant that many returned to pre-motor methods of getting about, such as using horses, walking and bicycling.[31]

Petrol rationing

Following stern warnings that all hoarders would be prosecuted, the government introduced limited rationing of non-branded 'pool-petrol' on 23 September 1939. At first the restrictions were not too onerous. The aim was to give each driver a ration to allow for approximately 200 miles' motoring a month. The scheme entitled every car owner to a basic ration, while those engaged in war work, such as Women's Land Army commissioners or Home Guard officers, received supplementary coupons. Allowances varied according to the car's horse-power, so those with a 7-horsepower engine were allowed 4 gallons (18.2 litres); 8 and 9 horsepower, 5 gallons (22.7 litres); 20 horsepower and above (45.5 litres).[32] The modern comparison would be for a smart car to be at a disadvantage when compared to a Chelsea tractor. A good driver, however, in a well-maintained efficient car could make his or her petrol go almost twice as far again. Thus, from the outbreak of war organisations such as the Royal Automobile Club and motoring magazines were full of tips on coasting downhill, moving almost immediately into a higher gear and then remaining at a speed of 20 to 30 mph, and keeping spark plugs clean could save as much as a third of your tank of petrol. Much as today, driving magazines are full of tips on tricks such as 'hypermiling' to make your fuel go further.[33]

Gas converters – The biofuels of their day

Faced with the dismal prospect of having to sacrifice their precious vehicles to the gods of war, many of the more zealous 1940s car lovers turned to gas converters – the biofuels of their day. Proposed in a flurry of excitement and reported animatedly in the newspapers, the idea was to attach a barrage balloon of gas (which was still unrationed) and an auxiliary carburettor to the engine. At first this seemed a viable alternative to petrol and there were demands in the House of Commons for the country's bus fleet to be converted to gas immediately. Luckily, nobody quite got round to completing this task before the absolute unviability of gas conversions became clear to everybody. For all the trouble gone to – and more than 1,000 cars underwent gas refittings – the barrages allowed for only about twenty to thirty miles of travelling before needing to be refilled. And the immense bulk of the gas bag and crate – nine feet long, six feet wide and four feet high – could make the vehicle hard to manoeuvre. Then, from October 1942, they were banned anyway. Others experimented, with modest success, by thinning out their existing petrol ration with paraffin.[34, 35]

Further petrol rationing

Petrol prices rose continually throughout the war. In September 1939 a gallon of petrol would have set a customer back 1s 6d. In November 1939 prices rose again. Then, in March 1940, there was a halfpenny increase to 1s 11d. By 1942 a gallon of petrol cost 2s 1½d, almost twice what it had been in the pre-war era. Each price rise was coupled with a cut in the ration.[36]

For some it must almost have been a relief when in July 1942 the government banned driving for pleasure. For those who couldn't live without driving there was the Black Market. In 1942 a gallon could have been found illegally, though it would have cost just over three times the price of its legal equivalent: 6s 6d. In an attempt to beat the Black Market all legal commercial fuel was dyed red.[37, 38]

Further vicissitudes for wartime motorists

It was not just the difficulties in eking out one's petrol ration that put the brakes on wartime motoring. Driving itself became dangerous because of the blackout and the need for headlamp masks. In 1939, 8,272 people were killed on Britain's roads, an increase of 1,624 from the 6,648 who had died in road accidents the previous year. And the war had only started in September. Despite the speed limit being reduced to 28 mph in built-up areas, the increase in deaths on the roads continued. In 1941, 9,200 people were killed in road accidents. The Army forbade soldiers to hitchhike, stating as their reason that it was too dangerous. To shed some light in the gloom, white lines were painted on the roads and car bumpers were also painted white, but the number of accidents still continued to rise – with almost twice as many pedestrians being knocked down as before the war. In an effort to confine most journeys to daylight hours the government tried to get the nation an hour ahead of itself with the introduction of British Summer Time on 25 February 1940. This increased to Double Summer Time in 1941, announced with the memorable claim that 'Summer Time will continue through Winter'.[39, 40]

After the fall of France a German invasion became a very real threat. All road signs were removed and huge tracts of the eastern and southern coasts were cordoned off as restricted areas. Getting lost wasted a huge amount of your precious petrol supply and often led to drivers being stranded not just in the middle of nowhere, but in the middle of an unidentified nowhere, which must have been all the more frightening. Checkpoints were also established with permission to shoot at any motorist who failed to stop. It was forbidden to listen to a car radio or to fail to immobilise your vehicle (recommended methods were to cross the spark plug leads, or to remove the rotor arm or high-tension leads). The roads held one further terror: driving tests having been suspended, unidentified learners were given free rein on the – admittedly much quieter – roads.[41, 42]

And as if blundering about in dangerous darkness without even the comforting burble of the Home Service for company – eyes peeled for a pedestrian on a suicide mission to the post box, an out-of-control learner or a trigger-happy Home Guard on checkpoint duty – were not nerve-racking enough to put off the diehard driver, there was also the hard fact of 'pleasure motorists' having become hate figures. Truly, the lady in the Rolls-Royce was to wartime society what the lady in the Chelsea tractor is to today's. Those who went to race meetings became a particular target because of 'the continued use of motor cars for what seemed to be more or less selfish purposes'. One MP stated, 'Every gallon of petrol used in this country is mixed with the blood of seamen.' Herbert Morrison acknowledged that 'the large accumulation of cars at sports functions . . . has undoubtedly been offensive to public feeling'. *The Times* welcomed his comments, responding: 'The further restrictions on the private use of petrol will be warmly welcomed by public opinion . . . distaste at the sight of a large number of cars used for purposes which have not the remotest connection with the war.'[43, 44]

The anti-driving lobby won. On 13 March 1942 the government announced: 'As from 1 July the basic ration will cease to exist,' adding, 'These measures are designed to end pleasure motoring . . . The government wants all unessential cars taken off the road.'[45] For wartime diarists the news, while being accepted without a murmur of dissent, brought gloom. A release for Nella Last and her husband had been a restorative Sunday excursion to her beloved Coniston Lake. But the loss of their petrol ration ended all that. Clara Milburn suddenly introduced a bicycle to her diaries, whereas before she and her husband had been enthusiastic motorists.

After the basic ration was dropped, any driver could be stopped and asked to prove that he was on a necessary journey and taking the shortest possible route to complete it. The law was enforced, even by imprisonment. And there was a celebrity case when the songwriter and West End star Ivor Novello was imprisoned for four weeks after being caught driving from his home in Berkshire to the London theatre where he was appearing.[46] Doctors in rural areas were allowed to keep their cars, but even they could not get spare parts if they broke down. Many doctors reverted to antique methods of transportation such as riding a horse, using a pony and trap or, for shorter journeys, good old shank's pony. Many city doctors started making their regular rounds by bicycle. By 1944 expenditure per head of population on petrol was one-fiftieth of its pre-war average.[47]

Buses in wartime

Many bus drivers and conductors had responded to the initial call-up, and some buses had had to be taken off the road following bombing damage and natural wear and tear. Fuel supplies to London Transport were reduced by a quarter after war broke out. As a result of all this, more than 800 buses were withdrawn and some routes were cancelled altogether, while many others were to run only before 10 a.m. and after 4 p.m. (which wasn't helpful to shift workers of whom there were many during the war). From 1940 onwards the last London 'night bus' left at 10.30 p.m., but in other towns services often stopped at 9.30 p.m., leaving revellers with no choice but to go home early or to walk late. From 1942 few places ran a Sunday service before 1 p.m., which caused distress to some churchgoers (though the old and infirm were often given an extra petrol ration to provide for this spiritual journey) but for the less observant provided a perfect excuse for a lie-in.

At the end of a shift in London, bus drivers would park up under a canopy of trees in a place like Hyde Park, both because they did not want to waste petrol driving back to the depot, but also to try to protect their buses against German bombs. Nonetheless, within the first two months of the blitz, London lost so many of its red buses it had to make a nationwide appeal for replacement stock. Nearly 500 arrived within the week and, to add to the general oddity of life in a city besieged from the skies, those who had stayed in London found themselves commuting to work on buses that displayed quite different routes and wore a different city's branding.

Housewives!
PLEASE FINISH TRAVELLING BY
4 O'CLOCK
and leave the buses, trams and trains free for war workers
Issued by the MINISTRY OF TRANSPORT and the MINISTRY OF LABOUR AND NATIONAL SERVICE

When the Nazi bombers moved on to other cities, London Transport repaid its debt in kind by then providing the bombed-out citizenry of Coventry and Bristol with London Transport buses. But some old antagonisms still festered. Liverpudlians called the buses lent to them by Manchester 'red devils'. As the war progressed, any new buses were painted a uniform battle-ship grey, wherever they were destined to work.

The British queuing habit is apparently a hangover from the wartime period. Before the war, boarding a bus had been a free for all – as it appears to have become again – but during the conflict queuing became obligatory. Servicemen and the uniformed war workforce were let on to buses and trains before non-uniformed citizens. Buses were kitted out plainly inside to provide more space for standing. But even then space was short and often a conductor would appeal to those whose journey was brief to make their way on foot. And again, night-time travel was made more difficult for both passengers and bus staff by the blackout regulations.[48]

Bicycling

The war at least made things safer for cyclists who found themselves briefly kings of the road again. Prior to the war, bikes had fallen down the social scale with cars being seen as a symbol of wealth. The redundancy of cars in wartime put bikes back in the ascendant as the ethical choice – as they are now. Near the start of the war *The Times* reported 'an exceptional demand by well-to-do people for machines'. There was a shortage of the red rear lamps that had become compulsory when the blackout began. There was also a revival in cycling holidays – as there is today – with many families taking the 'two wheels good, four wheels bad' option, and hotels, hostels and hostelries being more amenable about providing bicycle sheds. Cyclists also suffered from shortages of new parts, however, and in particular of pumps and rubber for wheels. New bicycles, for which many children had to wait a long time, compared badly with pre-war models in terms of frames, wheels, gears and equipment.[49]

Post-war

An AA survey of 1948 revealed that road traffic was half what it had been in 1937.[50] That year Britain held its first ever Motor Show at Earls Court. Inundated with visitors, reported widely in the press, the Motor Show proved the country's fascination with cars. For most British families, however, a car – a small family one like the Ford Anglia might cost £229, or the Ford Prefect £275 – was then even more of an unobtainable luxury than it had been ten years earlier. British car firms such as Austin and Riley, had returned to production as early as 1945, but with post-war Britain being bankrupted by repayments and reconstruction, these companies were encouraged to produce for the export market. By law, 50 per cent of the cars manufactured in Britain had to go abroad. The remaining ones, after years of rocketing inflation and with high purchase taxes, were priced way beyond the pockets of most British householders. The continuing petrol ration only reinforced the idea that a car must be a costly and nigh unusable extravagance. Though a basic petrol ration of five gallons had been restored on 1 June 1945, it was withdrawn again in the summer of 1947 following widespread industrial unrest. When it was restored in June 1948, it was still only a third of the previous basic ration.[51]

With the public feeling more shared disgruntlement than shared sacrifice, the Black Market strengthened. And it was in an attempt to curb its growth that the government introduced the Motor Spirit regulation, euphemistically known as the Red Petrol Act. By this ruling petrol stations were to dispense red fuel for commercial vehicles and yellow fuel for private ones. A private motorist caught with red fuel risked a £1,000 fine, the loss of his licence and imprisonment, while guilty garage owners could lose their businesses. For many the last straw came when petrol rationing ended in Germany before Britain.

The petrol pumps of the United Kingdom were finally liberated from austerity regulations on 26 May 1950.[52] With Suez and the OPEC crisis the threat of petrol rationing loomed again. However, it has never seemed more of a permanent possibility than it does now.

How to apply wartime lessons to today

The wartime era proves that we can if we have to make huge changes in how we travel. However, to return to a time when we were effectively forbidden to visit loved ones or could only do so after undertaking an expensive, time-consuming and precarious journey which made us feel like a pariah would be undesirable. The obvious solution is for each of us to be self-rationing – to take stock of how much fuel we expend through day-to-day trips and travelling, and then to decide which of those journeys are our priority and which can be adapted to be more fuel-efficient or even cut out. For example, if you are an Australian living in Britain, your top priority might be to return home every two years to visit your family. To justify that kind of fuel splurge – especially if you wished to take your partner and children with you – you would ideally be living fuel frugally on a day-to-day basis. You might, for example, get all your shopping delivered, commute by public transport, do the school run on foot, not maintain a car and only holiday in places that could be easily reached by train. All in order for you to justify the one journey home you regarded as necessary. Or, for example, if you were determined to keep running a car daily that might be what you prioritised over foreign holidays. Peak oil is coming – if we self-ration now we might delay an era of government-imposed rationing where little room will be left for personal choice.

The government should be doing a far better job of making fuel-efficient travel more attractive to the voting public. Our public transport networks should be fully integrated, quicker than most journeys made by car, more reliable and cheaper for the general user. Having improved the public transport network, the government would then be more justified in penalising road users, so that driving one's car became the exception rather than the rule.

Sucking Eggs:
How to apply your wartime granny's travel savvy to today

- Audit your own carbon output. See where you could make cuts and set yourself fuel targets, which you try to improve year on year.
- Before booking any journey ask yourself, 'Is it really necessary?' If it is, first research the most fuel-efficient means of making that journey. Don't fly automatically, but perhaps instead try to find the time to make getting there an adventure in itself. Most parts of Europe, and indeed the near Middle East and even the Far East, are accessible by train. There is good national and inter-national train advice on the website, www.seat61.com. While you can research rail options nearer to home at www.nationalrailenquiries.com. And remember, the earlier you book a train ticket the less you pay.
- If you do have to fly at least offset (it surely must help a bit to plant those trees?) and also investigate the most fuel-efficient flights and airlines.
- And if you've flown for a family holiday one year, maybe consider holidaying at home the next. If you are lucky with the weather – or even if you aren't – it could be revelatory.
- Do you need a car? Shops will deliver; buses and trains run; occasional short car journeys can be organised through car clubs like www.streetcar.co.uk and longer ones by more traditional hire firms. Find out more about car shares, car clubs and ethical car use at www.carplus.org.uk, a charity investigating such things. Or set up your own car club, to share the burden of a necessary school run or commute.
- And if you really can't give up your car, at least ration your petrol supply: eke out a tank of petrol so that you use it only for the trips that you really can't see making any other way.
- Get on your bike.

- Walk more.
- Politicise yourself: if greener transport solutions are a priority for you, tell your MP, local authority and anyone who comes canvassing your opinion.
- Are your products making unnecessary journeys? Curb food miles, and especially air miles, by trying to buy locally and seasonally, or at least Fair Trade.

PART FOUR

REBELLION

CHAPTER TEN

A PARADISE FOR SPIVS: *Cheating, disillusion and the Black Market*

Like all other modern peoples, the English are in process of being numbered, labelled, conscripted, 'co-ordinated'. But the pull of their impulses is in the other direction, and the kind of regimentation that can be imposed on them will be modified in consequence.

George Orwell, *The Lion and the Unicorn*, 1941[1]

The restriction not only of rationing of individuals but of the rationing of all public catering exercised demands on the patriotism of those whom it concerned, and everybody was not equal to it.

Lord Woolton[2]

In the late spring of 2008 it became abundantly clear that what had been boom would soon become bust.

Listening to the radio, one evening in April, I heard a government spokesman thank the public for not buying more petrol than they needed. In Grangemouth, Scotland, the workers of an oil refinery were striking over changes to their pension scheme. At petrol stations throughout Scotland managers had hung signs forbidding drivers from hoarding and recommending motorists purchase no more than £50 of petrol per non-working vehicle. Meanwhile, in Southall, Middlesex, an ethnically Indian enclave on the western fringes of London, shopkeepers had started to limit the amount of rice their customers could buy at any one time. They were not acting in isolation. In the US, the country's biggest and best-known grocer, Wal-Mart, had also adopted this policy in what was being billed by pundits as 'rationing'. In Bangladesh the government had for the moment given up trying to obtain enough rice at affordable prices and was instead promoting a staple of Western cuisine: the potato. Again, they were not acting in isolation. China recently became the world's biggest producer of potatoes – yet I cannot think of even once seeing potatoes on a menu in a Chinese restaurant. Meanwhile in countries as far apart as Latvia and Peru (where, of course, it all started for the potato) potato flour has been suggested for bread-making as an alternative to wheat – another staple that has rocketed in price. These schemes come with a stamp of approval from the highest source: 2008 was the United Nations' International Year of the Potato.

The cost of wheat, rice and other staple grains had nearly doubled in the late 2000s and continues to escalate in response to increased biofuel production, a rising global population and, in some countries, an increased affluence, which has led to the cultivation – expensive in environmental terms – of more meat for the world. In the developing world, meat has traditionally been the preserve of the rich. Would rationing be the answer? Should the world's governments impose austerity schemes? And would the indulged and self-indulgent citizenry of a fatted developed country such as Britain accept such diktats from on high?

Woolton wrote, 'The success of any rationing scheme depends, in the long run, on two things; the first is its justice and impartiality, and secondly – and perhaps the more important factor – on the general public acceptance of the correctness of its purpose and the fairness of its administration.'[3] In Woolton's 452-page memoirs he writes just less than two pages under the heading of the Black Market. Nor did the official histories admit that illegal secretive trading went on to any demonstrable extent. But popular and oral histories tell a different story. Nobody who has read her lively and informative wartime diary would question the respectability of Clara Milburn, a gentlewoman whose good work through the WVS, WI and Women's Land Army included finding homes for evacuees, fundraising and overseeing land girls. She confesses, however, to many cheering under-the-counter delights. There is to these light-hearted reports a shamelessness about having done something illegal, which chimes with Mass Observation views that 'The existence of a Black Market was little disputed. Mass Observation found, indeed, that a surprising number of people were willing to admit quite freely that they had bought scarce goods through it.'[4]

> Saturday 17th June 1944
>
> The beautiful car bustled to the butcher and then Twink and I walked on our six feet to the grocer, where we picked up one or two unexpected oddments. One was a pound of suet! It's extraordinary how there's never a mite of suet in the winter, but in the middle of the summer out comes a packet of 'Cook's Suet' from under the counter! Then three tomatoes were put in a bag surreptitiously and placed quickly in my basket.[5]
>
> Saturday 16th December 1944
>
> The car took me to the butcher's and Twink afterwards took me to the grocer's! At the latter a mysterious small bag was put into my basket with the words 'twopence ha'penny'. I did not know what this under-the-counter treasure was until I got home and found *two lemons*! Great excitement![6]
>
> Tuesday 17th April 1945
>
> In Leamington today I wanted a bottle of sherry in case Alan John [her only son, a soon-to-be-liberated prisoner of war in Germany] should come home soon. I know it is like asking for gold, but eventually a bottle, duly concealed in a wrapping of newspaper, was obtained.[7]

It was Angus Calder in his landmark *The People's War: Britain 1939–45*, published in 1969, who first questioned the official record that there was almost no Black Market activity in wartime Britain. Calder's book was pioneering because it was not, as most previous historical studies had been, a history from the top down, starting with great men's memoirs and Cabinet minutes, but a citizens' history from the bottom up, which drew heavily on such sources as the Mass Observation archive; contemporary diaries and letters; and accounts in the popular press. As he writes, 'How big the latter [the Black Market] was, no one will ever know, it was in the nature of a successful black market transaction that it was left out of official statistics and evaded the courts of law.'[8]

What is indisputable is that there was more criminal activity during the war and that some of these crimes related to abuse of rationing regulations. Ina Zweiniger-Bargielowska argues in her academic economic study, *Austerity in Britain: Rationing, Controls and Consumption 1939–1945*, that crime casts 'doubt on the myth of shared sacrifice on the Home Front'.[9] Juliet Gardiner reports that in 1939 'there were 303,771 reported crimes in England and Wales; in 1945, 478,494, a rise of 57 per cent. And since there was a difficulty in collecting statistics in wartime, that latter figure should probably be higher.'[10] But the most simple explanation for a nationwide crime wave is that there were, almost overnight, in a suddenly extremely regulated country, many more laws to be broken. Thus the most dutiful and community-spirited citizens could find themselves on the wrong side of the law because they had flouted the blackout regulation by failing to draw a bathroom curtain or even given their sweet ration to a grandchild.

In the earliest months of the war, offences by career criminals fell by 10 per cent, though the Chief Constable of Essex believed this was down to many of the younger offenders who had been operating in the East End and Essex area having been called up. It did not take long, however, for the remaining criminals and those who became drawn into a life of petty pilfering to realise what rich pickings could be had from exploiting the prevailing conditions for personal gain.[11] The blackout offered huge scope for skulduggery. Many homes were deserted because of air raids, the call-up and evacuation. What could be crueller than to have returned to the traumatised shell of your home to discover that looters had ransacked your few remaining possessions? Many suffered this double blow. Two months into the blitz there had been 390 reported cases of home looting. By the end of 1940 that figure had risen to 4,584. Many of those crimes were opportunistic. Some were, however, planned in advance and perpetrated by those involved in official air raid duties. In 1941 thirty-three Royal Engineers, who had been working as a demolition squad, were tried at the

WANTED
FOR SABOTAGE
THE SQUANDERBUG ALIAS HITLER'S PAL
KNOWN TO BE AT LARGE IN CERTAIN PARTS OF THE KINGDOM
USUALLY FOUND IN THE COMPANY OF USELESS ARTICLES, HAS A TEMPTING LEER AND A FLATTERING MANNER
WANTED
ALSO FOR THE CRIME OF 'SHOPPERS DISEASE'
INFORMATION CONCERNING THIS PEST SHOULD BE REPORTED TO

Old Bailey for stealing more than nine tons of roofing lead that they had then sold on to a scrap-metal dealer.[12]

The first-time thief, passing a deserted, bombed-out house on his way home from a shift or the shelter, might opt to loot luxury booty such as a fur coat, a painting or jewellery, though he would also grab ration books found lying around. Some of the loot might find its way on to the Black Market, despite the difficulty in then offloading it. With wartime conditions prevailing, however, the real prize for the career criminal, often while posing as an emergency worker, was to use the cover of the blitz and blackout to rob to order items such as cigarettes and spirits from warehouses and shops – 14,000 ration books were stolen from a warehouse in Hertfordshire. Within days they were being sold on, for around £5 each, a profit of £70,000 for the gang at a time when a three-bedroomed home in the suburbs of London could be bought for £800. By 1944, so great had been the number of ration book heists, forgeries and scams that someone trying to sell a ration book in the pub would be lucky to get £1 for it.

The bulk of the offences against the austerity regulations were, however, petty crimes. A claim for a missing ration book might well be false. A staggering 800,000 clothes rationing books were claimed missing in the first year of the scheme.[13] The coupons of the dead mysteriously continued to circulate because no one handed them in. Those who kept hens surely never declared *all* their eggs. It was, of course, a questionable practice for a grocer to keep 'under the counter' goods for a favoured customer, or not to take a coupon for a points-value product and instead to charge a higher price. Yet these nod-and-a-wink under-the-counter transactions seem to have been a commonplace. Some months after the introduction of clothes rationing, a newspaper correspondent observed a brisk trade in clothes at Romford market in Essex, without seeing a single coupon change hands. In all likelihood the goods were themselves sourced from the Black Market and so had to remain coupon free.[14]

In surveys the public condemned the Black Market vociferously, even calling for heavier punishments to include 'the death penalty, the cat, and the abolition of the possibility of a fine without imprisonment' and describing Black Marketeers as 'traitors', 'fifth columnists' and 'highly anti-social and unpatriotic'.[15] Yet some of those surveyed would almost certainly, as consumers, have had some experience of the Black, or at least the Grey, Market.

Coupon scams were rife. One regular racket, in the early years of clothes rationing, involved a widespread abuse by clothes retailers of the Board of Trade's suggested method of cashing in coupons as an entitlement to further stocks. The initial recommendation was that the retailer should exchange at the post office envelopes containing batches of 500 coupons for vouchers with which to purchase replacement stock. Gambling that the understaffed post office would never have time to check each envelope, many retailers mixed in makeweight bits of waste paper and the like with their coupons, or even took in an envelope containing no coupons at all. This widespread brinksmanship was put a stop to by the introduction of rubber-stamping.[16]

Then there was profiteering. Sir Douglas Macraith, the chairman of the North Midland Region Food Price Investigation Committee, announced in the spring of 1941 that cans of soup sold by manufacturers at 6s 6d a dozen were being sold on to the public at 14s 6d a dozen, having changed hands in the interim as often as six times. In some cases the price of goods was rocketing through speculation without them having even moved from the warehouse. Also, there were scams such as selling, as 'milk substitutes', a paste of flour, salt and baking powder.[17]

In some workplaces pilfering became endemic. 'Sometimes such light-fingeredness was enmeshed in poor pre-war industrial relations, when war increased rather than diminished workers' suspicious that their employer was exploiting them for the company's profit rather than the good of the nation,'[18] argues Juliet Gardiner, citing the Liverpool docks as a particular example of this, where crates being loaded for export were often lightened. Obvious prizes were easily concealable bottles of spirits, cartons of cigarettes and even peroxide – almost impossible for bottle blondes to obtain by the war's endgame years.

To promote industrial relations many employers turned a blind eye until their lost margins made it impossible not to act. Thefts in the areas of Hackney and Romford alone included quantifiable amounts of shoes, handbags, nylons, sanitary towels, sugar, meat, electric fires, dolls, soap and, from the canteens of London Transport, 66,000 knives and forks, which cost £8,000 to replace.[19] As the war progressed, both employers and the authorities became less tolerant of petty thieving. Employers became increasingly likely to call in the police and decreasingly likely to show tolerance by taking back a first-time offender or speaking up for them in the magistrates' court. The magistrates themselves became more severe in their sentencing. In the early years of the war they had been lenient, on the basis that the impetus for first-time crimes was a failure of judgement brought on by the strain of the war. As the conflict progressed, however, they came to view pilfering as unpatriotic sabotaging of the war effort.

Zweiniger-Bargielowska insists: 'The Black Market was extensive during the war. The emphasis here is not on theft and receiving of stolen goods but on endemic circumvention of the emergency legislation which confronted many citizens with the prospect of law-breaking for the first time. There are countless examples of exploitation of loopholes.'[20] Others, however, such as the historian of consumerism Matthew Hilton, believe Zweiniger-Bargielowska's analysis is too negative. Surely, had such abuses become endemic, the Home Front would have buckled? The majority must have lived within the stringent regulations, albeit with some small excursions from the letter of the law. Other administrations were less successful at curbing rationing abuses. In Axis-occupied areas, including the Channel Islands, Black Markets flourished and in the US the wartime Black Market came to pose a genuine competitor to legal distribution – there, the majority of civilian meat was understood to have passed through Black Market channels.

Certainly Woolton believed in the British sense of right and their strength of character. The Ministry of Food, however, housed a secret department that tracked chains of supply and investigated what looked like heists, robberies to order and patterns in thieving. The courts were given the rights to impose 'a fine of up to £500, with or without two years' imprisonment, and an additional fine of three times the total capital involved in the transaction . . . The penalties for infringement of the food regulations were literally ruinous on the people convicted of breaking the law, and the consequence was that, however great the temptation to make money in this illicit manner might have been, it became so perilous an occupation that few indeed dared to embark on it – and most of those who did so subsequently had plenty of time for reflection, away from temptation.'[21] Woolton could be a little disingenuous here, though. By 1944 (by which time he was Minister of Reconstruction) the Ministry of Food had 900 inspectors reinforcing the department's 415 statutory orders. The Board of Trade, meanwhile, had undercover busybodies on its payroll. One of their methods of entrapping retailers reported as flouting the clothes rationing regulations was to try on clothes and then attempt to pay for them with loose coupons.[22]

The post-war period

Oh, won't it be wonderful after the war –
. . . We'll work for the state and we'll knock off at four
After the war – after the war.
We won't work at all if we find it a bore,
There won't be no rich and there won't be no pore
The beer will be better and quicker and more
But why didn't we have the old wa-er before?

A.P. Herbert, 'After the War', *Punch*, 8 July 1942

We may allow ourselves a brief period of rejoicing, but let us not forget for a moment the toil and effort that lies ahead . . .

Churchill's VE Day victory speech, 8 May 1945

We are going to have hell trying to get people to work the peace, trying to give people a worth-while-ness in their peace time lives comparable with the worth-while-ness of working together during the war. We shall probably fail.

Naomi Mitchison, writing immediately after the 1945 election in which her husband had usurped the sitting Tory MP, to become the Labour MP for Kettering, Northamptonshire

During the war our grandparents' generation had been largely biddable, understanding – even if they did sometimes grumble about it – the role of personal sacrifice in achieving the common good. Peace had been greeted with the entertaining Home Service radio announcement: 'Bunting is off the rationing.' In his victory speech on VE Day, Winston Churchill had declared, 'The evil-doers now lie prostrate before us. Advance Britannia.' Britain permitted itself, as instructed by Churchill, 'a brief period of rejoicing', allowing itself to bask in the warmth of a righteous victory.

Within weeks the surprise election of a truly radical, reforming Labour government seemed to promise a brave new world. From its first day in office Attlee's government set about implementing the Beveridge Report's blueprint for a more equal Britain that, with a National Health Service and National Insurance scheme, would look after its people from the cradle to the grave. After six years of slogging it out for their country it was time for the British people to find out what the country was prepared to do for them. Theirs, alas, was a hungry, threadbare victory. Britannia's empire was to be given away and six years of war had left it crippled by debt to its dominions and, to a far greater extent, the US, whose abrupt cessation of Lend-Lease in August 1945 came far sooner than the Labour government had expected. Almost everything Britain produced in the early post-war years would have to be for export only, to close the dollar gap. The government was also £765 million in hock to its citizens through National Savings and post-war credits, and it would not be until the 1970s that these debts could be redeemed.[23] Meanwhile, the international humanitarian effort to feed the world's starving meant that there was to be no slackening of the food-rationing regulations.

After the war . . . after the war . . . had been the bitter-sweet stuff of daydreams for every soldier fighting, every housewife queuing and every mother juggling war work with her commitments to her family. Young wives who had barely seen their husbands since they had gone off to fight had promised themselves a new outfit with peace. Others had thought they would eat better, drink wine, put their motor back on the road for a jaunt to the seaside. The reality, however, was that instead of

National Savings: the public were encouraged to invest in the country's post-war future.

becoming easier to do these things it was more difficult. In 1944 and 1945 there had been a noticeable improvement in the supply of food and therefore some relaxation of the controls. But between 1946 and 1948 the stringent economic measures of a heavily indebted government ushered in austerity regulations which were worse than anything during the war itself. Bread rationing; regulation controls for the first time on potatoes, four-day weeks and bans on domestic fires for six months of the year all came *after* the war.

Even the weather was worse: the winters of 1946 and 1947 remain two of the most severe on record. In July 1946 the Fuel Minister, Emmanuel Shinwell, warned that there would not be enough coal to see

There was no goodbye to queues in the post-war period.

Britain and its industries through that winter. Sure enough, come December several Midlands cotton factories were forced to close temporarily due to coal shortages. When they returned to work it was to a four-day week.[24] The Labour government nationalised the coal mines but in January 1947 several steelworks had to instruct their workforce to down tools because of lack of coal. Meanwhile, a strike by road haulage workers, with whom the dockers came out in sympathy, meant that vital meat supplies were left rotting on the quayside. Even after the Army was called in to maintain essential supplies, many still went without. Shops rationed potatoes and local councils reopened the emergency centres that had once fed people in the aftermath of bombing raids. Within a week of the hauliers voting to return to work the meat ration was cut again.[25]

The misery-inducing combination of cold, chaos and power cuts threatened to bring the country to its knees. The freezing conditions prevailed for more than a fortnight. On 12 February one remote Devon village, Widdecombe-in-the-Moor, sent a telegram: 'No bread since January 27. Starving.'

In the summer of 1947 came a full resumption of rationing – even worse than it had been in wartime. Rations of tobacco, petrol, sweets and tinned meats were cut down still further and newspapers had to revert to their wartime size. This was not how victory was meant to be.[26]

Morale, which had remained high during the war, now plummeted as the public grew increasingly resentful. Many began to feel that the enemy had triumphed while Britain was laid low. This rancour played into the hands of the Black Marketeers. Those who could afford it, especially if they were of a Conservative and therefore Free Market-supporting disposition, turned to their 'man in the know' as a morally permissible gesture of defiance against an over-controlling socialist government, whose restrictions and regulations they could barely keep track of, let alone fully understand. A 1947 Mass Observation report on shopping in London concluded that endemic practices included tipping to gain preferential treatment, off-ration purchases and under-the-counter sales. Certain sectors, like the catering industry, in particular in pricier hotels and restaurants, came to trade more and more with the Black Market in an effort to satisfy their austerity-weary customers. People resorted to stealing food – pilfering and looting – particularly from the docks. The annual cost of the stolen goods could still be valued at as much as £1 million.[27]

In May 1946 the Minister of Food expressed concern that food orders were 'generally being ignored and evaded more flagrantly now than at any time during the war'[28] and doubled the ministry's enforcement division. Staffing numbers at the Ministry of Food's flying squad were at their highest in 1948, a situation 'rendered necessary by the current food situation',[29] which involved a clampdown on illegal slaughter, following reports that butchers who were operating legally were being driven out of business by the loss of registered customers to competitors trading in Black Market rabbits and meat. At that time the French government's failure to combat illegal slaughter had made a mockery of its rationing system, with not just meat but also grain being traded on the Black Market. The government was anxious that Britain should not go the same way. Meanwhile, an investigation into Black Market petrol in January 1948 recorded '"that the moral standards of the country in regard to rationing had dropped amazingly" . . . that "many responsible people did not think it wrong to get extra petrol".'[30]

The Passionate Spiv to his Love

Come spiv with me and be my spove
And we will all the pleasures prove
That markets black and rackets bring;
Though shalt not lack for anything.

Thou shalt not queue yet shalt thou see
Food manna-like rain down on thee

Attendant spivs shall ply thy barrow
Through London's streets both wide and narrow
To ease the toils of thy housewifery
With a percentage from their spivvery;

And keep us safe from rivals' raids
With their protective razor blades.
If these delights thy mind may move,
Come spiv with me and be my spove.

By the female of the species, *New Statesman and Nation*, 27 September 1947 (compare with version in Chapter Four)

The figure of the spiv dates from the 1940s. The spiv is part of our cultural inheritance – as exemplified by the *Dad's Army* character Sid, in his co-respondent shoes. People were not only flouting authority but also mocking it, as in the British comic films so popular in the period. *Whisky Galore* is the riotous tale of a whisky-slaked Highland island galvanised by an export ship being wrecked on its shores. *Passport to Pimlico*, an Ealing Comedy, is the carnivalesque tale of a London borough that discovers in the post-blitz bomb wreckage a document that declares it a fiefdom of Burgundy and thus not governed by Britain's rationing regulations. It makes much of the lovable rogues and doggedness of the Cockney character: 'If the Nazis couldn't drive me out of my house with all their bombs and rockets and doodlebugs, you won't find me packing up now . . . We always were English, and we'll always be English. And it's just because we're English that we're sticking up for our right to be Burgundians.'[31]

The post-war Home Secretary, Chuter Ede, spoke truthfully in 1945 when he said, 'No one would have thought of stealing a second-hand shirt in 1939; today the sight of a shirt on a clothes-line has become a temptation.'[32] Eventually rationing had to be abandoned because the scheme had become unworkable. Clothes rationing came to an end in May 1949 because the high volume of loose coupons now flooding the market made it impossible for the Board of Trade to control. The lack of supply, especially in 'nylons', meant that a brisk Black Market in these items continued to trade. *Picture Post* carried a report on a London 'nylon racket' in 1950, which involved seconds and strays being sold at a price hike of between 50 and 80 per cent of their original value. The official response was: 'If only women didn't set such high store on getting nylons, if only they weren't prepared to pay extortionate prices, if only they would report overcharging to us, there wouldn't be a nylon black market.'[33]

Such a response rather typifies the Labour government's attitude to the women voters who were thoroughly fed up with queues, regulations and austerity. In June 1947 Harold Wilson, then a junior trade minister, attacked the extravagance of Christian Dior's New Look with its pretty swirly long skirts which used immense amounts of fabric. He counselled the women of Britain not to let it turn their heads. They ignored him in droves.

The post-war government lacked the chutzpah, salesmanship and empathetic sixth sense of someone like Woolton. The slogans of the day, 'Export or Die', 'Work or Want', lacked the charm of their wartime predecessors. The Ministry of Food's release of a recipe for squirrel pie*

* Interestingly, in 2008, recipes for grey squirrels were again being put forward as a diet that combined patriotism – they are predators of our native red squirrels – and economy during a world food crisis. I suspect the uptake will be similarly desultory.

Together . . .
we'll pull the
country round
HOW YOU CAN HELP
Put your heart into your job
Volunteer for mines, mills and farms
Save fuel — the factories must have it
Grow more food in gardens and allotments
Keep up National Savings
Get back the salvage habit

in February 1946 was seen as a desperate affront to a hungry nation rather than a left-field solution.

The government dreamed up big, brave schemes that promised popular appeal, including the hosting of the Olympics in London in 1948, soon billed the 'Austerity Olympics' because the British athletes were still on rationing, and 1951's Festival of Britain, conceived as 'a pat on the back' for the nation. But the continuation of rationing was much resented and the British Housewives' League, formed in protest in 1945, pursued its aims with a handbagging shrillness. When the Conservatives were re-elected in 1951 on a ticket that promised to end rationing and to promote prosperity not austerity, it was seen as a repudiation of those lean post-war years. The female vote had been key to the victory. In peacetime the public refused to accept the same level of government interference in their day-to-day lives as had been tolerated during wartime, even if that government's policies appeared to promise equality.

The story of rationing's success in wartime, but failure in peacetime, has lessons for today. If a recession-bound British government, seeking to eke out resources, were ever to reconsider rationing or government-imposed austerity measures, their planning would have to be meticulous. People will make shared national sacrifices, but only if they can see clearly that they are necessary. Emergency measures also need to be 'sold' to the public through propaganda – and how they are sold can make the difference between success and failure. In wartime the can-do community spiritedness of the propagandist's injunctions to 'Make Do and Mend' or 'Dig for Victory' fired the public's imagination. Post-war, however, bald bossy exhortations seemed an insult to a people who had endured six years of wartime working and wanting, only to experience, with peace, an apparent decline in living standards.

Fewer old maids hike to Holy Communion on autumn mornings than in George Orwell's day, but the portrait he painted of the national character in *The Lion and the Unicorn* is still a recognisable one. He presented a people who were stubbornly individualistic, anti-intellectual, rightly sceptical of government control but who, at times of national crises, could swing together. Britain did so in 1940 and I believe would do so again should a future global crisis threaten the essentials of our national life and culture. Should that need arise, our leaders today could do worse than look back to 1940, to our nation's darkest hour, to learn from our grandparents – and how they fought their way back towards peace and prosperity.

AFTERWORD

LESSONS FOR TODAY AND MY APPLICATION OF THEM

Macmillan described what he was doing as loosening the belt of austerity, allowing for good times to come. He refused to apologise for the affluent society but he did worry about the corrosive effects of materialism. That was an agenda that in a sense has gone on ever since and it has now become a political sin to make people feel discontented. It is not an option to tell people they're going to have to be less well off. Once the genie has been let out of the bottle, you can't put it back and we have become used to the promise that things are always going to be better and better.

Peter Hennessy, *Daily Express*, 15 December 2006[1]

Britain's days as the fastest growing economy in Europe were officially declared over yesterday as the deepest recession in a generation saw consumers turning off the lights and Poles returning home. The thousands of people being laid off each week and the hundreds of firms cutting production are reducing demand . . . The pound slumped. Brown admitted that the government had not seen what was coming: 'What we did not see, nobody saw, was the possibility of markets' failure. We are fighting this global recession with every weapon at our disposal. We need other countries to work with us.'

***Guardian*, 24 January 2009**[2]

I reached the end of writing the hardback edition of this book just as it was confirmed that Britain was officially in recession. Indeed, no sooner had that downbeat news been announced (in the same Friday morning bulletin as the gloomy information that ten days' worth of rain had fallen in the past twelve hours) than the pundits started arguing about whether 'recession' did our situation justice, when we might in fact be in a full-scale 'depression'. After a leading American financier urged investors 'to sell any sterling . . . it's finished', a member of the public asked the panellists on BBC Radio 4's *Any Questions* if Britain too was 'finished'.

A dark hour, certainly, but not our darkest. That surely came in the early 1940s, after the fall of France and the evacuation from Dunkirk.

Britain then was isolated, but not isolationist. In fact, it was precisely because of its engagement in a global conflict that its government embraced the self-sustaining policies into which the British people so willingly threw their energies.

A nagging concern of mine while writing *Sucking Eggs* has been that by urging people to take a leaf out of their wartime granny's book I might sound like a Little Englander (or technically a Little Scotlander living in voluntary exile in England). Nothing could be further from my aim. As our politicians have been so anxious to stress, the current financial mess is an international one. The challenge of global warming is universal, too. My objective was to look back on an earlier period of austerity to see if it held lessons for how we might live today in a more environmentally and financially responsible way. I believe it does and have tried to apply these lessons to my own life in a bid to become a better global citizen. And, as many school report cards used to say, there has been some improvement, but there is room for more.

On the **kitchen front** my household has changed its buying, cooking and eating habits. Our basic needs (fruit, seasonal vegetables, bread, milk and eggs) now get left in our hallway each week by an organic delivery firm. We no longer go out specifically to buy food but supplement the main delivery either by ordering more off the site or by quick, one-off purchases from local shops or supermarkets on the way home from work. The different seasonal vegetables that we have been left each week dictate what we eat in the evenings. We eat more vegetarian meals, or more meals where meat or fish is an extra rather than the main attraction, plus the thrown-together concoctions that my husband dubs 'madness'. We eat no 'luxury' ready meals and few pre-packaged foods. We don't panic buy in the supermarkets or shop purposelessly for food without specific meals in mind. It is a healthier way of life and cheaper too. We do not throw away food.

What meat we buy is British and usually organic, or at least free range (it tastes better and makes us feel better about cultivating animals for food). We sometimes buy cheaper cuts such as ox cheek or pork belly. If we are going to roast a chicken, we get our money's worth from an eye-wateringly expensive bird, eking out its meat, carcass and juices over three or four subsequent meals. Our fish is labelled as being from sustainable sources and caught in national waters.

On the not so virtuous front we do, of course, consume food and drink that has been imported such as olive oil, spices, tea, coffee, wine, chocolate and non-native fruit in winter. Indeed, fruit is my guiltiest pleasure. The organic delivery firm leaves Free Trade bananas and citrus fruits. They come with the guarantee that they have been ethically sourced and never airfreighted, so I have never quite got around to cancelling them. I remind myself that as a 'priority class' pregnantee and then the mother of a baby I would have been given first dibs on what supplies of commodities such as bananas and oranges came into the country anyway. But pregnancy kyboshed one project: when I told a GP and midwife my plans for living on wartime rationing for a month they looked so horrified that I feared my unborn baby might get put on an 'at risk' register. So remembering how keen Lord Woolton, the wartime Minister of Food, had been to look after the 'preggies', I adapted the ration. I ate more fat, meat and fish than many would have managed to source in wartime. Ambitions, going forward, are to continue trying to eat less meat and fish, and to try and cultivate salad vegetables and herbs on the unsafe-looking roof space beyond our stair window.

Make Do and Mend. Certainly from the autumn of 2007 to the spring of 2008 I spent more money on repairs and dry-cleaning than on buying new items. In January my intention was to get through the year on the 1941–2 allocation of sixty-six points, though my hope was not to actually use up more virtual coupons than the forty-eight points that were allotted in 1942–3 and again in 1944–5.

I hadn't bought shoes the previous winter, so in the January sale I bought two new pairs of boots (roughly seven ration points each). It was shoes again I needed in the summer, so in May I bought a new pair of trainers and some sandals (seven points each). I also purchased some undergarments to wear beneath an old frock to a wedding: tights, bra, pants, underslip (nine points). At the halfway point of the year I had used up the equivalent of thirty-seven points, in the happy knowledge that my winter wardrobe did not need much replenishing. Then, however, I received a marriage proposal and fell pregnant. I spent a further thirty-one coupons on my wedding outfit – evening dress (calculated at eleven points, though a silk dress would have been hard to come by in wartime); tights (two points); knickers (three); bra (one); wedding shoes (seven) and dancing pumps (seven). Luckily the Board of Trade handed out sixty extra coupons to pregnant women. I did not get knocked up in order to lay my hands on them, but I certainly needed them. With few of my old clothes fitting by the time we got married in November – by which point I was more than five months pregnant – the rest of the allocation went on maternity wear: a dress (seven); two pairs of trousers (eight each); a jumper (five); three tops (five each); two vests (three each); two bras (one each); one swimsuit (I guessed at three) and two pairs of tights (four). And I might have needed more had I not been the beneficiary of some very generous hand-me-downs. So in the end it was not such a virtuous year at all. I had spent a full 1941–2 and a full maternity allowance by the end of December. In 2009 I managed for myself on forty-eight points. And my baby was exemplary in his hand-me-downs.

On the **Home Front** we cooked more fuel-efficiently, ate more salads in the summer and consistently put out more rubbish to be recycled than could not be recycled. In the early autumn we even had a week or so of experimenting with wartime-like amounts of hot water when our boiler broke down. But though we tried not to have the heating on until 1 November, a bout of cold weather in October broke our resolve. We put down carpet where once had been some cold floorboards. We know that what our flat would really benefit from is better floor insulation throughout and a more modern boiler. But since we intend to move soon these may be plans we shall put into place in our next home.

Away from home, we asked **Is Our Journey Really Necessary?** but quite often our resolve broke and we took the trip anyway. We don't have a car, which scores us some Brownie points. And, heroically, we honeymooned in Cornwall, *in November*, which I would recommend to any bright-eyed couple who want a romantic honeymoon that they won't be paying back for the whole of the following year (that's what the wedding is all about surely . . .). Earlier in 2008 we had spent our summer break in Devon. Less heroically, having allowed ourselves a flight to Switzerland in the spring, we did then take more European and short-haul flights than we had originally anticipated. One friend married an Italian in Venice, another a Bulgarian in Plovdiv. We attended both weddings, carbon-offsetting our flights (though I think this achieves far less than just not taking them) and travelling one way to Venice by train, which was a highlight of my year. Most annoyingly, I also flew home to Scotland three times. On every occasion I looked into catching the train and on every occasion rail travel would have cost almost twice as much as air travel, and there were major weekend works ongoing on the line that would have almost doubled the journey time. In 2009, when I had more time and flexibility on maternity leave, we did do things differently: no international travel and one sleeper train to Scotland, though the prohibitive costs of the rail option, left us little choice but to return home by plane. Later in the year, the same problem meant we flew both ways

Would we all do things differently if the government helped us to make true our good intentions? I believe so. During the war people lived less wastefully because of moral pressure and legislative enforcement. And if needs must, we could do so again, learning from our past to emerge stronger, without depleting the world's resources unnecessarily.

ACKNOWLEDGEMENTS

I am indebted to a number of people. I would like to thank my agent, Cathryn Summerhayes at the William Morris agency, for first embracing my idea. I am grateful to all those at Chatto & Windus who have been involved in producing and promoting this book. I owe special thanks to my two insightful, sensitive and patient editors, Poppy Hampson and Penny Hoare, and to Parisa Ebrahimi, who has assisted them; Peter Ward for the design and typesetting; and Greg Heinimann for the cover.

For help with the images, thanks are due to the picture departments of the National Archives and the Imperial War Museum. I would like to thank the sources credited throughout the book (see Endnotes and Bibliography) for text material, and the staff of the Imperial War Museum and the London Library.

My colleagues at the *Culture* desk of the *Sunday Times*, Helen Hawkins, Adrienne Connors and David Mills, accepted my taking holidays at funny times and sometimes at short notice with remarkable forbearance. Patience has also been shown by my family and friends, who have been wonderfully understanding and supportive of social arrangements being changed late in the day and of holidays where my laptop and research notes have gone too. Friends, including Jo Littler, Harriet Atkinson, Susanna Rustin, Sarah Quarmby, Justine Walton, Victoria Hopkinson, Matthew and Mary Grenby, and Richard Clayton, have suggested books and ideas, while the photographer Belinda Lawley deserves thanks for allowing me to use a picture she took of me for the book's jacket. John Lloyd very helpfully returned overdue library books. Others have offered peaceful havens in which to write: Justine Walton and Peter Skelton, James and Rachel Aldrige, George and Anna Butler, Siobhan and Nick Tindal and my brother and sister-in-law, Andrew and Mary Nicol.

The greatest personal debt of thanks, however, is owed to my unstintingly generous and patient husband, Al Philp. There have been many

Saturdays and Sundays when I have felt quite defeated by the task ahead, but have been eased into it by his gentle coercion and superb at-desk catering. This book has been with us since we first started seeing one another and even had to come on our honeymoon. Frankly, there are not many men who would have put up with it and I'm very lucky to have found one who would. This is humble acknowledgement of that fact.

P. N.

LIST OF ILLUSTRATIONS

My thanks to Hugh Alexander at the National Archives in Kew, for facilitating a happy day trawling through their collections. At the Imperial War Museum, I owe gratitude to Yvonne Oliver and David Bell in the Photography Department and Pauline Allwright in the Art Department (although in the end we sourced the works she helped with from the National Archives). For assistance in sourcing and gaining permission to use images I would like to acknowledge the following.

Dig for Victory poster. (HMSO/Crown copyright)
Dining in a British Restaurant. (Courtesy of the Imperial War Museum IWM D 12268).
The British Restaurant at London's Fishmonger's Hall. (Courtesy of the Imperial War Museum IWM D 10506)
A mobile canteen. (HMSO/Crown copyright)
Canteen food preparation. (HMSO/Crown copyright)
A crowded grill room in London's West End. (Courtesy of the Imperial War Museum IWM D 6577)
Make Do and Mend booklet cover. (HMSO/Crown copyright)
Clothes rationing in Britain. (HMSO/Crown copyright)
Useful Jobs that Girls Can Do. (HMSO/Crown copyright)
Make Do and Mend Advice Centre. (HMSO/Crown copyright)
Fight the Moth. (HMSO/Crown copyright)
Utility fashions. (Courtesy of the Imperial War Museum IWM D 14818 (*left*) and D 14826 (*right*))
Female war worker applying lipstick. (Courtesy of the Imperial War Museum IWM D 176)
Cover Your Hair for Safety. (Courtesy of the Imperial War Museum IWM MH 13802)
Victory in Your Hands. (HMSO/Crown copyright)
Up Housewives and at 'em. (HMSO/Crown copyright)
Weapons from school's scrap metal poster. (HMSO/Crown copyright)
Your Books are Wanted. (HMSO/Crown copyright)
Schoolboys collecting salvage. (Courtesy of the Imperial War Museum IWM HU 36208)
Little girl putting out waste for pigs. (Courtesy of the Imperial War Museum IWM HU 36203)
Save Fuel for Battle poster. (HMSO/Crown copyright)
Save Fuel for Battle poster. (HMSO/Crown copyright)
The Battle for Fuel targets poster. (HMSO/Crown copyright)
Lag to Keep Heat In. (HMSO/Crown copyright)
One Pot Meals. (HMSO/Crown copyright)
Is Your Journey Really Necessary poster. (HMSO/Crown copyright)
Is Your Journey Really Necessary poster. (HMSO/Crown copyright)
Transport of Flowers By Rail. (HMSO/Crown copyright)
Walk Short Distances. (HMSO/Crown copyright)
Housewives!. (HMSO/Crown copyright)
Wanted for Sabotage. (HMSO/Crown copyright)
National Savings. (HMSO/Crown copyright)
People queuing at a greengrocers. (Courtesy of the Imperial War Museum IWM D 25035)
Together We'll Pull the Country Around. (HMSO/Crown copyright)

Every effort has been made to trace the holders of copyright in text quotations and illustrations, but any inadvertant mistakes or omissions may be corrected in future editions.

ENDNOTES

INTRODUCTION
(Pages 1–7)

1 Professor Peter Hennessy, author of *Having it so Good*, quoted in the *Daily Express*, 15 December 2006.
2 Jane Grigson, *English Food* (London: Penguin, 1974).
3 http://www.esrcsocietytoday.ac.uk.
4 http://www.timesonline.co.uk/tol/news/world/article624201.ece.
5 http://www.guardian.co.uk.
6 What Britain Has Done 1939–45 (Ministry of Information, 1945, reissued p. 44.
7 Ina Zweiniger-Bargielowska, *Austerity in Britain: Rationing, Controls and Consumption 1939–1955*, (Oxford: Oxford University Press, 2000), p.33.
8 Simms, quoted in the *Guardian*, 16 May 2001.

PREFACE
(Pages 11–20)

1 F. J. M. Woolton, *Memoirs* (London: Cassell & Company, 1959), p. 192.
2 http://www.telegraph.co.uk/health/3269479/Fife-diet-requires-local-food.html.
3 Carolyn Steel, *Hungry City: How Food Shapes Our Lives* (London: Chatto & Windus, 2008), p. x.
4 Ibid., p. 49.
5 Ibid., p. 49.
6 http://www.guardian.co.uk/lifeandstyle/2008/dec/27/2008-the-year-in-review.
7 http://www.telegraph.co.uk/news/uknews/1575614/Food-cost-increase-adds-andpound750-to-annual-bill.html.
8 http://www.nationalobesityforum.org.uk/component/content/article/1-nof-in-the-media/277-experts-say-many-briton-malnourished.html.
9 *Healthy Weight, Healthy Lives: A cross-government strategy for England* (2008), p. 5.
10 *Statistics on Obesity, Physical Activity and Diet: England* (Information Centre, January 2008), p. 33.
11 *Healthy Weight, Healthy Lives* p. 5.
12 Ibid.
13 *Statistics on Obesity, Physical Activity and Diet*, p. ii.

14 Ibid., p. 9.
15 http://www.finemb.org.uk/public/default.aspx?nodeid=35366&contentlan=2&culture=en-GB.
16 http://www.guardian.co.uk/befit/story/0,15652,1385645,00.html.
17 Ibid.
18 Ibid.
19 Zweiniger-Bargielowska, op. cit., p. 36.
20 http://news.bbc.co.uk/1/hi/health/6225450.stm.
21 *Home Front Handbook* (London: Ministry of Information, 1945), pp. 31–3.

CHAPTER ONE
Go To It: Towards victory on the kitchen front
(*Pages 21–42*)

1 Zweiniger-Bargielowska, op. cit., p. 13.
2 Quoted in Juliet Gardiner, *Wartime Britain 1939–1945* (London: Headline, 2004), p. 144.
3 Ibid.
4 Woolton, op. cit., p. 131.
5 Ibid., p. 193.
6 Ibid., pp. 193–4.
7 Ibid., p. 228.
8 Ibid., p. 226.
9 Ibid., p. 228.
10 Ibid., p. 184.
11 Ibid., p. 185.
12 Ibid., pp. 194–5.
13 Ibid., p. 207.
14 Ibid., pp. 229–30.

CHAPTER TWO
Wise Eating in Wartime
(*Pages 43–61*)

1 George Orwell, *The Lion and the Unicorn: Socialism and the English Genius* (London: Secker & Warburg, 1941), pp. 15–16.
2 Woolton, op. cit, p. 186.
3 Ibid., pp. 171–2.
4 Norman Longmate, *How We Lived Then: A History of Everyday Life During the Second World War* (London: Hutchinson, 1971; republished by Pimlico, 2002), p. 140.
5 *The Letters of Vita Sackville-West to Virginia Woolf*, Louise DeSalvo and Mitchell A.

Leaska, eds (London: Virago, 1992; first published in Great Britain by Hutchinson, 1984), p. 467.
6 Woolton, op. cit., p. 190.
7 Ibid., p. 209.
8 Ibid., p. 212.
9 Meyer, quoted in the *Guardian*, 16 May 2001.
10 Woolton, op. cit., pp. 208–9.

CHAPTER THREE
Dig for Victory: Towards a more self-sustaining nation
(Pages 62–98)

1 Quoted in the *Home Front Handbook*, printed by the Ministry of Information (London) in April 1945, reprinted by the Ministry of Information in 2005.
2 On Talking Heads' *Naked*, 1988.
3 Steel, op. cit., p. 44.
4 From the DEFRA report, 'The Validity of Food Miles as an indicator of Sustainable Development' (2005), pp. 6–7, https://statistics.defra.gov.uk/esg/reports/foodmiles/final.pdf.
5 Steel, op. cit., pp. 4–5.
6 Juliet Gardiner, op. cit., p. 140.
7 Statistics from Juliet Gardiner, op. cit., p. 141.
8 Angus Calder, *The People's War* (London: Jonathan Cape, 1969), p. 423.
9 Longmate, op. cit., p. 235.
10 Ibid.
11 Ibid.
12 *Home Front Handbook*, p. 7.
13 *Land at War: The Official Story of British Farming 1939–1944* (Ministry of Information, 1945), Chapter 10: New Life on the Land, p. 92.
14 Ibid., pp. 91–2.
15 Ibid., pp. 92–4.
16 Vita Sackville-West, *The Women's Land Army* (London: Michael Joseph, 1944), pp. 7–8.
17 *Home Front Handbook*, p. 6.
18 Longmate, op. cit., p. 239.
19 *Land At War*, p. 88.
20 Longmate, op. cit., p. 244.
21 *Land At War*, p. 89.
22 Calder, op. cit., p. 429.
23 Details given in Juliet Gardiner, op. cit., p. 452.
24 Mary Tetlow, left at the IWM on 25 October 1985 (IWM Catalogue Number, 3824).

25 Mrs Mary Dowzell (IWM Catalogue Number, 116).
26 Quoted in Longmate, op. cit., p. 244.
27 http://www.guardian.co.uk/uk/2007/apr/09/foodanddrink.food.
28 http://www.guardian.co.uk/environment/2008/mar/22/food.gardens.
29 Juliet Gardiner, op. cit., p. 143.
30 Details from Juliet Gardiner, op. cit., pp. 142–3.
31 *Home Front Handbook*, p. 6.
32 Details from Juliet Gardiner, op. cit., p. 143.
33 Clara Milburn, *Mrs Milburn's Diaries, An Englishwoman's Day-to-Day Reflections 1939–45* (London: Harrap 1979), p. 147.
34 Ibid., p. 145.
35 Ibid., p. 145.
36 Calder, op. cit., p. 430.
37 *Home Front Handbook*, p. 6.
38 Ibid., p. 6.
39 Steel, op. cit., p. 6.
40 FAO statistics quoted in Steel, op.cit., p. 5.
41 Ibid., p. 8.
42 Ibid., pp. 8–9.
43 Ibid., pp. 9–10.
44 http://www.metro.co.uk/metrolife/food/article.html?in_article_id=270498&in_page_id=26&in_a_source=.
45 http://www.guardian.co.uk/lifeandstyle/2008/jun/30/gardens.food.
46 Ibid.
47 Steel, op. cit., p. 313.
48 Ibid., p. 313.
49 http://www.timesonline.co.uk/tol/life_and_style/food_and_drink/real_food/article4039968.ece.
50 www.mvrdv.nl.
51 www.verticalfarm.com.

CHAPTER FOUR
The British Restaurant and Canteen: How your wartime granny pioneered today's eating-out and drinking culture

(*Pages 99–120*)

1 Patrick Hamilton, *The Slaves of Solitude* (London: Constable & Robinson, 1947), p. 61.
2 http://www.statistics.gov.uk/cci/nugget.asp?id=946.
3 http://www.guardian.co.uk/business/2009/jan/08/fooddrinks-foodanddrink.
4 *Home Front Handbook*, p. 43.

5 Juliet Gardiner, op. cit., p. 470.
6 Quoted in ibid., p. 152.
7 Hamilton, op. cit., p. 61.
8 Brian Glover, *Brewing for Victory: Brewers, Beer and Pubs in World War II* (Cambridge: Lutterworth Press, 1995), from the chapter Ally on the Home Front, p. 9.
9 Ibid., pp. 14–15.
10 Quoted in Calder, op. cit., p. 174.
11 Glover, op. cit., p. 27.
12 Quoted in Calder, op. cit., p. 186.
13 Woolton, op. cit., pp. 222–5.
14 Ibid., pp. 222–5.
15 From the private papers of Miss R. C. Desch, IWM 89/19/1, Catalogue Number 179.
16 C. G. Gardiner, *Canteens At Work* (Oxford: Oxford University Press, 1941), pp. ix–xii.
17 Woolton, op. cit., p. 219.
18 Gardiner C.G., op. cit., pp. ix–xii.
19 'Quivers Choice', 1945, quoted in A. Sinclair, *The War Decade: An anthology of the 1940s* (London: 1989), p. 220.
20 *Chips, The Diaries of Sir Henry Channon*, Robert Rhodes James, ed. (London: Weidenfeld & Nicolson, 1967), p. 221.
21 Ibid., p. 272.
22 Woolton, op. cit., pp. 220–21.
23 Statistics and quotes from Zweiniger-Bargielowska, op. cit., pp. 78–9.

CHAPTER FIVE
Make Do and Mend: Wartime fashion
(Pages 123–155)

1 Quoted in Longmate, op. cit., p. 127.
2 Julie Clapperton, MD of Financial Direction for Women, quoted in the *Daily Mail*, 10 July 2006, p. 37.
3 Cited in the *Daily Express*, 28 November 2006, p. 6.
4 Cited in the *Daily Mail*, 10 July 2006, p. 37.
5 Cited in the *Scotsman*, 9 August 2007, p. 22.
6 http://www.telegraph.co.uk/news/uknews/3516158/Primark-effect-lead-to-throwaway-fashion-turning-up-in-landfill.html.
7 Quoted in Clobbered!, an article on how limited-range clothing lines have changed the way we shop, by the journalist Simon Mills, *Guardian*, 5 February 2007.
8 Quoted in Longmate, op. cit., p. 246.
9 Ibid.

10 Quoted in ibid., p. 245.
11 *Mrs Milburn's Diaries*, p. 99.
12 *Nella Last's War: A Mother's Diary 1939–1945*, Richard Broad and Suzie Fleming, eds (London: Falling Wall Press, 1981) p. 156.
13 *Chips*, p. 307.
14 The unpublished letters of Elizabeth Hudson are in the archive of the Imperial War Museum. This letter was first dated 27 May 1941. (IWM Catalogue Number 7790).
15 Longmate, op. cit., p. 245.
16 Ibid., p. 246.
17 Quoted in Sadie Ward, *War in the Countryside* (London: Cameron Books, in association with David & Charles, 1988), p. 7.
18 Longmate, op. cit., p. 247.
19 Ibid.
20 Board of Trade, (HMSO) Clothing Coupon Quiz (London, 1941), p. xxiii, point 89.
21 Longmate, op. cit., p. 253.
22 Board of Trade, Make Do and Mend Leaflet No. 2, Heat Plays Havoc With Shoe Leather.
23 Ibid.
24 Ibid.
25 Board of Trade (HMSO), Clothing Coupon Quiz, p. xiv, p. 40.
26 Quoted in Jane Waller and Michael Vaughan-Rees, *Women in Wartime: The Role of Women's Magazines 1939–1945* (London: Optima, 1977), p. 90.
27 Longmate, op. cit., p. 249.
28 Elizabeth Hudson letters, dated 8 June 1941.
29 http://www.guardian.co.uk/lifeandstyle/2008/apr/28/fashion.ethicalliving
30 Rosa Silverman, 'Sewing Machines Make a Comeback', *Independent*, 21 April 2008.
31 The Association of Teachers of Domestic Subjects, with the Approval of the Board of Trade, Make Do and Mend Leaflet 11.
32 Board of Trade newspaper advertisement, April 1944.
33 Wartime ATS recruitment poster, cited in George Begley, *Advertising Goes to War* (London: Lemon Tree, 1975), p. 27.
34 Board of Trade, Make Do and Mend Booklet, Foreword.
35 *Nella Last's War*, p. 194.
36 Colin McDowell, *Forties Fashion and the New Look* (London: Bloomsbury, 1947). From Sir Hardy Amies's Introduction, p. 11.
37 *Chips*, p. 277, from 29 November 1940.
38 Quoted in Juliet Gardiner, op. cit., p. 493.
39 McDowell, op. cit., p. 92.
40 Quoted in Juliet Gardiner, op. cit., p. 490.

CHAPTER SIX
Best Face Forward: Beauty and keeping up appearances
(Pages 156–170)

1 Alice Hart-Davis, *Daily Telegraph*, 21 November 2008, http://www.telegraph.co.uk/fashion/beauty/3489999/Good-value-cosmetics-that-gloss-over-the-credit-crunch.html.
2 http://www.premiumbeautynews.com/Credit-crunch-who-believes-in-the,425.
3 http://www.marieclaire.co.uk/news/beauty/276313/credit-crunch-doesn-t-effect-cosmetic-sales.html.
4 *Nella Last's War*, p. 64.
5 Ibid., pp. 57–8.
6 Elizabeth Hudson letters, letter dated 8 June 1941.
7 Quoted in McDowell, op. cit., p. 70.
8 Ibid. p. 72.
9 Ibid., p. 61.
10 Waller and Vaughan-Rees, op. cit., p. 80.
11 Quoted in Juliet Gardiner, op. cit., p. 498.
12 Quoted in Waller and Vaughan-Rees, op. cit., p. 80.
13 Quoted in McDowell, op. cit., p. 94.
14 Ibid.
15 Maggie Wood, *We Wore What We'd Got: Women's Clothes in World War II* (Warwickshire Books, 1989).
16 Ursula Bloom, *Woman's Own*, 29 May 1942, quoted in Waller and Vaughan-Rees, op. cit., p. 83.

CHAPTER SEVEN
The Great Saucepan Offensive: Our grandparents' forgotten victory in the war on waste
(Pages 173–200)

1 The Mayor of Lewisham addressing his borough's housewives in a salvage pamphlet, January 1942.
2 British Prime Minister Gordon Brown declaring war on waste at the Tokyo G8 summit, July 2008, quoted in *The Times*.
3 'What Britain Has Done 1939–1945', issued by the Ministry of Information 1945, reissued by the Department of Printed Books, Imperial War Museum, London, 2005, p. 48.
4 Statistics found in Longmate, op. cit., p. 288.

5 Raynes Minns, *Bombers and Mash: The Domestic Front, 1939–45* (London: Virago, 1980), p. 143.
6 Sir David Attenborough giving evidence to the House of Commons Rural Affairs Committee, Climate Change: The Citizens Agenda, Wednesday, 13 December 2006.
7 http://www.foe.co.uk/campaigns/waste/issues/what_a_mess_index.html.
8 http://www.defra.gov.uk/environment/statistics/waste/kf/wrkf04.htm.
9 http://www.defra.gov.uk/ENVIRONMENT/waste/topics/index.htm.
10 http://www.wrap.org.uk/wrap_corporate/news/wasted_food_now.html.
11 http://www.defra.gov.uk/environment/localenv/litter/bags/index.htm.
12 *Guardian* 'Weekend', 31 March 2007, pp. 30–39.
13 http://www.defra.gov.uk/environment/localenv/litter/bags/index.htm.
14 http://www.foe.co.uk/campaigns/waste/issues/reduce_reuse_recycle_index.html.
15 http://www.resource.co.uk/do/ecco.py/view_item?listid=37&listcatid=217&listitemid=9718.
16 http://www.recycling-guide.org.uk/blog/2008/09/mixed-messages-in-dumping-scandal/.
17 *Guardian* 'Weekend', 31 March 2007, pp. 30–39.
18 Woolton, op. cit., pp. 171–2.
19 Quoted in Calder, op. cit., p. 149.
20 From the BBC archives and quoted in Longmate, op. cit., p. 281.
21 Ibid., p. 282.
22 Minns, op. cit., p. 147.
23 Longmate, op. cit., pp. 283–4.
24 Ibid., p. 284.
25 Text for Ministry of Supply advert.
26 Ibid.
27 Ibid.
28 Ibid.
29 Mike Brown and Carol Harris, *The Wartime House: Home Life in Wartime Britain 1939–1945* (Stroud: Sutton Publishing, 2001), p. 92.
30 Ibid.
31 Ibid.
32 Longmate, op. cit., pp. 286–7.
33 'What Britain Has Done 1939–1945', p. 48.
34 Longmate, op. cit., p. 289.
35 Ibid., p. 291.
36 *Home Front Handbook*, p. 49.
37 All statistics from 'What Britain Has Done 1939–1945'.
38 Longmate, op. cit., p. 285.
39 *Welsh Schools Prizewinning Essays: Salvage as munitions of war* (1943), (IWM Catalogue Number 86/2693).
40 *Daily Express*, 25 May 2007.

41 *Daily Mail*, 6 September 2008.
42 http://www.defra.gov.uk/environment/waste/about/index.htm.
43 http://www.menvcity.org.uk.

CHAPTER EIGHT
The Battle for Fuel

(*Pages 201–230*)

1 Eleanor Roosevelt, *The Autobiography of Eleanor Roosevelt* (London: Hutchinson, 1962), pp. 185–6
2 Longmate, op. cit., pp. 325–6.
3 Andrew Lane, *Austerity Motoring 1939–1950* (Oxford: Shire Publications, 1987), p. 3.
4 Ibid.
5 *Oil for Victory: The Story of Petroleum in War and Peace* (1946), Editors of *Look*.
6 Longmate, op. cit., p. 315.
7 Ibid., p. 321.
8 Ibid., p. 321.
9 Ibid., p. 321.
10 George Monbiot, *Heat: How We Can Stop the Planet Burning* (London: Penguin, 2006, revised 2007), p. 65.
11 Ibid.
12 Ibid.
13 http://www.energysavingtrust.org.uk/Your-impact-on-climate-change/How-we-contribute-to-climate-change.
14 http://www.communities.gov.uk/planningandbuilding/theenvironment/zerocarbonhomes.
15 Monbiot, op. cit., p. 46.
16 http://www.energysavingtrust.org.uk/content/download/2804...
17 Ibid.
18 http://en.wikipedia.org/wiki/Smart_meter.
19 Ibid.
20 http://www.guardian.co.uk/money/2008/jun/02/householdbills.consumeraffairs.
21 Ministry of Fuel and Power, 'Here Are Your Battle Orders'.
22 Longmate, op. cit., p. 323.
23 Ministry of Fuel and Power, 'Save Fuel for Battle'.
24 Fuel Communiqué No. 3, September 1942.
25 Fuel Communiqué No. 6.
26 http://www.energysavingtrust.org.uk/Your-impact-on-climate-change/Surprising-statistics/Home-and-the-environment.
27 Ibid.

28 Monbiot, op. cit., pp. 65–73.
29 http://www.energysavingtrust.org.uk/Your-impact-on-climate-change/Surprising-statistics/Home-and-the-environment.
30 Monbiot, op. cit., pp. 66–7.
31 http://www.energysavingtrust.org.uk/Your-impact-on-climate-change/Surprising-statistics/Home-and-the-environment.
32 Monbiot, op. cit., p. 68.
33 http://www.energysavingtrust.org.uk/Your-impact-on-climate-change/Surprising-statistics/Home-and-the-environment.
34 Monbiot, op. cit., pp. 59–78.
35 Ministry of Fuel and Power, 'Here Are Your Battle Orders'.
36 Longmate, op. cit., p. 324.
37 Ministry of Fuel and Power, 'Here Are Your Battle Orders'.
38 Ministry of Fuel and Power, 'Save Fuel: Food and Fuel Planning'.
39 Ministry of Fuel and Power, 'Here Are Your Battle Orders'.
40 Ministry of Food, Cookery Leaflet No. 12: 'A Salad a Day All Year Round'.
41 Ministry of Fuel and Power, 'Fuel Sense Saves Money in the Home, 65 Easy Ways of Saving Money'.
42 Ministry of Fuel and Power, 'Save Fuel for Battle'.
43 Ministry of Food Leaflet No. 35.
44 Longmate, op. cit., p. 325.
45 http://www.energysavingtrust.org.uk/Resources/Useful-statistics.
46 Ministry of Fuel and Power, 'Fuel Sense Saves Money in the Home, 65 Easy Ways of Saving Money'.
47 Ibid.
48 Ministry of Fuel and Power, 'Save Fuel for Battle'.
49 http://www.energysavingtrust.org.uk/What-can-I-do-today/Save-water.
50 Ibid.
51 Ibid.
52 Longmate, op. cit., p. 331–2.
53 Ibid., p. 332.
54 Ministry of Fuel and Power, 'All Along the Line'.
55 Ministry of Fuel and Power, 'Save Fuel for Battle'.
56 Ministry of Fuel and Power, 'Gas Makes Munitions'.

CHAPTER NINE
Is Your Journey Really Necessary?
(Pages 231–256)

1 Sir David Attenborough, giving evidence to the House of Commons Rural Affairs Committee in Climate Change: the Citizen's Agenda, Wednesday, 13 December 2006.

2 Monbiot, op. cit., p. 174.
3 Ibid., p. 195.
4 Ibid.
5 Report on BBC1 *News at Ten*, Friday, 21 November 2008.
6 http://www.energysavingtrust.org.uk/Travel/Driven-a-review-of-the-passenger-car-market.
7 Wartime Railway Executive Committee Poster.
8 Ibid.
9 *Home Front Handbook*, p. 65.
10 Both statistics from Longmate, op. cit., pp. 293–4.
11 *Home Front Handbook*, p. 65.
12 Ibid.
13 Longmate, op. cit., p. 294.
14 *Home Front Handbook*, p. 43.
15 Ibid. p. 65.
16 Longmate, op. cit., p. 294.
17 *Home Front Handbook*, p. 65.
18 Wartime Railway Executive Committee Poster.
19 Longmate, op. cit., p. 294.
20 Ibid. p. 295.
21 *Home Front Handbook*, p. 65.
22 Longmate, op. cit., p. 297.
23 Ibid., pp. 296–7.
24 *Home Front Handbook*, p. 66.
25 Orwell, op. cit.
26 *The Letters of Vita Sackville-West to Virginia Woolf*, p. 463.
27 Lane, op. cit.
28 Ibid.
29 Ibid.
30 Ibid.
31 Longmate, op. cit., pp. 313–5.
32 Lane, op. cit.
33 Longmate, op. cit., pp. 308–10.
34 Ibid., p. 309.
35 Ibid., p. 308.
36 Lane, op. cit.
37 Longmate, op. cit., p. 307.
38 Lane, op. cit.
39 Longmate, op. cit., pp. 310–12.
40 Lane, op. cit.
41 Longmate, op. cit., pp. 310–13.
42 Ibid., pp. 310–11.
43 Lane, op. cit.

44 Ibid.
45 Longmate, op. cit., pp. 312–13.
46 Ibid.
47 Ibid., p. 315.
48 Ibid., pp. 316–18.
49 Ibid., pp. 319–20.
50 Ibid.
51 Lane, op. cit.
52 Ibid.

CHAPTER TEN

A Paradise for Spivs: cheating, disillusion and the Black Market

(Pages 259–276)

1 Orwell, op. cit., pp. 15–16.
2 Woolton, op. cit., p. 230.
3 Ibid.
4 Calder, op. cit., p. 66.
5 *Mrs Milburn's Diaries*, p. 220.
6 Ibid., p. 257.
7 Ibid., p. 287.
8 Calder, op. cit., p. 406.
9 Zweiniger-Bargielowska, op. cit., p. 151.
10 Juliet Gardiner, op. cit., p. 504.
11 Ibid., p. 510.
12 Ibid., p. 514.
13 Ibid., p. 506.
14 Ibid.
15 Mass Observation, Food Rationing 1781, 'Some Notes on popular Feeling about Black Markets', 17 May 1943 (emphasis in original). Quoted in Zweiniger-Bargielowska, op. cit., p. 157.
16 Juliet Gardiner, op. cit., p. 506.
17 Calder, op. cit., p. 254.
18 Juliet Gardiner, op. cit., p. 509.
19 Ibid.
20 Zweiniger-Bargielowska, op. cit., p. 151.
21 Woolton, op. cit., p. 231.
22 Zweiniger-Bargielowska, op. cit., p. 179.
23 Juliet Gardiner, op. cit., p. 586.
24 *Chronicle of the 20th Century* (London: Longman, 1988), p. 649.
25 Ibid., pp. 650–51.
26 Ibid., p. 657, p. 660.

27 Zweiniger-Bargielowska, op. cit., pp. 157–8.
28 PRO MAF, 100/45 Minute 3 May 1946; MAF 100/52 Enforcement – Policy and Organisation: Interim Report, 1 July 1946; Minute 23 October 1946, quoted in Zweiniger-Bargielowska, op. cit., p. 161.
29 PRO MAF, 100/57 Enforcement Review, vol. 2, no. 2 (February 1948), quoted in Zweiniger-Bargielowska, op. cit., p. 161.
30 PRO, POWE 33/1440, Committee of Inquiry into Evasion of Petrol Rationing Control, Meeting, 29 January 1948, quoted in Zweiniger-Bargielowska, op. cit., p. 151.
31 A character in *Passport to Pimlico*, 1949.
32 Quoted in Zweiniger-Bargielowska, op. cit., pp. 155–6.
33 *Picture Post*, 'Behind the Nylon Racket', 10 February 1951, quoted in Zweiniger-Bargielowska, op. cit., p. 180.

AFTERWORD

(*Pages 277–283*)

1 Peter Hennessy, author of *Having it so Good*, quoted in the *Daily Express*, 15 December 2006.
2 http://www.guardian.co.uk/business/2009/jan/24/recession-britain.

BIBLIOGRAPHY

Begley, George, *Advertising Goes to War* (London: Lemon Tree, 1975).
Brown, Mike, and Carol Harris, *The Wartime House: Home Life in Wartime Britain 1939–1945* (Stroud: Sutton Publishing, 2001).
Calder, Angus, *The People's War* (London: Jonathan Cape, 1969).
Channon, Chips, *Chips, The Diaries of Sir Henry Channon*, ed. Robert Rhodes James (London: Weidenfeld & Nicolson, 1967).
Chronicle of the 20th Century (London: Longman, 1988).
The papers of Miss RC Desch (IWM Catalogue Number 179).
The papers of Miss Mary Dowzell (IWM Catalogue Number 116).
Gardiner, C. G., *Canteens at Work* (Oxford: Oxford University Press, 1941).
Gardiner, Juliet, *Wartime Britain 1939–1945* (London: Headline, 2004).
Glover, Brian, *Brewing for Victory: Brewers, Beer and Pubs in World War II* (Cambridge: Lutterworth Press, 1995).
Grigson, Jane, *English Food* (London: Penguin, 1974).
Hamilton, Patrick, *The Slaves of Solitude* (London: Constable & Robinson, 1947).
Healthy Weight, Healthy Lives: A cross-government strategy for England (2008).
The papers of Miss Elizabeth Hudson (IWM Catalogue Number 7790).
Imperial War Museum Department of Documents.
Lane, Andrew, *Austerity Motoring, 1939–1950* (Oxford: Shire Publications, 1987).
Last, Nella, *Nella Last's War: A Mother's Diary 1939–1945*, ed Richard Broad and Suzie Fleming (London: Falling Wall Press, 1981).
Longmate, Norman, *How We Lived Then: A History of Everyday Life During the Second World War* (London: Hutchinson, 1971; republished by Pimlico, 2002).
McDowell, Colin, *Forties Fashion and the New Look* (London: Bloomsbury, 1947).
Milburn, Clara, *Mrs Milburn's Diaries An Englishwoman's Day-to-Day Reflections 1939–1945*, ed. Peter Donnelly (London: Harrap, 1979).
Ministry of Information, Home Front Handbook (London: 1945); reprinted by the Ministry of Information, 2005.
— *Land at War: The Official Story of British Farming 1939–1944* (London: 1945).
— *What Britain Has Done 1939–1945* (London: 1945); reissued by the Department of Printed Books, Imperial War Museum, London, 2005.
Minns, Raynes, *Bombers and Mash: The Domestic Front, 1939–1945* (London: Virago, 1980).
Monbiot, George, *Heat: How We Can Stop the Planet Burning* (London: Penguin, 2006, revised 2007).
Orwell, George, *The Lion and the Unicorn: Socialism and the English Genius* (London: Secker & Warburg, 1941).

Roosevelt, Eleanor, *The Autobiography of Eleanor Roosevelt* (London: Hutchinson, 1962).
Sackville-West, Vita, *The Letters of Vita Sackville-West to Virginia Woolf*, ed. Louise DeSalvo and Mitchell A Leaska (London: Virago, 1992; first published in Great Britain by Hutchinson, 1984).
— *The Women's Land Army* (London: Michael Joseph, 1944).
Sinclair, Andrew, *The War Decade: An Anthology of the 1940s* (London: Hamish Hamilton, 1989).
Statistics on Obesity, Physical Activity and Diet: England (Information Centre, January 2008).
Steel, Carolyn, *Hungry City: How Food Shapes Our Lives* (London: Chatto & Windus, 2008).
The papers of Miss Mary Tetlow (IWM Catalogue Number 3824).
Waller, Jane, and Michael Vaughan-Rees, *Women in Wartime: The Role of Women's Magazines 1939–1945* (London: Optima, 1977).
Ward, Sadie, *War in the Countryside* (London: Cameron Books, in association with David Charles, 1988).
Whyl Bogard, Eva, *Useful Hints from Odds & Ends* (London: John Gifford, 1944).
Wood, Maggie, *We Wore What We'd Got: Women's Clothes in World War II* (Warwickshire Books, 1989).
Woolton, F. J. M., *Memoirs* (London: Cassell & Company, 1959).
Zweiniger-Bargielowska, Ina, *Austerity in Britain: Rationing, Controls and Consumption 1939–1955* (Oxford: Oxford University Press, 2000).

Some useful web addresses:

Department for Environment, Food and Rural Affairs www.defra.gov.uk
Economics Research Council www.esrsocietytoday.ac.uk
Energy Saving Trust www.energysavingtrust.org.uk
Friends of the Earth www.foe.co.uk
Love Food Hate Waste www.lovefoodhatewaste.com
National Obesity Forum www.nationalobesityforum.org.uk
Selfsufficientish.com www.selfsufficientish.com
UK Statistics Authority http://www.statistics.gov.uk

INDEX